THE DAILY DU'A BOOK

PRAYERS TO RECITE EVERY MORNING & EVENING

COMPILED BY

The Imam, Mufassir, Muḥaddith, and Shaykh
ʿAbdullāh Sirāj al-Dīn al-Ḥusaynī

Imam Ghazali PUBLISHING

TITLE: THE DAILY DU'A BOOK
ISBN: 978-1-952306-24-2 (STANDARD PB)

979-8-8691-0504-2 (INTERNATIONAL PB)

FIRST EDITION | JANUARY 2024

AUTHOR: ʿABDULLĀH SIRĀJ AL-DĪN AL-ḤUSAYNĪ
TYPESETTING: IGP CONSULTING | WWW.IGPCONSULTING.COM
DISTRIBUTION: WWW.SATTAURPUBLISHING.COM

www.imamghazali.co

CONTENTS

The Life & Legacy of the Shaykh

Shaykh ʿAbdullāh ibn Muhammad Najīb Sirāj al-Dīn al-Ḥusaynī al-Ḥalabī was an eminent Islamic scholar, spiritual master, and ḥāfiẓ recognized for his profound knowledge, unparalleled piety, and dedicated service to Islam. Born in 1923 CE into a prestigious and devout family during the twilight of the Ottoman Caliphate, Shaykh ʿAbdullāh's spiritual journey was shaped by a nurturing environment rooted in Islamic values and scholarship.

The early years of Shaykh ʿAbdullāh's education were guided by his father, the esteemed Shaykh Muhammad Najīb Sirāj al-Dīn al-Ḥusaynī, who in his own right was a renowned scholar and spiritual guide. As a young man, Shaykh ʿAbdullāh was fortunate to study under a number of distinguished scholars of his time, including Imam Muhammad Ibrāhīm al-Salqīnī, Shaykh ʿĪsā al-Bayānūnī, Shaykh ʿUmar Masʿūd al-Ḥarīrī, Shaykh Fayḍullāh al-Ayyubī al-Kurdī, Shaykh Aḥmad al-Shammā', and the highly respected historian of Aleppo, Shaykh Muhammad Rāghib al-Ṭabbākh. The latter, who recognized Shaykh ʿAbdullāh's intellect and devotion, would ultimately become his mentor.

Shaykh ʿAbdullāh's knowledge and spiritual insight led him to become an influential figure in the Islamic world, and his teachings produced a generation of scholars, such as Shaykh Dr. Aḥmad Sirāj al-Dīn, Shaykh Dr. Nūr al-Dīn ʿItr, Shaykh Dr. Sāmir al-Naṣṣ, and Shaykh Muhammad ʿAwwāmah, all of whom have carried forward his scholarly legacy.

The Shaykh's spiritual life was marked by extraordinary moments. His profound connection with the Prophet Muhammad ﷺ, as manifested in his dreams and visions, was a testament to his spiritual stature. Shaykh ʿAbdullāh had a deep-seated love for al-Madinah al-Munawwarah, the city of the Prophet ﷺ, where he stayed for a significant period teaching, writing, and worshipping. His numerous visits to the Mosque of the Prophet ﷺ, fervent prayers, and respect for the sacred space were indicative of his unwavering devotion.

Despite his towering accomplishments, Shaykh ʿAbdullāh was a man of profound humility. He was known to conduct his lessons with an emphasis on dhikr (remembrance of Allah) and good manners. He treated others with the utmost level of respect and kindness, thereby demonstrating the Islamic values he espoused. His humility notwithstanding his spiritual and scholarly stature – was stunning and exemplary. In one story, those accompanying him noted his refusal to let a caretaker of the Ḥaram kiss his hand, citing the sanctity of the land of the Prophet ﷺ, thereby epitomizing his humble nature. This humility, combined with his scholarly prowess and spiritual depth, made him a revered figure, both during his lifetime and beyond.

In 2002, after a surgical operation, Shaykh ʿAbdullāh's health rapidly declined; he tragically passed away on the 4th of March during the same year. His passing was a significant loss for the Muslim world, casting a veil of sorrow across communities that revered him. He was laid to rest in the Shaʿbāniyyah complex, next to the graves of its Ottoman founders, ultimately marking the end of an era of spiritual enlightenment.

Shaykh ʿAbdullāh ibn Muhammad Najīb Sirāj al-Dīn al-Ḥusaynī al-Ḥalabī's life and legacy continue to be an inspiration for many. His profound understanding of Islamic jurisprudence, exceptional scholarship of Hadith, and brilliant exegesis of the Qur'an remain relevant in the domain of contemporary Islamic thought. His teachings continue to guide scholars and spiritual seekers alike, making him a timeless beacon in the ocean of Islamic wisdom.

SELECTED LIST OF THE SHAYKH'S WORKS

1. Ḥawla Tafsīr Sūrah al-Fātiḥah
2. Ḥawla Tafsīr Sūrah al-Ḥujurāt
3. Ḥawla Tafsīr Sūrah Qāf
4. Ḥawla Tafsīr Sūrah al-Mulk
5. Ḥawla Tafsīr Sūrah al-Insān
6. Ḥawla Tafsīr Sūrah al-ʿAlaq

7. Ḥawla Tafsīr Sūrah al-Kawthar
8. Ḥawla Tafsīr Sūrah al-Ikhlāṣ
9. Hadī al-Qur'ān al-Karīm ilā Ḥujjah al-Burhān
10. Hadī al-Qur'ān ilā Maʿrifah al-ʿUlūm wa al-Tafakkur
11. Tilāwah al-Qur'ān al-Majīd
12. al-Taqarrub ilā Allāh Taʿālā
13. Shahādah Lā Ilāha Illā Allāh, Muḥammad Rasūl Allāh
14. Sayyidunā Muḥammad Rasūl Allāh
15. al-Hadī al-Nabawī wa al-Irshādāt al-Muḥamadiyyah
16. al-Ṣalāh fī al-Islām
17. al-Ṣalāh ʿalā al-Nabī
18. Ṣuʿūd al-Aqwāl wa-Rafʿ al-ʿAmāl
19. al-Duʿā'
20. al-Imān bi-ʿAwalim al-Ukhrā wa-Mawāqifuhā
21. al-Adʿiyyah wa al-Adhkār al-Wāridah
22. Adaʿiyyah al-Ṣabāḥ wa al-Masā'
23. Manāsik al-Ḥajj wa al-ʿUmrah
24. al-Isrā' wa al-Miʿraj
25. Hijrah Rasūl Allāh

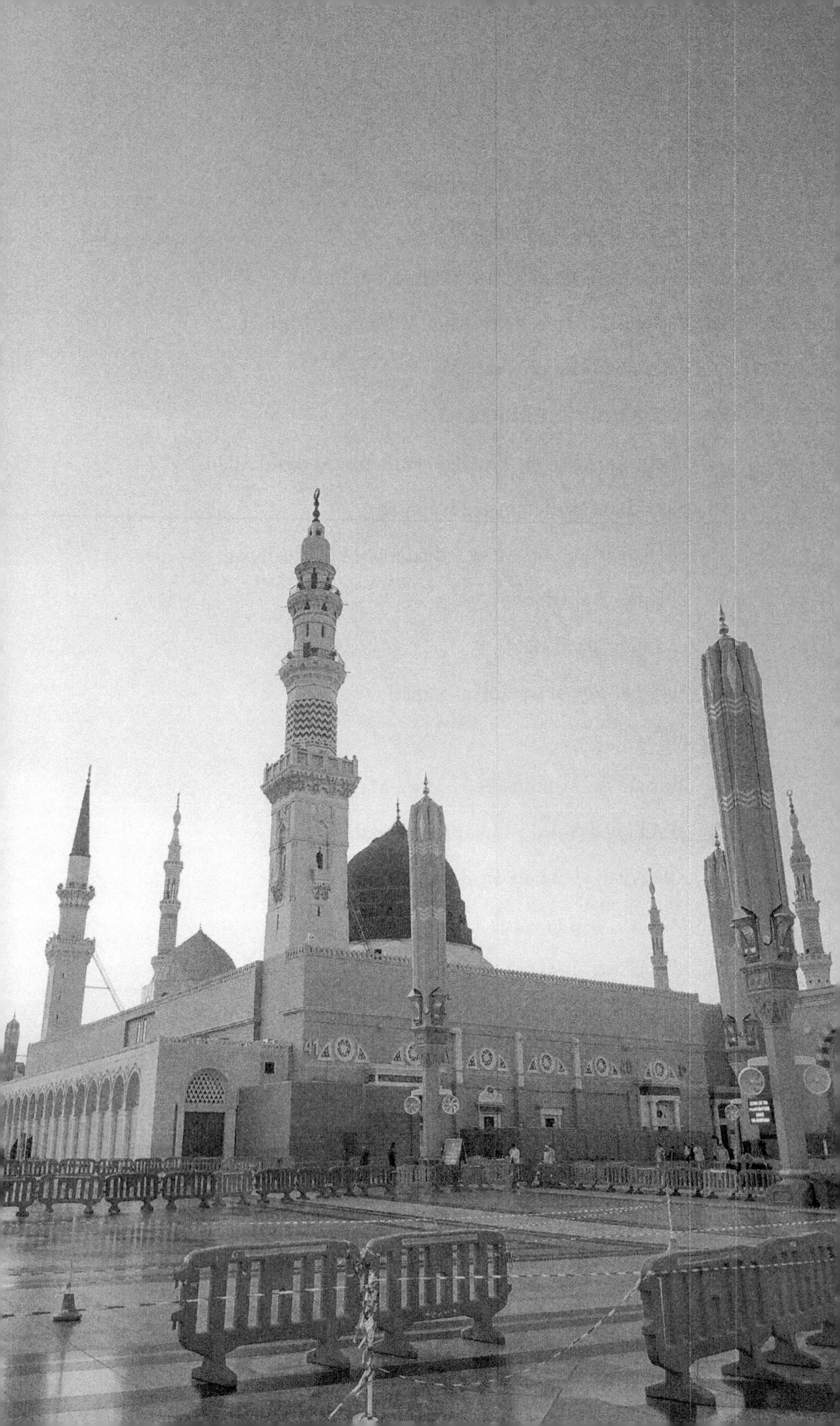

THE DAILY DU'A BOOK

PRAYERS TO RECITE EVERY MORNING & EVENING

COMPILED BY

The Imam, Mufassir, Muḥaddith, and Shaykh
ʿAbdullāh Sirāj al-Dīn al-Ḥusaynī

In the Name of Allah the Beneficent, the Merciful

Praise be to Allah, Lord of the worlds. May the best blessings and most perfect peace be upon our master Muhammad the Seal of the Prophets, and upon his family and Companions, all of them.

To proceed:

The following is an important collection of the morning and evening supplications. I have ordered them and mentioned what each has of unique features in the tradition, highlighting the narrations whence they are sourced.

By Allah, these supplications have secrets, light, distinct features, and effects which the believing slave benefits from in this world and the next. Be diligent, therefore, my Muslim brother and sister in reciting them, and supplicate for goodness to the one who spread and compiled them.

بِسْمِ اللهِ الرَّحْمٰنِ الرَّحِيمِ

اَلْحَمْدُ لِلهِ رَبِّ الْعَالَمِينَ، وَأَفْضَلُ الصَّلَاةِ وَأَتَمُّ التَّسْلِيمِ عَلَى سَيِّدِنَا مُحَمَّدٍ خَاتَمِ النَّبِيِّينَ، وَعَلَى آلِهِ وَصَحْبِهِ أَجْمَعِينَ.

وَبَعْدُ:

فَهَذِهِ جُمْلَةٌ مُهِمَّةٌ مِنْ أَدْعِيَةِ الصَّبَاحِ وَالْمَسَاءِ؛ رَتَّبْتُهَا وَذَكَرْتُ مَا لَهَا مِنْ خَصَائِصَ مَأْثُورَةٍ، مَعَ بَيَانِ مُسْنَدِهَا وَمَأْخَذِهَا.

وَأَيْمُ اللهِ إِنَّ لَهَا أَسْرَارًا وَأَنْوَارًا وَخَصَائِصَ وَآثَارًا، يَنْتَفِعُ بِهَا الْعَبْدُ الْمُؤْمِنُ فِي الدُّنْيَا وَالْآخِرَةِ - فَوَاظِبْ أَيُّهَا الْأَخُ الْمُسْلِمُ عَلَى قِرَاءَتِهَا، وَادْعُ خَيْرًا لِنَاشِرِهَا وَجَامِعِهَا.

The Morning and Evening Remembrance

Once you have concluded the ṣubḥ (Fajr) and Maghrib prayers, say:

Allāhumma ajirnī min al-nār - seven times.[1]

Allah, save me from the Fire.

Allāhumma saddidnī bil-īmāni wa-iḥfaẓhu ʿalayya fī ḥayātī wa ʿinda wafātī wa baʿda mamātī. Allāhumma innī uqaddimu ilayka bayna yaday kulli nafasin wa lamḥatin wa laḥẓatin wa ṭarfatin yaṭrifu bihā ahlu al-samāwāti wa al-arḍi wa kulli shay'in huwa fī ʿilmika kā'inun aw qad kān. Allāhumma innī uqaddimu ilayka bayna dhālika kullih.

Allah, keep me steadfast through faith, and preserve it for me throughout my life, upon my passing, and after my death. Allah, I come forth to You with every breath, glance, moment, and blink of an eye by those in the heavens and Earth, and with everything in Your knowledge that is or was. Allah, I come forth to You through all this.[2]

Bismillāhi al-Raḥmāni al-Raḥīm. Al-ḥamdu lillāhi Rabbi al-ʿālamīn, al-Raḥmāni al-Raḥīm, Māliki yawmi al-dīn. Iyyāka naʿbudu wa iyyāka nastaʿīn. Ihdinā al-ṣirāṭa al-mustaqīm, ṣirāṭa alladhīna anʿamta ʿalayhim ghayri al-maghḍubi ʿalayhim wa lā al-ḍāllīn. Āmīn.

"In the Name of Allah, Most Compassionate, Most Merciful. All praise is for Allah, Lord of all worlds, the Most Compassionate, Most Merciful, Master of the Day of Judgment. You [alone] we worship and You [alone] we ask for help. Guide us along the Straight Path, the Path of those You have blessed - not those You are displeased with, or those who are astray."[3] Āmīn.

---

1 In the narration of Abū Dāwūd, whoever says this during the day then dies, they will be spared from it (Hellfire), and whoever says it during the night and dies, they will be spared from it.

2 al-Sheikh al-Akbar mentioned this in his *Waṣāyā*.

3 *al-Fātiḥah*, 1-7.

أَذْكَارُ الصَّبَاحِ وَالْمَسَاءِ

إِذَا فَرَغْتَ مِنْ صَلَاةِ الصُّبْحِ وَالْمَغْرِبِ فَقُلْ: اَللّٰهُمَّ أَجِرْنِي مِنَ النَّارِ – سَبْعَ مَرَّاتٍ[1].

اَللّٰهُمَّ سَدِّدْنِيْ بِالْإِيْمَانِ وَاحْفَظْهُ عَلَيَّ فِي حَيَاتِيْ وَعِنْدَ وَفَاتِيْ؛ وَبَعْدَ مَمَاتِيْ، اَللّٰهُمَّ إِنِّي أُقَدِّمُ إِلَيْكَ بَيْنَ يَدَيْ كُلِّ نَفَسٍ وَلَمْحَةٍ وَلَحْظَةٍ وَطَرْفَةٍ يَطْرِفُ بِهَا أَهْلُ السَّمٰوَاتِ وَأَهْلُ الْأَرْضِ وَكُلُّ شَيْءٍ هُوَ فِي عِلْمِكَ كَائِنٌ أَوْ قَدْ كَانَ اَللّٰهُمَّ إِنِّي أُقَدِّمُ إِلَيْكَ بَيْنَ يَدَيْ ذٰلِكَ كُلِّهِ[2]:

﴿بِسۡمِ ٱللَّهِ ٱلرَّحۡمَٰنِ ٱلرَّحِيمِ ١ ٱلۡحَمۡدُ لِلَّهِ رَبِّ ٱلۡعَٰلَمِينَ ٢ ٱلرَّحۡمَٰنِ ٱلرَّحِيمِ ٣ مَٰلِكِ يَوۡمِ ٱلدِّينِ ٤ إِيَّاكَ نَعۡبُدُ وَإِيَّاكَ نَسۡتَعِينُ ٥ ٱهۡدِنَا ٱلصِّرَٰطَ ٱلۡمُسۡتَقِيمَ ٦ صِرَٰطَ ٱلَّذِينَ أَنۡعَمۡتَ عَلَيۡهِمۡ غَيۡرِ ٱلۡمَغۡضُوبِ عَلَيۡهِمۡ وَلَا ٱلضَّآلِّينَ ٧﴾ آمِين.

---

(١) فَفِي الْحَدِيْثِ الَّذِيْ رَوَاهُ أَبُوْ دَاوُدَ أَنَّ مَنْ قَالَ ذٰلِكَ فِيْ يَوْمِهِ ثُمَّ مَاتَ كُتِبَ لَهُ جِوَارٌ مِنْهَا، وَمَنْ قَالَ ذٰلِكَ مِنْ لَيْلَتِهِ وَمَاتَ كُتِبَ لَهُ جِوَارٌ مِنْهَا.

(٢) ذَكَرَهُ الشَّيْخُ الْأَكْبَرُ رَضِيَ اللهُ عَنْهُ فِي الْوَصَايَا.

Then:

Bismillāhi al-Raḥmāni al-Raḥīm. Alif-Lām-Mīm. Dhālika al-kitābu lā rayba fīhi hudan lil-muttaqīn. Alladhīna yu'minūna bil-ghaybi wa yuqīmūna al-ṣalāta wa min mā razaqnāhum yunfiqūn, wa alladhīna yu'minūna bimā unzila ilayka wa mā unzila min qablika wa bil-ākhirati hum yūqinūn. Ulā'ika alā hudan min Rabbihim wa ulā'ika humu al-mufliḥūn.

"In the Name of Allah, the Most Compassionate, Most Merciful. Alif Lām Mīm. This is the Book! There is no doubt about it – a guide for those mindful [of Allah], who believe in the unseen, establish prayer, and donate from what We have provided for them, and who believe in what has been revealed to you [O Prophet] and what was revealed before you, and have sure faith in the Hereafter. It is they who are [truly] guided by their Lord, and it is they who will be successful."[4]

Bismillāhi al-Raḥmāni al-Raḥīm. Allāhu lā ilāha illā huwa al-Ḥayyu al-Qayyūm. Lā ta'khudhuhū sinatun wa lā nawm. Lahū mā fī al-samawāti wa mā fī al-arḍ. Man dhā alladhī yashfaʿu ʿindahū illā bi'idhnih. Yaʿlamu mā bayna aydīhim wa mā khalfahum wa lā yuḥīṭūna bi-shay'in min ʿilmihī illā bimā shā'. Wasiʿa kursiyyuhū al-samāwāti wa al-arḍa wa lā ya'ūduhū ḥifẓuhumā, wa huwa al-ʿAliyyu al-ʿAẓīm.

"In the Name of Allah, the Most Compassionate, Most Merciful. Allah! There is no god [worthy of worship] except Him, the Ever-Living, All-Sustaining. Neither drowsiness nor sleep overtakes Him. To Him belongs whatever is in the heavens and whatever is on the earth. Who could possibly intercede with Him without His permission? He [fully] knows what is ahead of them and what is behind them, but no one can grasp any of His knowledge – except what He wills [to reveal]. His Seat encompasses the heavens and the earth, and the preservation of both does not tire Him. For He is the Most High, the Greatest."[5]

---

4 *al-Baqarah*, 1-5.

5 *al-Baqarah*, 255.

ثُمَّ: ﴿بِسۡمِ ٱللَّهِ ٱلرَّحۡمَٰنِ ٱلرَّحِيمِ: الٓمٓ ١ ذَٰلِكَ ٱلۡكِتَٰبُ لَا رَيۡبَۛ فِيهِۛ
هُدٗى لِّلۡمُتَّقِينَ ٢ ٱلَّذِينَ يُؤۡمِنُونَ بِٱلۡغَيۡبِ وَيُقِيمُونَ ٱلصَّلَوٰةَ وَمِمَّا
رَزَقۡنَٰهُمۡ يُنفِقُونَ ٣ وَٱلَّذِينَ يُؤۡمِنُونَ بِمَآ أُنزِلَ إِلَيۡكَ وَمَآ أُنزِلَ
مِن قَبۡلِكَ وَبِٱلۡأٓخِرَةِ هُمۡ يُوقِنُونَ ٤ أُوْلَٰٓئِكَ عَلَىٰ هُدٗى مِّن رَّبِّهِمۡۖ
وَأُوْلَٰٓئِكَ هُمُ ٱلۡمُفۡلِحُونَ ٥﴾.

﴿بِسۡمِ ٱللَّهِ ٱلرَّحۡمَٰنِ ٱلرَّحِيمِ: ٱللَّهُ لَآ إِلَٰهَ إِلَّا هُوَ ٱلۡحَيُّ ٱلۡقَيُّومُۚ لَا
تَأۡخُذُهُۥ سِنَةٞ وَلَا نَوۡمٞۚ لَّهُۥ مَا فِي ٱلسَّمَٰوَٰتِ وَمَا فِي ٱلۡأَرۡضِۗ مَن
ذَا ٱلَّذِي يَشۡفَعُ عِندَهُۥٓ إِلَّا بِإِذۡنِهِۦۚ يَعۡلَمُ مَا بَيۡنَ أَيۡدِيهِمۡ وَمَا
خَلۡفَهُمۡۖ وَلَا يُحِيطُونَ بِشَيۡءٖ مِّنۡ عِلۡمِهِۦٓ إِلَّا بِمَا شَآءَۚ وَسِعَ كُرۡسِيُّهُ
ٱلسَّمَٰوَٰتِ وَٱلۡأَرۡضَۖ وَلَا يَـُٔودُهُۥ حِفۡظُهُمَاۚ وَهُوَ ٱلۡعَلِيُّ ٱلۡعَظِيمُ﴾

Then say:

Subḥān Allāh – thirty-three times.

Glory be to Allah. Likewise:

Al-ḥamdu lillāh.

Praise be to Allah. Likewise:

Allāhu Akbar.

Allah is Greatest. Then say:

Lā ilāha illā Allāhu waḥdahū lā sharīka lah, lahū al-mulku wa lahū al-ḥamd, yuḥyī wa yumīt, wa huwa Ḥayyun lā yamūt, wa huwa ʿalā kulli shay'in Qadīr – ten times.

There is no god but Allah, only He, without associates. Praise and dominion are His. He gives life and death, and He is Ever Living and never dies. He is Powerful over all things.

Allahumma lā mâniʿa limā aʿṭayta, wa lā muʿṭiya limā manaʿta wa lā rādda limā qaḍayta wa lā yanfaʿu dhā al-jaddi minka al-jadd, tabārakta wa taʿālayt. Lā ilāha illā Allāhu waḥdahū lā sharīka lah, lahū al-mulku wa lahū al-ḥamd, yuḥyī wa yumīt, wa huwa ʿalā kulli shay'in Qadīr. Lā ḥawla wa lā quwwata illā billāh. Lā ilāha illā Allāhu wa lā naʿbudu illā iyyāh, lahū al-niʿmatu wa lahū al-faḍlu wa lahū al-thanā'u al-ḥasanu al-jamīl. Lā ilāha illā Allāhu mukhliṣīna lahū al-dīna wa law kariha al-kāfirūn.

Allah, there is no one who can withhold what You give, nor one who can give what You withhold, nor one who can reject what You decree. The affluence of the affluent cannot benefit them against You, Blessed and Exalted You are. There is no god but Allah, only He, without associates. Praise and dominion are His. He gives life and death, and He is Ever Living and never dies. He is Powerful over all things. There is no might nor strength save through Allah. There is no god but Allah, we worship none but Him. To Him are all blessings, bounties, and beautiful, goodly praises. There is no god but Allah, we dedicate our devotion solely to Him, however much the disbelievers hate it.

- ثُمَّ قُلْ: سُبْحَانَ اللهِ - ثَلَاثًا وَثَلَاثِينَ، وَكَذَلِكَ ٱلْحَمْدُ لِلهِ، وَكَذَلِكَ اَللهُ أَكْبَرُ، ثُمَّ قُلْ: لَا إِلٰهَ إِلَّا اللهُ وَحْدَهُ لَا شَرِيكَ لَهُ، لَهُ الْمُلْكُ وَلَهُ الْحَمْدُ، يُحْيِي وَيُمِيتُ، وَهُوَ حَيٌّ لَا يَمُوتُ، بِيَدِهِ الْخَيْرُ، وَهُوَ عَلَى كُلِّ شَيْءٍ قَدِيرٌ - عَشْرًا.

اَللّٰهُمَّ لَا مَانِعَ لِمَا أَعْطَيْتَ، وَلَا مُعْطِيَ لِمَا مَنَعْتَ، وَلَا رَادَّ لِمَا قَضَيْتَ، وَلَا يَنْفَعُ ذَا الْجَدِّ مِنْكَ الْجَدُّ، تَبَارَكْتَ وَتَعَالَيْتَ؛ لَا إِلٰهَ إِلَّا اللهُ وَحْدَهُ لَا شَرِيكَ لَهُ، لَهُ الْمُلْكُ، وَلَهُ الْحَمْدُ، يُحْيِي وَيُمِيتُ، وَهُوَ عَلَى كُلِّ شَيْءٍ قَدِيرٌ، لَا حَوْلَ وَلَا قُوَّةَ إِلَّا بِاللهِ، لَا إِلٰهَ إِلَّا اللهُ وَلَا نَعْبُدُ إِلَّا إِيَّاهُ، لَهُ النِّعْمَةُ وَلَهُ الْفَضْلُ وَلَهُ الثَّنَاءُ الْحَسَنُ الْجَمِيلُ، لَا إِلٰهَ إِلَّا اللهُ مُخْلِصِينَ لَهُ الدِّينَ وَلَوْ كَرِهَ الْكَافِرُونَ.

Bismillāhi al-Raḥmāni al-Raḥīm. Lillāhi mā fī al-samawāti wa mā fī al-arḍ, wa in tubdū mā fī anfusikum aw tukhfūhu yuḥāsibkum bihī Allāh, fa-yaghfiru li-man yashā'u wa yuʿadhdhibu man yashā', wa Allāhu alā kulli shay'in Qadīr. Āmana al-rasūlu bimā unzila ilayhi min Rabbihī wa al-mu'minūn. Kullun āmana billāhi wa malā'ikatihī wa kutubihī wa rusulihī lā nufarriqu bayna aḥadin min rusulih, wa qālū samiʿnā wa aṭaʿnā ghufrānaka Rabbanā wa ilayka al-maṣīr. Lā yukallifu Allāhu nafsan illā wusʿahā, lahā mā kasabat wa ʿalayhā mā iktasabat. Rabbanā lā tu'ākhidhnā in nasīnā aw akhṭa'nā, Rabbanā wa lā taḥmil ʿalaynā iṣran kamā ḥamaltahū ʿalā alladhīna min qablinā, Rabbanā wa lā tuḥammilnā mā lā ṭāqata lanā bih; wa uʿfu annā wa ighfir lanā wa irḥamnā. Anta Mawlānā fa-unṣurnā alā al-qawmi al-kāfirīn.

"To Allah [alone] belongs whatever is in the heavens and whatever is on the earth. Whether you reveal what is in your hearts or conceal it, Allah will call you to account for it. He forgives whoever He wills, and punishes whoever He wills. And Allah is Most Capable of everything. The Messenger [firmly] believes in what has been revealed to him from his Lord, and so do the believers. They [all] believe in Allah, His angels, His Books, and His messengers. [They proclaim] 'We make no distinction between any of His Messengers.' And they say, 'We hear and obey. [We seek] Your forgiveness, our Lord! And to you [alone] is the final return.' Allah does not require of any soul more than what it can afford. All good will be for its own benefit, and all evil will be to its own loss. [The believers pray] 'Our Lord! Do not punish us if we forget or make a mistake. Our Lord! Do not place a burden on us like the one you placed on those before us. Our Lord! Do not burden us with what we cannot bear. Pardon us, forgive us, and have mercy on us. You are our [only] Guardian. So grant us victory over the disbelieving people.'"[6]

---

6 *al-Baqarah*, 284-286.

﴿بِسۡمِ ٱللَّهِ ٱلرَّحۡمَٰنِ ٱلرَّحِيمِ:

لِّلَّهِ مَا فِي ٱلسَّمَٰوَٰتِ وَمَا فِي ٱلۡأَرۡضِۗ وَإِن تُبۡدُواْ مَا فِيٓ أَنفُسِكُمۡ
أَوۡ تُخۡفُوهُ يُحَاسِبۡكُم بِهِ ٱللَّهُۖ فَيَغۡفِرُ لِمَن يَشَآءُ وَيُعَذِّبُ مَن يَشَآءُۗ
وَٱللَّهُ عَلَىٰ كُلِّ شَيۡءٖ قَدِيرٌ ٢٨٤

ءَامَنَ ٱلرَّسُولُ بِمَآ أُنزِلَ إِلَيۡهِ مِن رَّبِّهِۦ وَٱلۡمُؤۡمِنُونَۚ كُلٌّ ءَامَنَ بِٱللَّهِ
وَمَلَٰٓئِكَتِهِۦ وَكُتُبِهِۦ وَرُسُلِهِۦ لَا نُفَرِّقُ بَيۡنَ أَحَدٖ مِّن رُّسُلِهِۦۚ وَقَالُواْ
سَمِعۡنَا وَأَطَعۡنَاۖ غُفۡرَانَكَ رَبَّنَا وَإِلَيۡكَ ٱلۡمَصِيرُ ٢٨٥

لَا يُكَلِّفُ ٱللَّهُ نَفۡسًا إِلَّا وُسۡعَهَاۚ لَهَا مَا كَسَبَتۡ وَعَلَيۡهَا مَا
ٱكۡتَسَبَتۡۗ رَبَّنَا لَا تُؤَاخِذۡنَآ إِن نَّسِينَآ أَوۡ أَخۡطَأۡنَاۚ رَبَّنَا وَلَا تَحۡمِلۡ
عَلَيۡنَآ إِصۡرٗا كَمَا حَمَلۡتَهُۥ عَلَى ٱلَّذِينَ مِن قَبۡلِنَاۚ رَبَّنَا وَلَا تُحَمِّلۡنَا
مَا لَا طَاقَةَ لَنَا بِهِۦۖ وَٱعۡفُ عَنَّا وَٱغۡفِرۡ لَنَا وَٱرۡحَمۡنَآۚ أَنتَ مَوۡلَىٰنَا
فَٱنصُرۡنَا عَلَى ٱلۡقَوۡمِ ٱلۡكَٰفِرِينَ ٢٨٦﴾.

Bismillāhi al-Raḥmāni al-Raḥīm. Shahida Allāhu annahū lā ilāha illā huwa wa al-malā'ikatu wa ulū al-ʿilmi qā'iman bil-qisṭ, lā ilāha illā huwa al-ʿAzīzu al-Ḥakīm. Wa ana ashhadu bimā shahida Allāhu taʿālā bih, wa astawdiʿu Allāha taʿālā hādhihī al-shahādah, wa hiya lī wadīʿatun ʿinda Allāhi taʿālā.

"Allah [Himself] is a Witness that there is no god [worthy of worship] except Him – and so are the angels and people of knowledge. He is the Maintainer of justice. There is no god [worthy of worship] except Him – the Almighty, All-Wise."[7] I bear witness to what Allah, Exalted, bore witness to. I deposit this testimony to Allah, Exalted, and it is a trust for me with Allah.[8]

Allāhumma uktubnā maʿa al-shāhidīn.

Allah, write us among those who bear witness [to truth].

Allāhumma Rabbanā wa Rabba kulli shay', ana shahīdun annaka al-Rabbu waḥdaka lā sharīka lak.

Allah, our Lord and the Lord of all things, I am a witness that You are the Lord, only You, without associates.

Allāhumma Rabbanā wa Rabba kulli shay', ana shahīdun anna sayyidanā Muḥammadan ṣallā Allāhu ʿalayhi wa sallama ʿabduka wa rasūluk.

Allah, our Lord and the Lord of all things, I am a witness that our Master Muhammad ﷺ is Your slave and Messenger.

Allāhumma Rabbanā wa Rabba kulli shay', ana shahīdun anna al-ʿibāda kullahum ikhwah.

Allah, our Lord and the Lord of all things, I am a witness that the slaves are all brothers.

---

7 Āl *Imrān*, 18

8 It is reported in Ṭabarānī and others, that he ﷺ said: "The one who made this testimony is brought forth on the Day of Reckoning, then Allah says: 'My slave has made a vow with me, and I have most right to fulfil vows – enter my slave into the Garden.'"

﴿بِسۡمِ ٱللَّهِ ٱلرَّحۡمَٰنِ ٱلرَّحِيمِ: شَهِدَ ٱللَّهُ أَنَّهُۥ لَآ إِلَٰهَ إِلَّا هُوَ وَٱلۡمَلَٰٓئِكَةُ وَأُوْلُواْ ٱلۡعِلۡمِ قَآئِمَۢا بِٱلۡقِسۡطِۚ لَآ إِلَٰهَ إِلَّا هُوَ ٱلۡعَزِيزُ ٱلۡحَكِيمُ﴾

وَأَنَا أَشْهَدُ بِمَا شَهِدَ اللهُ تَعَالَىٰ بِهِ، وَأَسْتَوْدِعُ اللهَ تَعَالَىٰ هَذِهِ الشَّهَادَةَ، وَهِيَ لِي وَدِيعَةٌ عِنْدَ اللهِ تَعَالَىٰ[٣].

اَللّٰهُمَ اكْتُبْنَا مَعَ الشَّاهِدِينَ.

اَللّٰهُمَّ رَبَّنَا وَرَبَّ كُلِّ شَيْءٍ أَنَا شَهِيدٌ أَنَّكَ الرَّبُّ وَحْدَكَ لَا شَرِيكَ لَكَ.
اَللّٰهُمَّ رَبَّنَا وَرَبَّ كُلِّ شَيْءٍ أَنَا شَهِيدٌ أَنَّ سَيِّدَنَا مُحَمَّدًا ﷺ عَبْدُكَ وَرَسُولُكَ.

اَللّٰهُمَّ رَبَّنَا وَرَبَّ كُلِّ شَيْءٍ أَنَا شَهِيدٌ أَنَّ الْعِبَادَ كُلَّهُمْ إِخْوَةٌ.

---

(٣) جَاءَ فِي الطَّبَرَانِيِّ وَغَيْرِهِ عَنْهُ ﷺ: « أَنَّ هَذِهِ الشَّهَادَةَ يُجَاءُ بِصَاحِبِهَا يَوْمَ الْقِيَامَةِ فَيَقُولُ اللهُ عَزَّ وَجَلَّ: عَبْدِي عَهِدَ إِلَيَّ وَأَنَا أَحَقُّ مَنْ وَفَّى بِالْعَهْدِ - أَدْخِلُوا عَبْدِي الْجَنَّةَ ».

Allāhumma Rabbanā wa Rabba kulli shay', ijʿalnī mukhliṣan laka wa ahlī fī kulli sāʿatin min al-dunyā wa al-ākhirah. Yā Dhā al-jalāli wa al-ikrām, ismaʿ wa-istajib. Allāhu Akbar, Allāhu Akbar, Allāhu Akbar. Allāhu Nūru al-samāwāti wal-arḍ. Allāhu Akbar, ḥasbiya Allāhu wa niʿma al-Wakīl. Allāhu Akbar, Allāhu Akbar.

Allah, our Lord and the Lord of all things, make me and my family sincere to You in every hour of this life and the next. Owner of majesty and generosity, hear [my call] and answer [it]. Allah is Greatest, Allah is Greatest, Allah is Greatest. "Allah is the Light of the heavens and the earth." Allah is Most Grand, Allah is sufficient for us, most excellent is He in Whom we trust. Allah is Greatest, Allah is Greatest.

Allāhumma innī aṣbaḥtu ushhiduka wa ushhidu ḥamalata ʿarshika wa malā'ikataka wa jamīʿa khalqika annaka anta Allāh, lā ilāha illā anta waḥdaka lā sharīka lak, wa anna sayyidanā Muḥammadan ʿabduka wa rasūluk – four times.

Allah, I enter a new morning calling upon You, the bearers of Your Throne, Your angels, and all of creation to bear witness that surely You are Allah, there is none worthy of worship but You alone without partners; and that our Master Muhammad ﷺ is Your slave and Messenger.

Bismillāhi al-Raḥmāni al-Raḥīm. Qul Allāhumma Mālika al-mulki tu'tī al-mulka man tashā'u wa tanziʿu al-mulka min man tashā', wa tuʿizzu man tashā'u wa tudhillu man tashā'u bi-yadika al-khayru innaka ʿalā kulli shay'in Qadīr. Tūliju al-layla fī al-nahāri wa tūliju al-nahāra fī al-layli wa tukhriju al-ḥayya min al-mayyiti wa tukhriju al-mayyita min al-ḥayyi wa tarzuqu man tashā'u bi-ghayri ḥisāb.

"Say [O Prophet], 'O Allah! Lord over all authorities! You give authority to whoever You please and remove it from who You please; You honour whoever You please and disgrace who You please – all good is in Your Hands. Surely You [alone] are Most Capable of everything. You cause the night to pass into the day and the day into the night. You bring forth the living from the dead and the dead from the living. And You provide for whoever You will without limit.'"

اَللّٰهُمَّ رَبَّنَا وَرَبَّ كُلِّ شَيْءٍ اجْعَلْنِي مُخْلِصًا لَكَ وَأَهْلِي فِي كُلِّ سَاعَةٍ مِنَ الدُّنْيَا وَالْآخِرَةِ؛ يَا ذَا الْجَلَالِ وَالْإِكْرَامِ اسْمَعْ وَاسْتَجِبْ، اَللّٰهُ أَكْبَرُ، اَللّٰهُ أَكْبَرُ، اَللّٰهُ أَكْبَرُ، ﴿ٱللَّهُ نُورُ ٱلسَّمَٰوَٰتِ وَٱلْأَرْضِ﴾، اَللّٰهُ أَكْبَرُ، حَسْبِيَ اللّٰهُ وَنِعْمَ الْوَكِيلُ، اَللّٰهُ أَكْبَرُ اَللّٰهُ أَكْبَرُ.

اَللّٰهُمَّ إِنِّيْ أَصْبَحْتُ أُشْهِدُكَ وَأُشْهِدُ حَمَلَةَ عَرْشِكَ وَمَلَائِكَتَكَ وَجَمِيعَ خَلْقِكَ؛ أَنَّكَ أَنْتَ اللّٰهُ لَا إِلَهَ إِلَّا أَنْتَ وَحْدَكَ لَا شَرِيكَ لَكَ، وَأَنَّ سَيِّدَنَا مُحَمَّدًا عَبْدُكَ وَرَسُولُكَ(٤) - أَرْبَعَ مَرَّاتٍ.

﴿بِسْمِ ٱللَّهِ ٱلرَّحْمَٰنِ ٱلرَّحِيمِ: قُلِ ٱللَّهُمَّ مَٰلِكَ ٱلْمُلْكِ تُؤْتِى ٱلْمُلْكَ مَن تَشَآءُ وَتَنزِعُ ٱلْمُلْكَ مِمَّن تَشَآءُ وَتُعِزُّ مَن تَشَآءُ وَتُذِلُّ مَن تَشَآءُ ۖ بِيَدِكَ ٱلْخَيْرُ ۖ إِنَّكَ عَلَىٰ كُلِّ شَىْءٍ قَدِيرٌ ﴿٢٦﴾ تُولِجُ ٱلَّيْلَ فِى ٱلنَّهَارِ وَتُولِجُ ٱلنَّهَارَ فِى ٱلَّيْلِ ۖ وَتُخْرِجُ ٱلْحَىَّ مِنَ ٱلْمَيِّتِ وَتُخْرِجُ ٱلْمَيِّتَ مِنَ ٱلْحَىِّ ۖ وَتَرْزُقُ مَن تَشَآءُ بِغَيْرِ حِسَابٍ ﴿٢٧﴾﴾.

(٤) رَوَاهُ أَبُوْ دَاوُدَ وَالتِّرْمِذِيُّ عَنْ أَنَسٍ رَضِيَ اللّٰهُ عَنْهُ مَرْفُوعًا، وَفِي رِوَايَةِ أَبِي دَاوُدَ أَنَّ مَنْ قَالَهَا أَرْبَعًا أَعْتَقَهُ اللّٰهُ مِنَ النَّارِ.

Allāhumma urzuqnā wa anta Khayru al-rāziqīn.

Allah, provide for us; You are surely the Best Provider.

Bismillāhi al-Raḥmāni al-Raḥīm. Ḥasbiya Allāhu lā ilāha illā huwa ʿalayhi tawakkaltu wa huwa Rabbu al-ʿarshi al-ʿaẓīm - seven times.[9]

"Allah is sufficient for me. There is no god [worthy of worship] except Him. In Him I put my trust. And He is the Lord of the Mighty Throne."[10]

Bismillāhi al-Raḥmāni al-Raḥīm. Innī tawakkaltu ʿalā Allāhi Rabbī wa Rabbikum mā min dābbatin illā huwa ākhidhun bi-nāṣiyatihā, inna Rabbī ʿalā ṣirāṭin mustaqīm. Tawakkaltu ʿala al-Ḥayyi alladhī lā yamūt. Al-ḥamdu lillāhi alladhī lam yattakhidh waladan wa lam yakun lahū sharīkun fī al-mulki wa lam yakun lahū waliyyun min al-dhulli wa kabbirhu takbīrā.[11]

"I have put my trust in Allah - my Lord and your Lord. There is no living creature that is not completely under His control. Surely my Lord's Way is perfect justice."[12] "I put my trust in the Ever-Living, Who never dies."[13] "All praise is for Allah. Who has never had [any] offspring; nor does He have a partner in [governing] the kingdom; nor is He pathetic, needing a protector. And revere Him immensely."[14]

---

9 Whoever says this in the day or night seven times, Allah will suffice him from his concerns. Abū Dāwūd on the authority of Abū al-Dardā' ﷺ.

10 *al-Tawbah*, 129.

11 Whoever recites this, Allah will do away with his ailments and afflictions (Abū Yaʿlā and others).

12 *Hūd*, 56.

13 *al-Furqān*, 58.

14 *al-Isrā'*, 111.

اَللّٰهُمَّ ارْزُقْنَا وَأَنْتَ خَيْرُ الرَّازِقِينَ.

﴿بِسۡمِ ٱللَّهِ ٱلرَّحۡمَٰنِ ٱلرَّحِيمِ: حَسۡبِيَ ٱللَّهُ لَآ إِلَٰهَ إِلَّا هُوَۖ عَلَيۡهِ تَوَكَّلۡتُۖ وَهُوَ رَبُّ ٱلۡعَرۡشِ ٱلۡعَظِيمِ﴾ - سَبْعَ مَرَّاتٍ -(٥).

﴿بِسۡمِ ٱللَّهِ ٱلرَّحۡمَٰنِ ٱلرَّحِيمِ: إِنِّي تَوَكَّلۡتُ عَلَى ٱللَّهِ رَبِّي وَرَبِّكُمۚ مَّا مِن دَآبَّةٍ إِلَّا هُوَ ءَاخِذُۢ بِنَاصِيَتِهَآۚ إِنَّ رَبِّي عَلَىٰ صِرَٰطٖ مُّسۡتَقِيمٖ﴾

• ﴿وَتَوَكَّلۡ عَلَى ٱلۡحَيِّ ٱلَّذِي لَا يَمُوتُ﴾ •

﴿ٱلۡحَمۡدُ لِلَّهِ ٱلَّذِي لَمۡ يَتَّخِذۡ وَلَدٗا وَلَمۡ يَكُن لَّهُۥ شَرِيكٞ فِي ٱلۡمُلۡكِ وَلَمۡ يَكُن لَّهُۥ وَلِيّٞ مِّنَ ٱلذُّلِّۖ وَكَبِّرۡهُ تَكۡبِيرَۢا﴾(٦).

---

(٥) مَنْ قَالَهَا حِينَ يُصْبِحُ وَحِينَ يُمْسِي - سَبْعاً - كَفَاهُ اللهُ مَا أَهَمَّهُ، كَمَا فِي أَبِي دَاوُدَ عَنْ أَبِي الدَّرْدَاءِ رضي الله عنه.

(٦) مَنْ قَرَأَ ذَلِكَ أَذْهَبَ اللهُ عَنْهُ السَّقَمَ وَالضُّرَّ كَمَا رَوَاهُ أَبُو يَعْلَى وَغَيْرُهُ.

Bismillāhi al-Raḥmāni al-Raḥīm. Fa-subḥān Allāhi ḥīna tumsūna wa ḥīna tuṣbiḥūn, wa lahū al-ḥamdu fī al-samāwati wa al-arḍi wa ʿashiyyan wa ḥīna tuẓhirūn. Yukhriju al-ḥayya min al-mayyiti wa yukhriju al-mayyita min al-ḥayyi wa yuḥyī al-arḍa baʿda mawtihā wa kadhālika tukhrajūn.[15]

"So glorify Allah in the evening and in the morning – all praise is for Him in the heavens and the earth – as well as in the afternoon, and at noon. He brings forth the living from the dead and the dead from the living. And He gives life to the earth after its death. And so will you be brought forth [from the grave]."[16]

Bismillāhi al-Raḥmāni al-Raḥīm. Inna Allāha wa malā'ikatahū yuṣallūna ʿala al-nabiyy; yā ayyuha alladhīna āmanū ṣallū ʿalayhi wa sallimū taslīmā.

"Indeed, Allah showers His blessings upon the Prophet, and His angels pray for him. O believers! Invoke Allah's blessings upon him, and salute him with worthy greetings of peace."[17]

Allāhumma ṣalli ʿalā sayyidinā Muḥammadin wa ʿalā āli sayyidinā Muḥammadin kamā ṣallayta ʿalā sayyidinā Ibrāhīm wa ʿalā āli sayyidinā Ibrāhīm, fī al-ʿālamīna innaka Ḥamīdun Majīd; wa bārik ʿalā sayyidinā Muḥammadin wa ʿalā āli sayyidinā Muḥammadin kamā bārakta ʿalā sayyidinā Ibrāhīm wa ʿalā āli sayyidinā Ibrāhīm, fī al-ʿālamīna innaka Ḥamīdun Majīd – ʿadada khalqika wa riḍā'a nafsika wa zinata ʿarshika wa midāda kalimātika kullamā dhakaraka al-dhākirūna wa ghafala an dhikrika al-ghāfilūn, wa kamā tuḥibbuhū wa tarḍāhu li-ḥabībika wa ālihī wa khalīlika wa ālih.

Allah, confer Your exaltations in all worlds upon our Master Muhammad and the family of our Master Muhammad as you have conferred upon our Master Ibrāhīm and the family of our Master Ibrāhīm. Truly, You are Praiseworthy and Glorious. Allah, confer your blessings in all worlds upon

15 Whoever recites this during the day will reap what he missed out on from it, and whoever recites it during the night will apprehend what he missed out on from it. Ṭabarānī and others.

16 *al-Rūm*, 17-19.

17 *al-Aḥzāb*, 56.

﴿بِسۡمِ ٱللَّهِ ٱلرَّحۡمَٰنِ ٱلرَّحِيمِ: فَسُبۡحَٰنَ ٱللَّهِ حِينَ تُمۡسُونَ وَحِينَ
تُصۡبِحُونَ ١٧ وَلَهُ ٱلۡحَمۡدُ فِي ٱلسَّمَٰوَٰتِ وَٱلۡأَرۡضِ وَعَشِيّٗا وَحِينَ
تُظۡهِرُونَ ١٨ يُخۡرِجُ ٱلۡحَيَّ مِنَ ٱلۡمَيِّتِ وَيُخۡرِجُ ٱلۡمَيِّتَ مِنَ ٱلۡحَيِّ
وَيُحۡيِ ٱلۡأَرۡضَ بَعۡدَ مَوۡتِهَاۚ وَكَذَٰلِكَ تُخۡرَجُونَ ١٩﴾(٧).

﴿بِسۡمِ ٱللَّهِ ٱلرَّحۡمَٰنِ ٱلرَّحِيمِ: إِنَّ ٱللَّهَ وَمَلَٰٓئِكَتَهُۥ يُصَلُّونَ عَلَى ٱلنَّبِيِّۚ
يَٰٓأَيُّهَا ٱلَّذِينَ ءَامَنُواْ صَلُّواْ عَلَيۡهِ وَسَلِّمُواْ تَسۡلِيمًا﴾.

اَللّٰهُمَّ صَلِّ عَلَى سَيِّدِنا مُحَمَّدٍ وَعَلَى آلِ سَيِّدِنا مُحَمَّدٍ، كَمَا صَلَّيْتَ عَلَى إِبْرَاهِيمَ وَعَلَى آلِ سَيِّدِنَا إِبْرَاهِيمَ، إِنَّكَ حَمِيدٌ مَّجِيدٌ، وَبَارِكْ عَلَى سَيِّدِنَا مُحَمَّدٍ وَعَلَى آلِ سَيِّدِنَا مُحَمَّدٍ، كَمَا بَارَكْتَ عَلَى سَيِّدِنَا إِبْرَاهِيمَ وَعَلَى آلِ سَيِّدِنَا إِبْرَاهِيمَ، فِي الْعَالَمِينَ إِنَّكَ حَمِيدٌ مَّجِيدٌ - عَدَدَ خَلْقِكَ وَرِضَاءَ نَفْسِكَ، وَزِنَةَ عَرْشِكَ، وَمِدَادَ كَلِمَاتِكَ، كُلَّمَا ذَكَرَكَ الذَّاكِرُونَ وَغَفَلَ عَنْ ذِكْرِكَ الْغَافِلُونَ، وَكَمَا تُحِبُّهُ وَتَرْضَاهُ لِحَبِيبِكَ وَآلِهِ وَخَلِيلِكَ وَآلِهِ.

(٧) مَنْ قَرَأَ ذَلِكَ حِينَ يُصْبِحُ أَدْرَكَ مَا فَاتَهُ فِي يَوْمِهِ، وَمَنْ قَرَأَ ذَلِكَ حِينَ يُمْسِي أَدْرَكَ مَا فَاتَهُ فِي لَيْلَتِهِ؛ كَمَا فِي حَدِيثِ الطَّبَرَانِيِّ وَغَيْرِهِ.

our Master Muhammad and the family of our Master Muhammad, as you have blessed our Master Ibrāhīm and the family of our Master Ibrāhīm. Truly, You are Praiseworthy and Glorious. This, as many times as is equal to the number of Your creatures, the satisfaction of Your Self, the weight of Your Throne, and the ink-worth of all Your words – whenever the mindful remember You and the heedless forget You, as You love and please for Your Beloved and his family and Your Intimate Friend and his family.

Allāhumma innī as'aluka bi-nūri wajh Allāhi al-ʿAẓīm, alladhī mala'a arkāna ʿarshi Allāhi al-ʿAẓīm, wa qāmat bihī ʿawālimu Allāhi al-ʿAẓīm, an tuṣalliya alā mawlānā Muḥammadin dhī al-qadri al-ʿaẓīm, wa ʿalā āli nabiyyi Allāhi al-ʿaẓīm, bi-qadri ʿaẓamati dhāti Allāhi al-ʿAẓīm, fī kulli lamḥatin wa nafasin ʿadada mā fī ʿilmi Allāhi al-ʿAẓīm, ṣalātan dā'imatan bi-dawāmi Allahi al-ʿAẓīm, taʿẓīman li-ḥaqqika yā mawlānā yā Muḥammadu yā dhā al-khuluqi al-ʿaẓīm, wa sallim ʿalayhi wa ʿalā ālihī mithla dhālik, wa ijmaʿ baynī wa baynahū kamā jamaʿta bayna al-rūḥi wa al-nafs, ẓāhiran wa bāṭinā, yaqaẓatan wa manāmā, wa ijʿalhu yā Rabbi rūḥan li-dhātī min jamīʿi al-wujūhi fī al-dunyā wa al-ākhirah.

Allah, I ask you by the Light of Allah's Face, the Great, which has filled the corners of the Throne of Allah the Great, and through which the realms of Allah the Great are established, that you confer exaltations upon our Master Muhmmad, possessor of great status, and upon the family of the Great Prophet of Allah. I ask You to do this in a way that is befitting of Allah's mighty essence, the Great. That you do so at every moment and with every breath, in an amount equal to the knowledge of Allah the Great – an eternal exaltation that is as eternal as Allah the Great. This is an extolment of your right, our Master Muhammad, possessor of great character. Confer greetings upon him and his family in the same way, and gather us together as You have gathered between the spirit and the self, manifestly and inwardly, in wakefulness and sleep. Allah, Most Great, make him the spirit to my essence in every way, in this life before the next.

اَللّٰهُمَّ إِنِّي أَسْأَلُكَ بِنُورِ وَجْهِ اللّٰهِ الْعَظِيمِ، الَّذِي مَلَأَ أَرْكَانَ عَرْشِ اللّٰهِ الْعَظِيمِ، وَقَامَتْ بِهِ عَوَالِمُ اللّٰهِ الْعَظِيمِ، أَنْ تُصَلِّيَ عَلَى مَوْلَانَا مُحَمَّدٍ ذِي الْقَدْرِ الْعَظِيمِ،

وَعَلَى آلِ نَبِيِّ اللّٰهِ الْعَظِيمِ، بِقَدْرِ عَظَمَةِ ذَاتِ اللّٰهِ الْعَظِيمِ، فِي كُلِّ لَمْحَةٍ وَنَفَسٍ عَدَدَ مَا فِي عِلْمِ اللّٰهِ الْعَظِيمِ، صَلَاةً دَائِمَةً بِدَوَامِ اللّٰهِ الْعَظِيمِ، تَعْظِيمًا لِحَقِّكَ يَا مَوْلَانَا يَا مُحَمَّدُ يَا ذَا الْخُلُقِ الْعَظِيمِ،

وَسَلِّمْ عَلَيْهِ وَعَلَى آلِهِ مِثْلَ ذَلِكَ،

وَاجْمَعْ بَيْنِي وَبَيْنَهُ كَمَا جَمَعْتَ بَيْنَ الرُّوحِ وَالنَّفْسِ،

ظَاهِرًا وَبَاطِنًا يَقْظَةً وَمَنَامًا، وَاجْعَلْهُ يَا رَبِّ رُوحًا لِذَاتِي مِنْ جَمِيعِ الْوُجُوهِ فِي الدُّنْيَا قَبْلَ الْآخِرَةِ يَا عَظِيمُ.

Allāhumma ṣalli ṣalātan kāmilatan, wa sallim salāman tāmman ʿalā sayyidinā Muḥammadin alladhī tanḥallu bihī al-ʿuqad, wa tanfariju bihī al-kurab, wa tanqaḍī bihī al-ḥawāʾij, wa tunālu bihī al-raghāʾib, wa ḥusnu al-khawātim, wa yustasqā al-ghamāmu bi-wajhihī al-karīm, wa ʿalā ālihī wa ṣaḥbihī fī kulli lamḥatin wa nafasin bi-ʿadadi kulli maʿlūmin lak.

Allah, confer perfect exaltations and complete greetings of peace upon our Master Muhammad through whom knots are undone, calamities are uplifted, needs are fulfilled, and wants as well as good endings are realized. Through his noble face the release of rain clouds is sought. Likewise upon his family and Companions at every moment and with every breath, in accordance with all that is known to You.

Allāhumma ṣalli ʿalā sayyidinā Muḥammadin miftaḥi khazāʾinik. Allāhumma iftaḥ lanā bi-sayyidinā Muḥammadin mā ughliqa ʿalaynā.

Allah, confer Your exaltations upon our Master Muhammad, the key to Your stores. Allah, open for us through our Master Muhammad that which has been locked.

Allāhumma ṣalli ʿalā sayyidinā Muḥammadin al-nabiyyi al-ummiyyi wa ʿalā ālihī wa ṣaḥbihī wa sallim taslīmā.

Allah, confer Your exaltations upon our Master Muhammad the Unlettered Prophet, his family, and his Companions. Confer also upon them greetings of perfect peace.

Bismillāhi al-Raḥmāni al-Raḥīm. Ḥā-Mīm. Tanzīlu al-kitābi min Allāhi al-ʿAzizi al-ʿAlīm. Ghāfiri al-dhanbi wa Qābili al-tawbi Shadīdi al-ʿiqābi Dhī al-ṭawli lā ilāha illā huwa ilayi al-maṣīr.

"Ḥā Mīm. The revelation of this Book is from Allah – the Almighty, All-Knowing, the Forgiver of sin and Accepter of repentance, the Severe in punishment, and Infinite in bounty. There is no god [worthy of worship] except Him. To Him [alone] is the final return."[18]

---

18 *Ghāfir*, 1-3.

اَللّٰهُمَّ صَلِّ صَلَاةً كَامِلَةً، وَسَلِّمْ سَلَامًا تَامًّا عَلَى سَيِّدِنَا مُحَمَّدٍ الَّذِي تَنْحَلُّ بِهِ الْعُقَدُ، وَتَنْفَرِجُ بِهِ الْكُرَبُ، وَتُقْضَى بِهِ الْحَوَائِجُ، وَتُنَالُ بِهِ الرَّغَائِبُ، وَحُسْنُ الْخَوَاتِمِ، وَيُسْتَسْقَى الْغَمَامُ بِوَجْهِهِ الْكَرِيمِ، وَعَلَى آلِهِ وَصَحْبِهِ فِي كُلِّ لَمْحَةٍ وَنَفَسٍ بِعَدَدِ كُلِّ مَعْلُومٍ لَكَ.

اَللّٰهُمَّ صَلِّ عَلَى سَيِّدِنَا مُحَمَّدٍ مِفْتَاحِ خَزَائِنِكَ، اَللّٰهُمَّ افْتَحْ لَنَا بِسَيِّدِنَا مُحَمَّدٍ مَا أُغْلِقَ عَلَيْنَا.

اَللّٰهُمَّ صَلِّ عَلَى سَيِّدِنَا مُحَمَّدٍ النَّبِيِّ الْأُمِّيِّ وَعَلَى آلِهِ وَصَحْبِهِ وَسَلِّمْ تَسْلِيمًا.

﴿بِسۡمِ ٱللَّهِ ٱلرَّحۡمَٰنِ ٱلرَّحِيمِ: حمٓ ١ تَنزِيلُ ٱلۡكِتَٰبِ مِنَ ٱللَّهِ ٱلۡعَزِيزِ ٱلۡعَلِيمِ ٢ غَافِرِ ٱلذَّنۢبِ وَقَابِلِ ٱلتَّوۡبِ شَدِيدِ ٱلۡعِقَابِ ذِي ٱلطَّوۡلِۖ لَآ إِلَٰهَ إِلَّا هُوَۖ إِلَيۡهِ ٱلۡمَصِيرُ ٣﴾.

Yā Ghāfira al-dhanbi ighfir lī, yā Qābila al-tawbi taqabbal tawbatī, yā Shadīda al-ʿiqābi lā tuʿāqibnī, yā Dhā al-ṭawli taṭawwal ʿalayya bi-raḥmatin.[19]

Forgiver of sin, forgive my sins. Accepter of repentance, accept my repentance. Severe in punishment, do not punish me. Infinite in bounty, be bountiful towards me with mercy.

Bismillāhi al-Raḥmāni al-Raḥīm. Sabbaḥa lillāhi mā fī al-samāwāti wa al-arḍi wa huwa al-ʿAzīzu al-Ḥakīm; lahū mulku al-samāwāti wa al-arḍi wa huwa ʿalā kulli shayʾin Qadīr. Huwa al-Awwalu wa al-Ākhiru wa al-Ẓāhiru wa al-Bāṭinu wa huwa bi-kulli shayʾin ʿAlīm. Huwa alladhī khalaqa al-samāwāti wa al-arḍa fī sittati ayyāmin thumma istawā ʿalā al-ʿarsh; yaʿlamu mā yaliju fī al-arḍi wa mā yakhruju minhā wa mā yanzilu min al-samāʾi wa mā yaʿruju fīhā, wa huwa maʿakum aynamā kuntum; wa Allāhu bimā taʿmalūna Baṣīr. Lahū mulku al-samāwāti wa al-arḍi wa huwa ʿAlīmun bi-dhāti al-ṣudur.

"Whatever is in the heavens and the earth glorifies Allah, for He is the Almighty, All-Wise. To Him belongs the kingdom of the heavens and the earth. He gives life and causes death. And He is Most Capable of everything. He is the First and the Last, the Most High and Most Near, and He has [perfect] knowledge of all things. He is the One Who created the heavens and the earth in six Days, then established Himself on the Throne. He knows whatever goes into the earth and whatever comes out of it, and whatever descends from the sky and whatever ascends into it. And He is with you wherever you are. For Allah is All-Seeing of what you do."[20]

---

19   This wording was taught by Ilyās 🙴 to Thābit al-Bunānī whilst in a state of wakefulness (Ibn Abī al-Dunyā).

20   *al-Ḥadīd*, 1-4.

يَا غَافِرَ الذَّنْبِ اغْفِرْ لِي ذَنْبِي، يَا قَابِلَ التَّوْبِ تَقَبَّلْ تَوْبَتِي، يَا شَدِيدَ الْعِقَابِ لَا تُعَاقِبْنِي، يَا ذَا الطَّوْلِ تَطَوَّلْ عَلَيَّ بِرَحْمَةٍ(٨).

﴿بِسۡمِ ٱللَّهِ ٱلرَّحۡمَٰنِ ٱلرَّحِيمِ﴾

﴿سَبَّحَ لِلَّهِ مَا فِي ٱلسَّمَٰوَٰتِ وَٱلۡأَرۡضِۖ وَهُوَ ٱلۡعَزِيزُ ٱلۡحَكِيمُ ١
لَهُۥ مُلۡكُ ٱلسَّمَٰوَٰتِ وَٱلۡأَرۡضِۖ يُحۡيِۦ وَيُمِيتُۖ وَهُوَ عَلَىٰ كُلِّ شَيۡءٖ
قَدِيرٌ ٢ هُوَ ٱلۡأَوَّلُ وَٱلۡأٓخِرُ وَٱلظَّٰهِرُ وَٱلۡبَاطِنُۖ وَهُوَ بِكُلِّ شَيۡءٍ عَلِيمٌ
٣ هُوَ ٱلَّذِي خَلَقَ ٱلسَّمَٰوَٰتِ وَٱلۡأَرۡضَ فِي سِتَّةِ أَيَّامٖ ثُمَّ ٱسۡتَوَىٰ
عَلَى ٱلۡعَرۡشِۖ يَعۡلَمُ مَا يَلِجُ فِي ٱلۡأَرۡضِ وَمَا يَخۡرُجُ مِنۡهَا وَمَا يَنزِلُ
مِنَ ٱلسَّمَآءِ وَمَا يَعۡرُجُ فِيهَاۖ وَهُوَ مَعَكُمۡ أَيۡنَ مَا كُنتُمۡۚ وَٱللَّهُ بِمَا
تَعۡمَلُونَ بَصِيرٞ ٤ لَّهُۥ مُلۡكُ ٱلسَّمَٰوَٰتِ وَٱلۡأَرۡضِۚ وَإِلَى ٱللَّهِ تُرۡجَعُ
ٱلۡأُمُورُ ٥ يُولِجُ ٱلَّيۡلَ فِي ٱلنَّهَارِ وَيُولِجُ ٱلنَّهَارَ فِي ٱلَّيۡلِۚ وَهُوَ عَلِيمُۢ
بِذَاتِ ٱلصُّدُورِ ٦﴾.

(٨) هَذِهِ الصِّيْغَةُ عَلَّمَهَا إِلْيَاسُ عَلَيْهِ السَّلَامُ لِثَابِتٍ الْبَنَانِيِّ يَقْظَةً كَمَا رَوَاهُ ابْنُ أَبِي الدُّنْيَا.

Allāhumma Rabba al-samāwāti al-sabʿi wa Rabba al-ʿarshi al-ʿaẓīm, Rabbanā wa Rabba kulli shay', Munzila al-tawrāti wa al-injīli wa al-furqān, Fāliqa al-iṣbāḥi wa al-nawā, aʿūdhu bika min sharri kulli shay'in anta ākhidhun bi-nāṣiyatih, anta al-Awwalu fa-laysa qablaka shay', wa anta al-Ākhiru fa-laysa baʿdaka shay', wa anta al-Ẓāhiru fa-laysa fawqaka shay', wa anta al-Bāṭinu fa-laysa dūnaka shay', iqḍi ʿannī al-dayna wa aghninī min al-faqr.

Allah, Lord of the seven heavens and Lord of the Great Throne, our Lord and Lord of all things, You are the One Who revealed the Torah, the Gospel, and the Criterion (*Furqān*). You are the One Who causes seeds and fruit stones to sprout. I seek refuge in You from the evil of all things under Your control. You are the First, such that there is nothing before You, and You are the Last, such that there is nothing after You. You are the Most High, such that there is nothing above You, and You are The Most Near, such that there is nothing closer than You. Fulfill my debts for me and suffice me from poverty.

Aʿūdhu billāhi al-Samīʿi al-ʿAlīmi min al-shayṭāni al-rajīm – three times.

I seek refuge in Allah the All Hearing, the All Knowing, from the accursed devil.

Bismillāhi al-Raḥmāni al-Raḥīm. Huwa Allāhu alladhī lā ilāha illā huwa ʿĀlimu al-ghaybi wa al-shahādah, huwa al-Raḥmānu al-Raḥīm. Huwa Allāhu alladhī lā ilāha illā huwa al-Maliku al-Quddūsu al-Salāmu al-Mu'minu al-Muhayminu al-ʿAzīzu al-Jabbāru al-Mutakabbir, subḥān Allāhi ʿammā yushrikūn. Huwa Allāhu al-Khāliqu al-Bāri'u al-Muṣawwiru lahū al-asmā'u al-ḥusnā, yusabbiḥu lahū mā fī al-samawāti wa al-arḍi wa huwa al-ʿAzīzu al-Ḥakīm.

"He is Allah – there is no god [worthy of worship] except Him: Knower of the seen and unseen. He is the Most Compassionate, Most Merciful. He is Allah – there is no god except Him: the King, the Most Holy, the All-Perfect, the Source of Serenity, the Watcher [of all], the Almighty, the Supreme in Might, the Majestic. Glorified is Allah far above what they associate with Him [in worship]! He is Allah: the Creator, the Inventor, the Shaper. He [alone] has the Most Beautiful Names. Whatever is in the heavens and the earth [constantly] glorifies Him. And He is the Almighty, All-Wise."

اَللّٰهُمَّ رَبَّ السَّمٰوَاتِ السَّبْعِ وَرَبَّ الْعَرْشِ الْعَظِيمِ، رَبَّنَا وَرَبَّ كُلِّ شَيْءٍ؛ مُنْزِلَ التَّوْرَاةِ وَالْإِنْجِيلِ وَالْفُرْقَانِ؛ فَالِقَ الْحَبِّ وَالنَّوَىٰ؛ أَعُوذُ بِكَ مِنْ شَرِّ كُلِّ شَيْءٍ أَنْتَ آخِذٌ بِنَاصِيَتِهِ، أَنْتَ الْأَوَّلُ فَلَيْسَ قَبْلَكَ شَيْءٌ، وَأَنْتَ الْآخِرُ فَلَيْسَ بَعْدَكَ شَيْءٌ، وَأَنْتَ الظَّاهِرُ فَلَيْسَ فَوْقَكَ شَيْءٌ، وَأَنْتَ الْبَاطِنُ فَلَيْسَ دُونَكَ شَيْءٌ، اقْضِ عَنِّي الدَّيْنَ وَأَغْنِنِي مِنَ الْفَقْرِ (٩).

أَعُوذُ بِاللهِ السَّمِيعِ الْعَلِيمِ مِنَ الشَّيْطَانِ الرَّجِيمِ - ثَلَاثًا -.

﴿بِسۡمِ ٱللَّهِ ٱلرَّحۡمَٰنِ ٱلرَّحِيمِ: هُوَ ٱللَّهُ ٱلَّذِي لَآ إِلَٰهَ إِلَّا هُوَ ٱلۡمَلِكُ ٱلۡقُدُّوسُ ٱلسَّلَٰمُ ٱلۡمُؤۡمِنُ ٱلۡمُهَيۡمِنُ ٱلۡعَزِيزُ ٱلۡجَبَّارُ ٱلۡمُتَكَبِّرُۚ سُبۡحَٰنَ ٱللَّهِ عَمَّا يُشۡرِكُونَ ﴿٢٣﴾

هُوَ ٱللَّهُ ٱلۡخَٰلِقُ ٱلۡبَارِئُ ٱلۡمُصَوِّرُۖ لَهُ ٱلۡأَسۡمَآءُ ٱلۡحُسۡنَىٰۚ يُسَبِّحُ لَهُۥ مَا فِي ٱلسَّمَٰوَٰتِ وَٱلۡأَرۡضِۖ وَهُوَ ٱلۡعَزِيزُ ٱلۡحَكِيمُ ﴿٢٤﴾﴾(١٠).

---

(٩) هَذِهِ الصِّيغَةُ عَلَّمَهَا النَّبِيُّ ﷺ لِلسَّيِّدَةِ فَاطِمَةَ رَضِيَ اللهُ عَنْهَا.

(١٠) مَنْ قَرَأَ آخِرَ سُورَةِ الْحَشْرِ وَكَّلَ اللهُ بِهِ سَبْعِينَ أَلْفَ مَلَكٍ يُصَلُّونَ عَلَيْهِ حَتَّى يُمْسِيَ، أَوْ حَتَّى يُصْبِحَ، وَإِنْ مَاتَ فَهُوَ شَهِيدٌ - كَمَا فِي الْمُسْنَدِ وَغَيْرِهِ.

Whoever recites the ending of *Surah al-Hashr*, Allah appoints seventy-thousand angels to pray for him until he enters into the night or day. If he dies, he is a martyr. This is found in *al-Musnad* and other sources.

Then recite:

Bismillāhi al-Raḥmāni al-Raḥīm. Qul huwa Allāhu Aḥad, Allāhu al-Ṣamad, lam yalid wa lam yūlad, wa lam yakun lahū kufuwan aḥad.

"Say [O Prophet], 'He is Allah – One [and Indivisible]; Allah – the Sustainer [needed by all]. He has never had offspring, nor was He born. And there is none comparable to Him.'"[21]

Bismillāhi al-Raḥmāni al-Raḥīm. Qul aʿūdhu bi-Rabbi al-falaq, min sharri mā khalaq, wa min sharri ghāsiqin idhā waqab, wa min sharri al-naffāthāti fī al-ʿuqad, wa min sharri ḥāsidin idhā ḥasad.

"Say [O Prophet], 'I seek refuge in the Lord of the daybreak from the evil of whatever He has created, and from the evil of the night when it grows dark, and from the evil of those [witches casting spells by] blowing onto knots, and from the evil of an envier when they envy.'"[22]

Bismillāhi al-Raḥmāni al-Raḥīm. Qul aʿūdhu bi-Rabbi al-nās, Maliki al-nās, Ilāhi al-nās, min sharri al-waswāsi al-khannās, alladhī yuwaswisu fī ṣudūri al-nās, min al-jinnati wa al-nās - Each of them three times.

"Say [O Prophet], 'I seek refuge in the Lord of humankind, the Master of humankind, the God of humankind, from the evil of the lurking whisperer – who whispers into the hearts of humankind – from among jinn and humankind.'"[23]

---

21 *al-Ikhlāṣ*, 1-4.

22 *al-Falaq*, 1-5.

23 *al-Nās*, 1-6.

ثُمَّ اقْرَأْ

﴿بِسْمِ ٱللَّهِ ٱلرَّحْمَٰنِ ٱلرَّحِيمِ: قُلْ هُوَ ٱللَّهُ أَحَدٌ ۝١ ٱللَّهُ ٱلصَّمَدُ ۝٢ لَمْ
يَلِدْ وَلَمْ يُولَدْ ۝٣ وَلَمْ يَكُن لَّهُۥ كُفُوًا أَحَدٌۢ ۝٤﴾

﴿بِسْمِ ٱللَّهِ ٱلرَّحْمَٰنِ ٱلرَّحِيمِ: قُلْ أَعُوذُ بِرَبِّ ٱلْفَلَقِ ۝١ مِن شَرِّ
مَا خَلَقَ ۝٢ وَمِن شَرِّ غَاسِقٍ إِذَا وَقَبَ ۝٣ وَمِن شَرِّ ٱلنَّفَّٰثَٰتِ فِى
ٱلْعُقَدِ ۝٤ وَمِن شَرِّ حَاسِدٍ إِذَا حَسَدَ ۝٥﴾

﴿بِسْمِ ٱللَّهِ ٱلرَّحْمَٰنِ ٱلرَّحِيمِ: قُلْ أَعُوذُ بِرَبِّ ٱلنَّاسِ ۝١ مَلِكِ ٱلنَّاسِ
۝٢ إِلَٰهِ ٱلنَّاسِ ۝٣ مِن شَرِّ ٱلْوَسْوَاسِ ٱلْخَنَّاسِ ۝٤ ٱلَّذِى يُوَسْوِسُ فِى
صُدُورِ ٱلنَّاسِ ۝٥ مِنَ ٱلْجِنَّةِ وَٱلنَّاسِ ۝٦﴾ ثلاثاً - ثلاثاً.

Aṣbaḥnā wa aṣbaḥa al-mulku lillāh,[24] *wa al-ḥamdu lillāh, lā ilāha illā Allāhu waḥdahū lā sharīka lah, lahū al-mulku wa lahū al-ḥamdu wa huwa ʿalā kulli shay'in Qadīr. Rabbi as'aluka khayra mā fī hādhā al-yawm: fatḥahū wa naṣrahū wa nūrahū wa barakatahū wa hudāhu wa khayra mā baʿdah; wa aʿūdhu bika min sharri mā fī hādhā al-yawmi wa sharri mā baʿdah. Rabbi aʿūdhu bika min al-kasal wa sū'i al-kibar; Rabbi aʿūdhu bika min ʿadhābin fī al-nāri wa ʿadhābin fī al-qabri.*

We have entered a new day and with it all dominion is Allah's. Praise is to Allah. None has the right to be worshipped but Allah alone, without associates. To Him belongs dominion and praise, and He is Able to do all things. My Lord, I ask You for the goodness of this day: its openings, victory, light, and guidance; and for the goodness of the days that come after it. I seek refuge in You from the evil of this day and of the days that come after it. My Lord, I seek refuge in You from laziness and helpless old age. My Lord, I seek refuge in You from the punishment of the Fire and the punishment of the grave.

Raḍīnā billāhi Rabban wa bil-Islāmi dīnan wa bi-sayyidinā Muḥammadin ṣallā Allāhu ʿalayhi wa sallama rasūlā.

We are content with Allah as a Lord, with Islam as a religion, and with Muhammad ﷺ as a Messenger.

Allāhumma mā aṣbaḥa[25] *bī min niʿmatin aw bi-aḥadin min khalqika fa-minka waḥdaka lā sharīka lak, laka al-ḥamdu wa laka al-shukr.*[26]

Allah, whatever blessing has been received by me on this day, or by anyone of Your creation, it is from You alone, without associates. All praise and thanks are to You alone.

---

24 In the evening, one says instead: *amsaynā wa amsā al-mulku lillāh* – 'We have entered a new night'.

25 In the evening, one says instead: *mā amsā* – 'On this night'.

26 Whoever says this has fulfilled his day's or night's thanks.

أَصْبَحْنَا وَأَصْبَحَ الْمُلْكُ لِلّٰهِ[١١]، وَالْحَمْدُ لِلّٰهِ، لَا إِلٰهَ إِلَّا اللّٰهُ وَحْدَهُ لَا شَرِيكَ لَهُ، لَهُ الْمُلْكُ، وَلَهُ الْحَمْدُ وَهُوَ عَلَىٰ كُلِّ شَيْءٍ قَدِيرٌ، رَبِّ أَسْأَلُكَ خَيْرَ مَا فِي هَذَا الْيَوْمِ:

فَتْحَهُ وَنَصْرَهُ وَنُورَهُ وَبَرَكَتَهُ وَهُدَاهُ وَخَيْرَ مَا بَعْدَهُ، وَأَعُوذُ بِكَ مِنْ شَرِّ مَا فِي هَذَا الْيَوْمِ وَشَرِّ مَا بَعْدَهُ، رَبِّ أَعُوذُ بِكَ مِنَ الْكَسَلِ وَسُوءِ الْكِبَرِ، رَبِّ أَعُوذُ بِكَ مِنْ عَذَابٍ فِي النَّارِ وَعَذَابٍ فِي الْقَبْرِ.

رَضِينَا بِاللّٰهِ رَبًّا، وَبِالْإِسْلَامِ دِيناً، وَبِسَيِّدِنَا مُحَمَّدٍ ﷺ رَسُولاً.

اَللّٰهُمَّ مَا أَصْبَحَ[١٢] بِي مِنْ نِعْمَةٍ أَوْ بِأَحَدٍ مِنْ خَلْقِكَ فَمِنْكَ وَحْدَكَ لَا شَرِيكَ لَكَ، لَكَ الْحَمْدُ وَلَكَ الشُّكْرُ[١٣].

---

(١١) وَفِي الْمَسَاءِ تَقُولُ: أَمْسَيْنَا وَأَمْسَى الْمُلْكُ لِلّٰهِ.

(١٢) وَفِي الْمَسَاءِ تَقُولُ: مَا أَمْسَى.

(١٣) مَن قَالَ ذَلِكَ فَقَدْ أَدَّىٰ شُكْرَ يَوْمِهِ وَلَيْلَتِهِ.

Aṣbaḥnā ʿalā fiṭrati al-islām, wa kalimat al-ikhlāṣ, wa dīni nabiyyinā Muḥammadin ṣallā Allāhu ʿalayhi wa sallam, wa millati abīnā Ibrāhīma ḥanīfan musliman wa mā kāna min al-mushrikīn.

We have entered a new day upon the natural way of Islam, the statement of sincerity, the religion of our Prophet Muhammad ﷺ, and the path of our father Ibrāhīm. He was of pure disposition, and a Muslim. He was not of those who associate others with Allah.

Allāhumma anta Rabbī lā ilāha illā anta khalaqtanī wa ana ʿabduk, wa ana ʿalā ʿahdika wa waʿdika mā istaṭaʿt; aʿūdhu bika min sharri mā ṣanaʿt, abū'u laka bi-niʿmatika ʿalayya wa abū'u bi-dhanbī fa-ighfir lī, fa-innahū lā yaghfiru al-dhunūba illā ant.[27]

Allah, You are my Lord, there is none worthy of worship but You. You created me and I am your slave. I keep Your covenant and my pledge to You so far as I am able. I seek refuge in You from the evil of what I have done. I admit to Your blessings upon me, and I admit to my misdeeds. Forgive me, for there is none who may forgive sins but You.

Aʿūdhu bi-wajhi Allāhi al-karīm wa bi-kalimāti Allāhi al-tāmmāti allatī lā yujāwizuhunna barrun wa lā fājir min sharri mā yanzilu min al-samā'i wa sharri mā yaʿruju fīhā, wa min sharri mā dhara'a fī al-arḍi wa min sharri mā yakhruju minhā; wa min fitani al-layli wa al-nahār, wa min ṭawāriqi al-layli wa al-nahār; illā ṭāriqan yaṭruqu bi-khayrin yā Raḥmān.

I seek refuge in the Noble face of Allah and His perfect words that neither the righteous nor wicked may exceed, from the evil that descends from heaven and that which ascends thereto, from the evil of what multiplies on earth and that which grows therefrom, from the trials of the night and day and their emergencies – but for an unexpected arrival that comes with goodness, Lord of Mercy.[28]

---

27 Whoever says it during the day with conviction and then dies before that night will be from the inhabitants of the Garden. Whoever says it in the night with conviction and then dies before the next morning will be from the inhabitants of the Garden – this is in Bukhārī.

28 Jibrīl taught this to the Prophet ﷺ on the Night Journey, as is recorded in al-Muwaṭṭa'

أَصْبَحْنَا عَلَى فِطْرَةِ الْإِسْلَامِ، وَكَلِمَةِ الْإِخْلَاصِ، وَدِينِ نَبِيِّنَا مُحَمَّدٍ ﷺ، وَمِلَّةِ أَبِينَا إِبْرَاهِيمَ حَنِيفاً مُسْلِماً وَمَا كَانَ مِنَ الْمُشْرِكِينَ.

اَللّٰهُمَّ أَنْتَ رَبِّيْ لَا إِلٰهَ إِلَّا أَنْتَ خَلَقْتَنِي وَأَنَا عَبْدُكَ، وَأَنَا عَلَى عَهْدِكَ وَوَعْدِكَ مَا اسْتَطَعْتُ، أَعُوذُ بِكَ مِنْ شَرِّ مَا صَنَعْتُ، أَبُوءُ لَكَ بِنِعْمَتِكَ عَلَيَّ، وَأَبُوءُ بِذَنْبِي، فَاغْفِرْ لِي فَإِنَّهُ لَا يَغْفِرُ الذُّنُوبَ إِلَّا أَنْتَ(١٤).

أَعُوذُ بِوَجْهِ اللهِ الْكَرِيمِ وَبِكَلِمَاتِ اللهِ التَّامَّاتِ الَّتِي لَا يُجَاوِزُهُنَّ بَرٌّ وَلَا فَاجِرٌ مِن شَرِّ مَا يَنْزِلُ مِنَ السَّمَاءِ وَشَرِّ مَا يَعْرُجُ فِيهَا، وَمِن شَرِّ مَا ذَرَأَ فِي الْأَرْضِ وَمِنْ شَرِّ مَا يَخْرُجُ مِنهَا، وَمِنْ فِتَنِ اللَّيْلِ وَالنَّهَارِ، وَمِن طَوَارِقِ اللَّيْلِ وَالنَّهَارِ؛ إِلَّا طَارِقاً يَطْرُقُ بِخَيْرٍ يَا رَحْمٰنُ(١٥).

---

(١٤) مَن قَالَهَا مِنَ النَّهَارِ مُوْقِنًا بِهَا فَمَاتَ مِن يَوْمِهِ قَبْلَ أَن يُمْسِيَ فَهُوَ مِنْ أَهْلِ الْجُنَّةِ، وَمَن قَالَهَا مِنَ اللَّيْلِ وَهُوَ مُوْقِنٌ بِهَا فَمَاتَ قَبْلَ أَن يُصْبِحَ فَهُوَ مِنْ أَهْلِ الْجُنَّةِ - كَمَا فِي الْبُخَارِيِّ.

١٥) عَلَّمَ ذٰلِكَ جِبْرِيلُ لِلنَّبِيِّ ﷺ لَيْلَةَ الْإِسْرَاءِ كَمَا فِي الْمُوطَأِ وَغَيْرِهِ.

Aʿūdhu bi-kalimāti Allāhi al-tāmmati min ghaḍabihī waʿiqābihī wa sharri ʿibādih, wa min hamazāti al-shayāṭīni wa aʿūdhu bika Rabbi an yaḥḍurūn.[29]

I seek refuge in Allah's perfect words from His wrath, punishment, and the evil of His slaves; and from the evil of the devils' goading or that they even come near me.

Allāhumma Fāṭira al-samāwāti wa al-arḍ, ʿĀlima al-ghaybi wa al-shahādah, Rabba kulli shay'in wa malīkah, ashhadu an lā ilāha illā ant; aʿūdhu bika min sharri nafsī wa min sharri al-shayṭāni wa shirkihī, wa an aqtarifa ʿalā nafsī sū'an aw ajurrahū ilā muslim.

Allah, Originator of the heavens and the Earth, Knower of the unseen and the evident, Lord of everything and its Possessor, I bear witness that there is none worthy of worship but You. I seek refuge in You from the evil of my soul and from the evil of the devil and his helpers, and from incurring evil upon myself or that I bring its harm to any Muslim.

Allāhumma anta Rabbī lā ilāha illā anta ʿalayka tawakkaltu wa anta Rabbu al-ʿarshi al-ʿaẓīm, wa lā ḥawla wa lā quwwata illā billāhi al-ʿAliyyi al-ʿAẓīm. Mā shā'a Allāhu kāna wa mā lam yasha' lam yakun; aʿlamu anna Allāha ʿalā kulli shay'in Qadir, wa anna Allāha qad aḥāṭa bi-kulli shay'in ʿilmā, wa aḥṣā kulla shay'in ʿadadā. Aʿūdhu min sharri nafsī wa min sharri kulli dābbatin anta ākhidhun bi-nāṣiyatihā, inna Rabbī ʿalā ṣirāṭin mustaqīm.

Allah, You are my Lord, there is none worthy of worship but You. I entrust myself to You, and You are the Lord of the Great Throne. There is no might nor strength save through Allah the Most High, the Sublime. Whatever Allah wills is realized; and what he does not will is not. "I know that Allah is Most Capable of everything", "and that Allah certainly encompasses all things in [His] knowledge", "and keeps account of everything"[30]. I seek refuge from the evil of my own self, and the evil of every living creature You control; "Surely my Lord's Way is perfect justice."

---

and others.

29 Whoever says it as quoted will have nothing harm him, as is in Tirmidhī.

30 *al-Jinn*, 28.

أَعُوذُ بِكَلِمَاتِ اللهِ التَّامَّاتِ مِنْ غَضَبِهِ وَعِقَابِهِ وَشَرِّ عِبَادِهِ، وَمِنْ هَمَزَاتِ الشَّيَاطِينِ وَأَعُوذُ بِكَ رَبِّ أَنْ يَحْضُرُونَ(١٦).

اَللّٰهُمَّ فَاطِرَ السَّمٰوَاتِ وَالْأَرْضِ، عَالِمَ الْغَيْبِ وَالشَّهَادَةِ، رَبَّ كُلِّ شَيْءٍ وَمَلِيكَهُ، أَشْهَدُ أَنْ لَا إِلٰهَ إِلَّا أَنْتَ، أَعُوذُ بِكَ مِنْ شَرِّ نَفْسِي، وَمِنْ شَرِّ الشَّيْطَانِ وَشِرْكِهِ، وَأَنْ أَقْتَرِفَ سُوءاً عَلَى نَفْسِي أَوْ أَجُرَّهُ إِلَى مُسْلِمٍ(١٧). اَللّٰهُمَّ أَنْتَ رَبِّي لَا إِلٰهَ إِلَّا أَنْتَ عَلَيْكَ تَوَكَّلْتُ وَأَنْتَ رَبُّ الْعَرْشِ الْعَظِيمِ، وَلَا حَوْلَ وَلَا قُوَّةَ إِلَّا بِاللهِ الْعَلِيِّ الْعَظِيمِ، مَا شَاءَ اللهُ كَانَ وَمَا لَمْ يَشَأْ لَمْ يَكُنْ،

﴿أَعْلَمُ أَنَّ ٱللَّهَ عَلَىٰ كُلِّ شَيْءٍ قَدِيرٌ﴾[18]، ﴿وَأَنَّ ٱللَّهَ قَدْ أَحَاطَ بِكُلِّ شَيْءٍ عِلْمًا﴾[19]، ﴿وَأَحْصَىٰ كُلَّ شَيْءٍ عَدَدًا﴾[20]، أَعُوذُ مِنْ شَرِّ نَفْسِي، وَمِنْ شَرِّ كُلِّ دَابَّةٍ أَنْتَ آخِذٌ بِنَاصِيَتِهَا، ﴿إِنَّ رَبِّي عَلَىٰ صِرَٰطٍ مُّسْتَقِيمٍ﴾[21].

(١٦) مَنْ قَالَهَا كَذَلِكَ لَمْ يَضُرَّهُ شَيْءٌ، كَمَا فِي التِّرْمِذِيِّ.

(١٧) رَوَاهُ التِّرْمِذِيُّ عَنْ أَبِي هُرَيْرَةَ وَعَبْدِ اللهِ بْنِ عَمْرِو بْنِ الْعَاصِ رَضِيَ اللهُ عَنْهُمْ.

18 *al-Baqarah*, 259.

19 *al-Ṭalāq*, 12.

20 *al-Jinn*, 28.

21 *Hūd*, 56.

Bismillāhi alladhī lā yaḍurru maʿa ismihī shay'un fī al-arḍi wa lā fī al-samā' wa huwa al-Samīʿu al-ʿAlīm. - three times.[31]

In the Name of Allah, in Whose Name nothing can cause harm in the Earth nor in the heavens, and He is the All Hearing, the All Knowing.

Bismillāh, mā shā'a Allāh, lā yasūqu al-khayra illā Allāh, mā shā'a Allāhu lā yaṣrifu al-sharra illā Allāh, mā shā'a Allāhu mā kāna min niʿmatin fa-min Allāh, mā shā'a Allāhu lā ḥawla wa lā quwwata illā billāhi al-ʿAliyyi al-ʿAẓīm - three times.[32]

In the Name of Allah, whatever Allah wills [is realized], none bring about goodness but Allah. Whatever Allah wills [is realized], none averts evil but Allah. Whatever Allah wills [is realized], whatever there are of bounties are only from Allah. Whatever Allah wills [is realized], there is no might nor strength but through Allah.

Bismillāhi alladhī lā ilāha illā huwa al-Raḥmānu al-Raḥīm, allāhumma adhhib ʿannī al-hamma wa al-ḥazan,[33] *allāhumma innī as'aluka al-ʿāfiyata fī al-dunyā wa al-ākhirah. Allāhumma innī as'aluka al-ʿafwa wa al-ʿāfiyata fī dīnī wa dunyāya wa ahlī wa mālī. Allāhumma ustur ʿawrātī wa āmin rawʿātī.*

In the Name of Allah, there is no god but He, the Lord of Mercy, the Giver of Mercy. Allah, remove my worry and grief. Allah, I seek Your pardon and my wellbeing in this world and the next. Allah, I seek Your pardon and wellbeing in my religion, worldly affairs, family, and wealth. Allah, conceal my faults and preserve me from anguish.

---

31 The Messenger of Allah ﷺ taught it to Abū Bakr ؓ as found in Tirmidhī and others.

32 Our Master Ilyās and our Master Khiḍr meet and then separate upon these words every year (Ibn Abī al-Dunyā). Ibn Abbās ؓ said: "Whoever says these words when entering upon a new night or day thrice, Allah will keep him safe from drowning, burning, waning, the devil, tyrannical authority, and other evils."

33 One wipes with his right hand over his head one says: *bismillāh*. He ﷺ would do this upon concluding the prayer, as narrated in Abū Yaʿlā.

بِسْمِ اللهِ الَّذِي لَا يَضُرُّ مَعَ اسْمِهِ شَيْءٌ فِي الْأَرْضِ وَلَا فِي السَّمَاءِ وَهُوَ السَّمِيعُ الْعَلِيمُ – ثَلَاثًا[٢٢].

بِسْمِ اللهِ، مَا شَاءَ اللهُ، لَا يَسُوقُ الْخَيْرَ إِلَّا اللهُ، مَا شَاءَ اللهُ لَا يَصْرِفُ الشَّرَّ إِلَّا اللهُ، مَا شَاءَ اللهُ مَا كَانَ مِنْ نِعْمَةٍ فَمِنَ اللهِ، مَا شَاءَ اللهُ لَا حَوْلَ وَلَا قُوَّةَ إِلَّا بِاللهِ الْعَلِيِّ الْعَظِيمِ – ثَلَاثًا[٢٣].

بِسْمِ اللهِ الَّذِي لَا إِلَهَ إِلَّا هُوَ الرَّحْمَٰنُ الرَّحِيمُ، اَللّٰهُمَّ أَذْهِبْ عَنِّي الْهَمَّ وَالْحَزَنَ[٢٤]، اَللّٰهُمَّ إِنِّي أَسْأَلُكَ الْعَافِيَةَ فِي الدُّنْيَا وَالْآخِرَةِ.

اَللّٰهُمَّ إِنِّي أَسْأَلُكَ الْعَفْوَ وَالْعَافِيَةَ فِي دِينِي وَدُنْيَايَ وَأَهْلِي وَمَالِي. اَللّٰهُمَّ اسْتُرْ عَوْرَاتِي وَآمِنْ رَوْعَاتِي.

---

(٢٢) عَلَّمَهَا رَسُولُ اللهِ ﷺ لِأَبِي بَكْرٍ رضي الله عنه كَمَا فِي التِّرْمِذِيِّ وَغَيْرِهِ.

٢٣) هَذِهِ الْكَلِمَاتُ يَفْتَرِقُ عَنْهَا سَيِّدُنَا إِلْيَاسُ وَسَيِّدُنَا الْخَضِرُ كُلَّ عَامٍ كَمَا رَوَاهُ ابْنُ أَبِي الدُّنْيَا، قَالَ ابْنُ عَبَّاسٍ رضى الله عنه: (مَنْ قَالَهُنَّ حِينَ يُمْسِي وَحِينَ يُصْبِحُ – ثَلَاثًا، آمَنَهُ اللهُ مِنَ الْغَرَقِ وَالْحَرَقِ وَالسَّرَقِ وَمِنَ الشَّيْطَانِ وَالسُّلْطَانِ وَغَيْرِ ذَلِكَ).

(٢٤) وَيَمْسَحُ بِيَمِينِهِ عَلَى رَأْسِهِ عِنْدَ قَوْلِهِ: بِسْمِ اللهِ وَقَدْ كَانَ ﷺ يَفْعَلُ ذَلِكَ عِنْدَ فَرَاغِهِ مِنَ الصَّلَاةِ، كَمَا رَوَاهُ أَبُو يَعْلَى.

Allāhumma iḥfaẓnī min bayna yadayya wa min khalfī, wa ʿan yamīnī wa ʿan shimālī wa min fawqī, wa aʿūdhu bi-ʿaẓamatika an ughtāla min taḥtī.[34]

Allah, guard me from what is in front of me and behind me, from my left, and from my right, and from above me. I seek refuge in Your Greatness from being struck from beneath me – meaning, from being swallowed up by the Earth.

Allāhumma ʿāfinī fī badanī, Allāhumma ʿāfinī fī samʿī, Allāhumma ʿāfinī fī baṣarī, lā ilāha illā ant. Allāhumma innī aʿūdhu bika min al-kufr wa al-faqr, wa Aʿūdhu bika min ʿadhābin fī al-qabr, lā ilāha illā ant – three times.[35]

Allah, grant me well-being in my body. Allah, grant me wellness in my hearing. Allah, grant me wellness in my sight. There is none worthy of worship but You. Allah, I seek refuge in You from disbelief and poverty, and I seek refuge in You from the punishment of the grave. There is none worthy of worship but You.

Allāhumma innī aʿūdhu bika min al-hammi wa al-ḥazan, wa aʿūdhu bika min al-ʿajzi wa al-kasal, wa aʿūdhu bika min al-jubni wa al-bukhl, wa aʿūdhu bika min ghalabati al-dayni wa qahri al-rijāl.[36]

Allah, I seek refuge in You from worry and grief. I seek refuge in You from incapacity and laziness. I seek refuge in You from cowardice and miserliness. I seek refuge in You from overwhelming debt and the tyranny of men.

Yā Ḥayyu yā Qayyūmu bi-raḥmatika astaghīth, fa-aṣliḥ lī sha'nī kullah, wa lā takilnī ilā nafsī ṭarfata ʿayn.

Ever Living, Sustainer of all, by Your mercy I beseech You to set right all my affairs. Do not place me in charge of my soul even for the blink of an eye.

---

34 Abū Dāwūd and others.

35 As found in the *Sunan* of Abū Dāwūd.

36 This supplication removes worries and settles debts. The Prophet ﷺ taught it to Abū Umāmah, Allah be pleased with him when he was overcome with worry and debt.

اَللّٰهُمَّ احْفَظْنِي مِنْ بَيْنِ يَدَيَّ وَمِنْ خَلْفِي، وَعَنْ يَمِينِي وَعَنْ شِمَالِي وَمِنْ فَوْقِي، وَأَعُوذُ بِعَظَمَتِكَ أَنْ أُغْتَالَ مِنْ تَحْتِي(٢٥) - يَعْنِي الْخَسْفَ -

اَللّٰهُمَّ عَافِنِي فِي بَدَنِي، اَللّٰهُمَّ عَافِنِي فِي سَمْعِي، اَللّٰهُمَّ عَافِنِي فِي بَصَرِي، لَا إِلٰهَ إِلَّا أَنْتَ، اَللّٰهُمَّ إِنِّي أَعُوذُ بِكَ مِنَ الْكُفْرِ وَالْفَقْرِ، اَللّٰهُمَّ إِنِّي أَعُوذُ بِكَ مِنْ عَذَابِ الْقَبْرِ؛ لَا إِلٰهَ إِلَّا أَنْتَ(٢٦) - ثَلَاثاً.

اَللّٰهُمَّ إِنِّي أَعُوذُ بِكَ مِنَ الْهَمِّ وَالْحَزَنِ، وَأَعُوذُ بِكَ مِنَ الْعَجْزِ وَالْكَسَلِ، وَأَعُوذُ بِكَ مِنَ الْجُبْنِ وَالْبُخْلِ، وَأَعُوذُ بِكَ مِنْ غَلَبَةِ الدَّيْنِ وَقَهْرِ الرِّجَالِ(٢٧).

يَا حَيُّ يَا قَيُّومُ بِرَحْمَتِكَ أَسْتَغِيثُ؛ فَأَصْلِحْ لِي شَأْنِي كُلَّهُ، وَلَا تَكِلْنِي إِلَى نَفْسِي طَرْفَةَ عَيْنٍ.

---

(٢٥) رَوَاهُ أَبُو دَاوُدَ وَغَيْرُهُ.

(٢٦) كَمَا فِي سُنَنِ أَبِي دَاوُدَ.

(٢٧) هَذَا الدُّعَاءُ يُزِيلُ الهُمُومَ وَيَقْضِي الدُّيُونَ فَقَدْ عَلَّمَهُ ﷺ لِأَبِي أُمَامَةَ ﵁ لَمَّا لَزِمَتْهُ الْهُمُومُ وَالدُّيُونُ، كَمَا رَوَاهُ أَبُو دَاوُدَ.

Allāhumma anta aḥaqqu man dhukir, wa aḥaqqu man ʿubid, wa anṣaru man ubtughiyā, wa ar'afu man malak, wa ajwadu man su'il, wa awsaʿu man aʿṭā. Anta al-Maliku lā sharīka lak, wa al-Fardu lā nidda lak, kullu shay'in hālikun illā wajhak. Lan tuṭāʿa illā bi-idhnika wa lam tuʿṣā illa bi-ʿilmik. Tuṭāʿu fa-tashkuru wa tuʿṣā fa-taghfir. Aqrabu Shahīdin wa Adnā Hafīẓ; ḥulta duna al-nufūs, wa akhadhta bi-nawāṣī, wa katabta al-āthār, wa nasakhta al-ājāl.

Allah, You have the most right to be remembered, and the most right to be worshipped. You give the best help to those who seek it. You are the Most Kind of those who own with whom they own. You are the Most Generous of those who are asked, and You are the Most Expansive in provision of those who give. You are the King without associates, the One without equal. Everything shall perish but Your Face. You are not worshipped save by Your leave, nor are You disobeyed except that You are aware. You are thankful to the worshipper, and forgiving to the disobedient. You are the closest of witnesses, and the most immediate of protectors. You come between us and our own selves, and guide us inexorably to our paths. You have written all deeds and You enact all decree.

Al-Qulūb laka mufḍiyah, wa al-sirru ʿindaka ʿalāniyah. Al-ḥalālu mā aḥlalt, wa al-ḥarāmu ma ḥarramt, wa al-dīnu mā sharaʿt, wa al-amru mā qaḍayt; al-khalqu khalquk, wa al-ʿabdu ʿabduk, wa anta Allāhu al-Ra'ūfu al-Raḥīm. As'aluka bi-nūri wajhika alladhī ashraqat lahū al-samāwatu wa al-arḍ, wa bi-kulli ḥaqqin huwa lak, wa bi-ḥaqqi al-sā'ilīn ʿalayk, an tuqīlanī fī hādhihī al-ghadāh, wa fī hādhihī al-ʿashiyyah, wa an tujīranī min al-nāri bi-qudratik.

Our hearts are outpouring to You. Secrets are known to You. The permissible is what You have deemed to be permissible, the unlawful is what You have deemed to be unlawful, the religion is what You have revealed, and our matters are what You decree. The creation is Yours; the slaves are Yours; and You are Allah, the Compassionate, the Merciful. I ask you by the light of Your Face which irradiates the heavens and the Earth, and by every right that is Yours, and by the right of those who ask upon You, that You acquit me on this morn and this eve, and that you save me from the Fire by Your leave.

اَللّٰهُمَّ أَنْتَ أَحَقُّ مَنْ ذُكِرَ، وَأَحَقُّ مَنْ عُبِدَ، وَأَنْصَرُ مَنِ ابْتُغِيَ، وَأَرْأَفُ مَنْ مَلَكَ، وَأَجْوَدُ مَنْ سُئِلَ، وَأَوْسَعُ مَنْ أَعْطَى، أَنْتَ الْمَلِكُ لَا شَرِيكَ لَكَ، وَالْفَرْدُ لَا نِدَّ لَكَ، كُلُّ شَيْءٍ هَالِكٌ إِلَّا وَجْهَكَ، لَنْ تُطَاعَ إِلَّا بِإِذْنِكَ، وَلَمْ تُعْصَ إِلَّا بِعِلْمِكَ، تُطَاعُ فَتَشْكُرُ، وَتُعْصَى فَتَغْفِرُ، أَقْرَبُ شَهِيدٍ وَأَدْنَى حَفِيظٍ، حُلْتَ دُونَ النُّفُوسِ وَأَخَذْتَ بِالنَّوَاصِي، وَكَتَبْتَ الْآثَارَ، وَنَسَخْتَ الْآجَالَ.

اَلْقُلُوبُ لَكَ مُفْضِيَةٌ وَالسِّرُّ عِنْدَكَ عَلَانِيَةٌ، اَلْحَلَالُ مَا أَحْلَلْتَ، وَالْحَرَامُ مَا حَرَّمْتَ، وَالدِّينُ مَا شَرَعْتَ، وَالْأَمْرُ مَا قَضَيْتَ، اَلْخَلْقُ خَلْقُكَ، وَالْعَبْدُ عَبْدُكَ، وَأَنْتَ اللّٰهُ الرَّؤُوفُ الرَّحِيمُ، أَسْأَلُكَ بِنُورِ وَجْهِكَ الَّذِي أَشْرَقَتْ لَهُ السَّمٰوَاتُ وَالْأَرْضُ، وَبِكُلِّ حَقٍّ هُوَ لَكَ، وَبِحَقِّ السَّائِلِينَ عَلَيْكَ: أَنْ تُقِيلَنِي فِي هَذِهِ الْغَدَاةِ، وَفِي هَذِهِ الْعَشِيَّةِ، وَأَنْ تُجِيرَنِي مِنَ النَّارِ بِقُدْرَتِكَ(٢٨).٢٩

(٢٨) رَوَاهُ الطَّبَرَانِيُّ مِنْ حَدِيثِ أُمَامَةَ رَضِيَ اللهُ عَنْهُ قَالَ: كَانَ رَسُولُ اللهِ ﷺ إِذَا أَصْبَحَ وَإِذَا أَمْسَى دَعَا بِهَذَا الدُّعَاءِ.

29 Ṭabarānī from the narration of Umāmah ﷺ who said: "Allah's Messenger ﷺ would make this supplication when he entered upon a day or night."

Labbayka Allāhumma labbayk, labbayka wa saʿdayk, wa al-khayru fī yadayka wa minka wa ilayk.

At Your beck and call, Allah. Here I am, at Your service. All goodness is in Your Hands – it is from You and it returns to You.

Allāhumma mā qultu min qawl, aw ḥalaftu min ḥilf, aw nadhartu min nadhr, fa-mashī'atuka bayna yaday dhālika kullih. Mā shi'ta kāna wa mā lam tasha' lam yakun, wa lā hawla wa lā quwwata illā bik, innaka ʿalā kulli shay'in Qadīr.

Allah, I do not utter a statement, nor swear by something, nor pledge some vow, but that Your will is dictating this all. What You will is realized, and what You do not will is not. There is no might nor strength but through You, You are Most Capable over all things.

Allāhumma mā ṣallaytu min ṣalātin fa-ʿalā man ṣallayta, wa mā laʿantu fa-ʿalā man laʿanta; innaka waliyyī fī al-dunyā wa al-ākhirah, tawaffanī musliman wa alḥiqnī bil-ṣāliḥīn.

Allah, I do not pray a prayer but it is for those upon whom You pray,[37] and I do not curse but it is upon those whom You curse. You are my Guardian in this life and the next, cause me to die as a Muslim and allow me to reach the righteous.

Allāhumma innī as'aluka al-riḍā baʿda al-qaḍā', wa barda al-ʿayshi baʿda al-mawt, wa ladhdhata al-naẓari ilā wajhik, wa shawqan ilā liqā'ik, min ghayri ḍarrā'in muḍirrah, wa lā fitnatin muḍillah, wa aʿūdhu bika an aẓlima aw uẓlam, aw aʿtadī aw yuʿtadā ʿalayy, aw aksiba khaṭī'atan aw dhanban lā yughfar.

Allah, I ask You for contentment after Your decree, blissful life after death, the sweetness of looking upon Your Face, the longing to meet You in neither a state that harms us nor a trial that misguides us. I seek refuge in You lest I oppress or am oppressed, or transgress or am transgressed against, or acquire a mistake or sin that is unforgivable.

---

37 i.e. 'Whatever I supplicate of mercy'.

لَبَّيْكَ اللّٰهُمَّ لَبَّيْكَ، لَبَّيْكَ وَسَعْدَيْكَ، وَالْخَيْرُ فِي يَدَيْكَ وَمِنْكَ وَإِلَيْكَ. اَللّٰهُمَّ مَا قُلْتُ مِنْ قَوْلٍ، أَوْ حَلَفْتُ مِنْ حَلْفٍ، أَوْ نَذَرْتُ مِنْ نَذْرٍ، فَمَشِيئَتُكَ بَيْنَ يَدَيْ ذَلِكَ كُلِّهِ، مَا شِئْتَ كَانَ وَمَا لَمْ تَشَأْ لَمْ يَكُنْ، وَلَا حَوْلَ وَلَا قُوَّةَ إِلَّا بِكَ، إِنَّكَ عَلَى كُلِّ شَيْءٍ قَدِيرٌ.

اَللّٰهُمَّ مَا صَلَّيْتُ مِنْ صَلَاةٍ[٣٠] فَعَلَى مَنْ صَلَّيْتَ، وَمَا لَعَنْتُ فَعَلَى مَنْ لَعَنْتَ، إِنَّكَ وَلِيِّي فِي الدُّنْيَا وَالْآخِرَةِ، تَوَفَّنِي مُسْلِمًا وَأَلْحِقْنِي بِالصَّالِحِينَ.

اَللّٰهُمَّ إِنِّي أَسْأَلُكَ الرِّضَا بَعْدَ الْقَضَاءِ، وَبَرْدَ الْعَيْشِ بَعْدَ الْمَوْتِ، وَلَذَّةَ النَّظَرِ إِلَى وَجْهِكَ، وَشَوْقاً إِلَى لِقَائِكَ مِنْ غَيْرِ ضَرَّاءَ مُضِرَّةٍ، وَلَا فِتْنَةٍ مُضِلَّةٍ، وَأَعُوذُ بِكَ أَنْ أَظْلِمَ، أَوْ أُظْلَمَ، أَوْ أَعْتَدِيَ، أَوْ يُعْتَدَىٰ عَلَيَّ، أَوْ أَكْسِبَ خَطِيئَةً أَوْ ذَنْباً لَا يُغْفَرُ.

(٣٠) أَيْ: مَا دَعَوْتُ بِهِ مِنْ رَحْمَةٍ.

Allāhumma Faṭira al-samāwāti wa al-arḍ, ʿĀlima al-ghaybi wa al-shahādah, Dhā al-jalāli wa al-ikrām, fa-innī aʿhadu ilayka fī hādhihī al-ḥayāti al-dunyā, wa ushhiduka wa kafā bika shahīdā: annī ashhadu an lā ilāha illā ant, waḥdaka lā sharīka lak, laka al-mulku wa laka al-ḥamdu wa anta ʿala kulli shay'in Qadīr; wa ashhadu anna Muḥammadan ʿabduka wa rasūluk, wa ashhadu anna waʿdaka ḥaqq, wa liqa'aka ḥaqq, wa al-sāʿata ātiyatun lā rayba fīhā, wa annaka tabʿathu man fī al-qubūr, wa innaka in takilnī ilā nafsī takilnī ilā ḍaʿfin wa ʿawazatin wa dhanbin wa khaṭī'ah, wa innī lā athiqu illā bi-raḥmatika fa-ighfir lī dhunūbī kullahā, innahū lā yaghfiru al-dhunūba illā ant, wa tub ʿalayya innaka anta al-Tawwābu al-Raḥīm. Subḥān Rabbika Rabbi al-ʿizzati ʿammā yaṣifūn, wa salāmun ʿalā al-mursalīn, wa al-ḥamdu lillāhi Rabbi al-ʿālamīn.

Allah, Originator of the heavens and the Earth, Knower of the unseen and the evident, Possessor of majesty and generosity, I take a pledge to You in this worldly life and seek You as a witness – and sufficient is Allah as a witness: that I bear witness that there is no god but You alone, without associates. To You belongs all dominion and praise, and you are Most Capable over all things. I bear witness that Muhammad is Your slave and Messenger. I bear witness that Your promise is true, meeting You is true, that the Hour is undoubtedly approaching, and that You resurrect people from their graves. I bear witness that if you entrust me to myself, then You entrust me to weakness, want, sin, and error. I do not trust but Your mercy, so forgive all my sins, for none may forgive sins save You; relent towards me, for You are the Ever Relenting, the Most Merciful. "Glorified is your Lord – the Lord of Honour and Power – above what they claim! Peace be upon the messengers. And praise be to Allah – Lord of all worlds."[38]

---

38 *al-Ṣāffāt*, 180-182.

اَللّٰهُمَّ فَاطِرَ السَّمٰوَاتِ وَالْأَرْضِ، عَالِمَ الْغَيْبِ وَالشَّهَادَةِ، ذَا الْجَلَالِ وَالْإِكْرَامِ، فَإِنِّي أَعْهَدُ إِلَيْكَ فِي هَذِهِ الْحَيَاةِ الدُّنْيَا، وَأُشْهِدُكَ وَكَفَى بِكَ شَهِيداً

: أَنِّي أَشْهَدُ أَنْ لَا إِلٰهَ إِلَّا أَنْتَ وَحْدَكَ لَا شَرِيكَ لَكَ، لَكَ الْمُلْكُ، وَلَكَ الْحَمْدُ، وَأَنْتَ عَلَى كُلِّ شَيْءٍ قَدِيرٌ، وَأَشْهَدُ أَنَّ مُحَمَّدًا عَبْدُكَ وَرَسُولُكَ، وَأَشْهَدُ أَنَّ وَعْدَكَ حَقٌّ، وَالسَّاعَةَ آتِيَةٌ لَّا رَيْبَ فِيهَا، وَأَنَّكَ تَبْعَثُ مَنْ فِي الْقُبُورِ، وَإِنَّكَ إِنْ تَكِلْنِي إِلَى نَفْسِي تَكِلْنِي إِلَى ضَيْعَةٍ وَعَوْرَةٍ وَذَنْبٍ وَخَطِيئَةٍ، وَإِنِّي لَا أَثِقُ إِلَّا بِرَحْمَتِكَ فَاغْفِرْ لِي ذُنُوبِي كُلَّهَا، إِنَّهُ لَا يَغْفِرُ الذُّنُوبَ إِلَّا أَنْتَ، وَتُبْ عَلَيَّ إِنَّكَ أَنْتَ التَّوَّابُ الرَّحِيمُ،

﴿سُبۡحَٰنَ رَبِّكَ رَبِّ ٱلۡعِزَّةِ عَمَّا يَصِفُونَ ۝١٨٠ وَسَلَٰمٌ عَلَى ٱلۡمُرۡسَلِينَ ۝١٨١ وَٱلۡحَمۡدُ لِلَّهِ رَبِّ ٱلۡعَٰلَمِينَ ۝١٨٢﴾ .

I came across in the manuscripts of my respected father, Allah have mercy upon him, a supplication attributed to al-Thawrī & Aḥmad ibn Ḥanbal 🌸:

Yā Rabba kulli shay', bi-qudratika ʿalā kulli shay'in ighfir lī kulla shay', wa lā tas'alnī ʿan shay'.

Lord of all things, by Your power over all things, forgive me everything, and take me not into account over anything.

My respected father said, Allah the Exalted show him mercy: "I added to it:

Allāhumma innā natawassulu ilayka bi-raḥmatika allatī wasiʿat kulla shay', an tuṣalliya ʿalā man faḍḍaltahū ʿalā kulli shay', wa khalaqta min nūrihī kulla shay', ṣallā Allāhu ʿalayhi wa sallam."

Allah, we seek proximity to You through Your mercy which encompasses all things, that You confer exaltations upon the one whom You favoured over all, and from whose light You created all things 🌸.

رَأَيْتُ فِي مَخْطُوطَاتِ سَيِّدِي الْوَالِدِ رَحِمَهُ اللهُ دُعَاءً مَأْثُورًا عَنِ الثَّوْرِيِّ وَأَحْمَدَ بْنِ حَنْبَلٍ رَضِيَ اللهُ تَعَالَىٰ عَنْهُمَا:

يَا رَبَّ كُلِّ شَيْءٍ، بِقُدْرَتِكَ عَلَى كُلِّ شَيْءٍ اغْفِرْ لِي كُلَّ شَيْءٍ، وَلَا تَسْأَلْنِي عَنْ شَيْءٍ.

قَالَ سَيِّدِي الْوَالِدُ رَحِمَهُ اللهُ تَعَالَىٰ:

وَزِدْتُ عَلَيْهِ:

اَللّٰهُمَّ إِنَّا نَتَوَسَّلُ إِلَيْكَ بِرَحْمَتِكَ الَّتِي وَسِعَتْ كُلَّ شَيْءٍ، أَنْ تُصَلِّيَ عَلَى مَنْ فَضَّلْتَهُ عَلَى كُلِّ شَيْءٍ، وَخَلَقْتَ مِن نُورِهِ كُلَّ شَيْءٍ صَلَّى اللهُ عَلَيْهِ وَآلِهِ وَسَلَّمَ.

Transmitted Supplications that Include the Greatest Name Through which Chests find Relief, Matters are Facilitated, Hearts Rejoice, and Tribulations are Uplifted

On the authority of Buraydah ﷺ: "The Prophet ﷺ heard a man saying:
Allāhumma innī as'aluka bi-annī ashhadu annaka anta Allāhu lā ilāha illā anta al-Aḥadu al-Ṣamad, alladhī lam yalid wa lam yūlad, wa lam yakun lahū kufuwan aḥad.

'Allah, I ask You by the fact that I testify You are Allah, there is no god but You; You are the One, the Eternal Refuge, Who neither had offspring nor was born, and there is no one comparable to Him.'

He ﷺ said upon hearing this: 'By the One in Whose Hands is my soul, he has asked Allah by His Greatest Name which He answers to if He is called by, and gives if He is supplicated through.'"[39]

On the authority of Anas ﷺ: "A man supplicated Allah saying:
Allāhumma innī as'aluka bi-anna laka al-ḥamd, lā ilāha illā anta al-Ḥannānu al-Mannān, Badīʿu al-samawāti wa al-arḍ, Dhū al-jalāli wa al-ikrām, yā Ḥayyu yā Qayyūm.

'Allah, I ask you that to You belongs all praise. There is no god but You, the Most Gentle, the Most Bountiful, the Inventor of the heavens and Earth, Possessor of all majesty and generosity; Ever Living, Sustainer of all things.' The Prophet ﷺ asked: 'Do you know what he supplicated by?' They replied: 'Allah and His Messenger know best.' He said: 'By the One in Whose Hands is my soul, he has asked Allah by His Greatest Name which He answers to if He is called by, and gives if He is supplicated through.'"[40]

---

39 Tirmidhī.

40 Authors of Hadith collections.

أَدْعِيَةٌ مَأْثُورَةٌ تَشْتَمِلُ عَلَى الِاسْمِ الْأَعْظَمِ وَبِهَا تَنْشَرِحُ الصُّدُورُ وَتَتَيَسَّرُ الْأُمُورُ وَتَفْرَحُ الْقُلُوبُ وَتُفَرَّجُ الْكُرُوبُ

عَنْ بُرَيْدَةَ رَضِيَ اللهُ تَعَالَىٰ عَنْهُ قَالَ: سَمِعَ النَّبِيُّ ﷺ رَجُلًا يَقُولُ: اَللّٰهُمَّ إِنِّيْ أَسْأَلُكَ بِأَنِّيْ أَشْهَدُ أَنَّكَ أَنْتَ اللهُ لَا إِلَهَ إِلَّا أَنْتَ الْأَحَدُ الصَّمَدُ الَّذِي لَمْ يَلِدْ وَلَمْ يُولَدْ، وَلَمْ يَكُنْ لَهُ كُفُواً أَحَدٌ. فَقَالَ ﷺ: «وَالَّذِيْ نَفْسِي بِيَدِهِ لَقَدْ سَأَلَ اللهَ بِاسْمِهِ الْأَعْظَمِ الَّذِي إِذَا دُعِيَ بِهِ أَجَابَ وإِذَا سُئِلَ بِهِ أَعْطَى»(٣١).

وَعَنْ أَنَسٍ رَضِيَ اللهُ تَعَالَىٰ عَنْهُ قَالَ: دَعَا رَجُلٌ فَقَالَ: اَللّٰهُمَّ إِنِّي أَسْأَلُكَ بِأَنَّ لَكَ الْحَمْدَ، لَا إِلَهَ إِلَّا أَنْتَ الْحَنَّانُ الْمَنَّانُ، بَدِيْعُ السَّمٰوَاتِ وَالْأَرْضِ، ذُوْ الْجَلَالِ وَالْإِكْرَامِ، يَا حَيُّ يَا قَيُّوْمُ، فَقَالَ النَّبِيُّ ﷺ: «أَتَدْرُوْنَ بِمَ دَعَا»؟ قَالُوا: اَللهُ وَرَسُوْلُهُ أَعْلَمُ. قَالَ: «وَالَّذِيْ نَفْسِي بِيَدِهِ لَقَدْ دَعَا اللهَ بِاسْمِهِ الْأَعْظَمِ الَّذِي إِذَا دُعِيَ بِهِ أَجَابَ وَإِذَا سُئِلَ بِهِ أَعْطَى»(٣٢).

---

(٣١) رَوَاهُ التِّرمِذِيُّ.

(٣٢) رَوَاهُ أَصْحَابُ السُّنَنِ.

ʿĀ'ishah ‎ said: "Allah's Messenger ‎ said: 'If the slave says:

Yā Rabb, yā Rabb, yā Rabb!

"My Lord, My Lord, My Lord!" Allah replies: "Here I am, My slave. Ask and you will be given."'"

On the authority of Ibn Abbās, the Prophet said: "Allah's Greatest Name which if He is asked by He answers is in this verse of *Āl Imrān*: *Bismillāhi al-Raḥmāni al-Raḥīm. Qul Allāhumma Mālika al-mulki tu'tī al-mulka man tashā'u wa tanziʿu al-mulka min man tashā', wa tuʿizzu man tashā'u wa tudhillu man tashā'u bi-yadika al-khayru innaka ʿalā kulli shay'in Qadīr. Tūliju al-layla fī al-nahāri wa tūliju al-nahāra fī al-layli wa tukhriju al-ḥayya min al-mayyiti wa tukhriju al-mayyita min al-ḥayyi wa tarzuqu man tashā'u bi-ghayri ḥisāb.*

'Say [O Prophet], "O Allah! Lord over all authorities! You give authority to whoever You please and remove it from who You please; You honour whoever You please and disgrace who You please – all good is in Your Hands. Surely You [alone] are Most Capable of everything. You cause the night to pass into the day and the day into the night. You bring forth the living from the dead and the dead from the living. And You provide for whoever You will without limit."'[41]"[42]

On the authority of Ibn ʿAbbās, a man asked: "Messenger of Allah, is there a portion of supplication that is never rejected?" He replied: "Yes. Say:

As'aluka bismika al-aʿlā al-aʿazzu al-ajallu al-akram.

'I ask You by Your Highest, Most Honourable, Most Majestic, and Most Noble Name.'"[43]

---

41 Āl *Imrān*, 26-27.

42 Ṭabarānī.

43 Ṭabarānī.

وَعَنْ عَائِشَةَ رَضِيَ اللهُ تَعَالَىٰ عَنْهَا قَالَتْ: قَالَ رَسُولُ اللهِ ﷺ: «إِذَا قَالَ الْعَبْدُ يَا رَبِّ يَا رَبِّ يَا رَبِّ، قَالَ اللهُ: لَبَّيْكَ عَبْدِي، سَلْ تُعْطَ»(٣٣).

وَعَنِ ابْنِ عَبَّاسٍ رَضِيَ اللهُ تَعَالَىٰ عَنْهُمَا عَنِ النَّبِيِّ ﷺ قَالَ: «اِسْمُ اللهِ الْأَعْظَمُ الَّذِيْ إِذَا دُعِيَ بِهِ أَجَابَ، فِي هَذِهِ الْآيَةِ مِنْ آلِ عِمْرَانَ: ﴿بِسۡمِ ٱللَّهِ ٱلرَّحۡمَٰنِ ٱلرَّحِيمِ: قُلِ ٱللَّهُمَّ مَٰلِكَ ٱلۡمُلۡكِ تُؤۡتِي ٱلۡمُلۡكَ مَن تَشَآءُ وَتَنزِعُ ٱلۡمُلۡكَ مِمَّن تَشَآءُ وَتُعِزُّ مَن تَشَآءُ وَتُذِلُّ مَن تَشَآءُۖ بِيَدِكَ ٱلۡخَيۡرُۖ إِنَّكَ عَلَىٰ كُلِّ شَيۡءٖ قَدِيرٞ ﴿٢٦﴾ تُولِجُ ٱلَّيۡلَ فِي ٱلنَّهَارِ وَتُولِجُ ٱلنَّهَارَ فِي ٱلَّيۡلِۖ وَتُخۡرِجُ ٱلۡحَيَّ مِنَ ٱلۡمَيِّتِ وَتُخۡرِجُ ٱلۡمَيِّتَ مِنَ ٱلۡحَيِّۖ وَتَرۡزُقُ مَن تَشَآءُ بِغَيۡرِ حِسَابٖ ﴿٢٧﴾﴾»(٣٤).

وَعَنِ ابْنِ عَبَّاسٍ رَضِيَ اللهُ عَنْهُمَا أَنَّ رَجُلًا قَالَ: يَا رَسُولَ اللهِ هَلْ مِنَ الدُّعَاءِ شَيْءٌ لَا يُرَدُّ؟

قَالَ نَعَمْ: «تَقُولُ أَسْأَلُكَ بِاسْمِكَ الْأَعْلَى الْأَعَزِّ الْأَجَلِّ الْأَكْرَمِ»(٣٥).

---

(٣٣) رَوَاهُ الْبَزَّارُ وَأَبُو الشَّيْخِ.

(٣٤) رَوَاهُ الطَّبَرَانِيُّ.

(٣٥) رَوَاهُ الطَّبَرَانِيُّ.

On the authority of Saʿīd 🙵, Allah's Messenger 🕌 said: "The supplication of Dhū al-Nūn (Yūnus) when he called out in the belly of the whale was:
Lā ilāha illā anta subḥānaka innī kuntu min al-ẓālimīn.
'There is no god [worthy of worship] except You. Glory be to You! I have certainly done wrong.'[44] No Muslim makes this supplication in any situation but that Allah answers him due to it."

On the authority of Ibn Masʿūd 🙵 he supplicated, saying:
Allāhumma innī as'aluka īmānan lā yartadd, wa naʿīman lā yanfad, wa murāfaqata nabiyyika Muḥammadin ṣallā Allāhu ʿalayhi wa sallama fī aʿlā daraji al-jannati jannati al-khuld.
'Allah, I ask You for unwavering faith, never-ending bliss, the Companionship of Your Prophet 🕌 in the highest stations of the Garden, the Garden of eternity.' The Prophet 🕌 said to Ibn Masʿūd: 'Ask, and you will be given.'[45]

On the authority of Anas 🙵: "Allah's Messenger 🕌 passed by a man who was saying:

Yā arḥama al-rāḥimīn.
'Most Merciful of those who show mercy.' He said to him: 'Ask, for Allah has looked upon You kindly.'"

On the authority of Abū Umāmah 🙵, "Allah's Messenger 🕌 said: 'Allah has prescribed a specific angel for those who say:
Yā arḥama al-rāḥimīn.
"Most Merciful of those who show mercy" – if a person says it thrice, the angel says to him: "The Most Merciful of the merciful comes forth to you, so ask."'"[46]

44   *al-Anbiyā'*, 87.
45   Ḥākim.
46   Ḥākim.

وَعَنْ سَعِيدٍ رَضِيَ اللهُ تَعَالَىٰ عَنْهُ أَنَّ رَسُولَ اللهِ ﷺ قَالَ: «دَعْوَةُ ذِي النُّونِ إِذَا دَعَا وَهُوَ فِي بَطْنِ الحُوتِ: ﴿لَّآ إِلَٰهَ إِلَّآ أَنتَ سُبۡحَٰنَكَ إِنِّي كُنتُ مِنَ ٱلظَّٰلِمِينَ﴾، فَإِنَّهُ لَمْ يَدْعُ بِهَا مُسْلِمٌ فِي شَيْءٍ قَطُّ إِلَّا اسْتَجَابَ اللهُ لَهُ بِهَا»[٣٦].

وَعَنِ ابْنِ مَسْعُودٍ رَضِيَ اللهُ تَعَالَىٰ عَنْهُ أَنَّهُ دَعَا فَقَالَ: (اَللّٰهُمَّ إِنِّي أَسْأَلُكَ: إِيمَانًا لَا يَرْتَدُّ، وَنَعِيمًا لَا يَنْفَدُ، وَمُرَافَقَةَ نَبِيِّكَ مُحَمَّدٍ ﷺ فِي أَعْلَى دَرَجِ الْجَنَّةِ جَنَّةِ الْخُلْدِ). فَقَالَ النَّبِيُّ ﷺ لِابْنِ مَسْعُودٍ: «سَلْ تُعْطَ»[٣٧].

وَعَنْ أَنَسٍ رَضِيَ اللهُ عَنْهُ قَالَ: مَرَّ رَسُولُ اللهِ ﷺ بِرَجُلٍ وَهُوَ يَقُولُ: يَا أَرْحَمَ الرَّاحِمِينَ، فَقَالَ: «سَلْ؛ فَقَدْ نَظَرَ اللهُ إِلَيْكَ». وَعَنْ أَبِي أُمَامَةَ رَضِيَ اللهُ عَنْهُ قَالَ: قَالَ رَسُولُ اللهِ ﷺ: «إِنَّ لِلَّهِ مَلَكًا مُوَكَّلًا بِمَنْ يَقُولُ يَا أَرْحَمَ الرَّاحِمِينَ، فَمَنْ قَالَهَا ثَلَاثًا - قَالَ لَهُ الْمَلَكُ: إِنَّ أَرْحَمَ الرَّاحِمِينَ قَدْ أَقْبَلَ عَلَيْكَ فَسَلْ»[٣٨].

---

(٣٦) رَوَاهُ التِّرْمِذِيُّ وَغَيْرُهُ.

(٣٧) رَوَاهُ الْحَاكِمُ.

(٣٨) رَوَاهُ الْحَاكِمُ.

ʿĀ'ishah ﵂ said: "I heard Allah's Messenger ﷺ say:

Allāhumma innī as'aluka bismika al-ṭāhiri al-ṭayyibi al-mubāraki al-aḥabbi ilayk, alladhī idhā duʿīta bihī ajabt, wa idhā su'ilta bihī aʿṭayt, wa idhā isturḥimta bihī raḥimt, wa idhā istufrijta bihī farrajt.

'Allah, I ask You by Your pure, good, blessed Name; the one that is most beloved to You. The Name that if You are called by, You answer; and if You are supplicated by, You give; and if Your mercy is besought by it, You give it; and if You are beseeched for relief through it, You relieve.'

He also said to me one day: 'Did you know that Allah has directed me to the Name by which He answers if He is called, ʿĀ'ishah?' I said: 'My mother and father are for your sake, Messenger of Allah. Teach me it.' He said: It is not for you to know, ʿĀ'ishah.' I sat away for a while, then came back, kissed his forehead, and then said: 'Messenger of Allah, teach me it.' He said: 'It is not for me to teach it to you, ʿĀ'ishah. You may not ask for any worldly matter through it.' So, I got up, made ablution, then prayed two units, and then said:

Allāhumma innī adʿūka al-Raḥmān, wa adʿūka al-Barra al-Raḥīm, wa adʿūka bi-asmā'ika al-ḥusnā kullihā mā ʿalimtu minhā wa mā lam aʿlam, an taghfira lī wa tarḥamanī.

'Allah, I call upon You as the Lord of Mercy, and I call upon You as the Beneficent, the Giver of Mercy. I call upon You with all Your Beautiful Names, what I know of them and what I do not know, that You forgive me and have mercy on me.' The Messenger of Allah ﷺ was brought to laughter by this and he said: 'It is among the Names that you supplicated with.'"[47]

Bayhaqī narrated from al-Ḍaḥḥāk that he said: "Mūsā supplicated the following when he made way to Pharaoh, and Allah's Messenger ﷺ supplicated on the day of the battle of Ḥunayn, with both of them saying:

47 Ibn Mājah.

وَعَنْ عَائِشَةَ رَضِيَ اللهُ تَعَالَىٰ عَنْهَا قَالَتْ: سَمِعْتُ رَسُولَ اللهِ ﷺ يَقُولُ: «اَللَّهُمَّ إِنِّي أَسْأَلُكَ بِاسْمِكَ الطَّاهِرِ الطَّيِّبِ الْمُبارَكِ الْأَحَبِّ إِلَيْكَ، الَّذِي إِذَا دُعِيتَ بِهِ أَجَبْتَ، وَإِذَا سُئِلْتَ بِهِ أَعْطَيْتَ، وَإِذَا اسْتُرْحِمْتَ بِهِ رَحِمْتَ، وَإِذَا اسْتُفْرِجْتَ بِهِ فَرَّجْتَ». وَقَالَ ذَاتَ يَوْمٍ: «يَا عَائِشَةُ هَلْ عَلِمْتِ أَنَّ اللهَ قَدْ دَلَّنِي عَلَى الْاِسْمِ الَّذِي إِذَا دُعِيَ بِهِ أَجَابَ»؟، قَالَتْ: قُلْتُ يَا رَسُولَ اللهِ بِأَبِي أَنْتَ وَأُمِّي فَعَلِّمْنِيهِ، قَالَ: «إِنَّهُ لَا يَنْبَغِي لَكِ يَا عَائِشَةُ»، قَالَتْ: فَتَنَحَّيْتُ وَجَلَسْتُ سَاعَةً ثُمَّ قُمْتُ فَقَبَّلْتُ رَأْسَهُ ثُمَّ قُلْتُ: يَا رَسُولَ اللهِ عَلِّمْنِيهِ، قَالَ: «إِنَّهُ لَا يَنْبَغِي لَكِ يَا عَائِشَةُ أَنْ أُعَلِّمَكِ، إِنَّهُ لَا يَنْبَغِي لَكِ أَنْ تَسْأَلِي بِهِ شَيْئاً مِنَ الدُّنْيَا»، قَالَت: فَقُمْتُ فَتَوَضَّأْتُ ثُمَّ صَلَّيْتُ رَكْعَتَيْنِ ثُمَّ قُلْتُ: اَللّٰهُمَّ إِنِّي أَدْعُوكَ اللهَ، وَأَدْعُوكَ الرَّحْمٰنَ، وَأَدْعُوكَ الْبَرَّ الرَّحِيمَ، وَأَدْعُوكَ بِأَسْمَائِكَ الْحُسْنَى كُلِّهَا مَا عَلِمْتُ مِنْهَا وَمَا لَمْ أَعْلَمْ؛ أَنْ تَغْفِرَ لِي وَتَرْحَمَنِي؛ فَاسْتَضْحَكَ رَسُولُ اللهِ ﷺ ثُمَّ قَالَ: «إِنَّهُ لَفِي الْأَسْمَاءِ الَّتِي دَعَوْتِ بِهَا»(٣٩). وَفِي التِّرْمِذِيِّ كَانَ ﷺ إِذَا كَرَبَهُ أَمْرٌ يَقُولُ: «يَا حَيُّ يَا قَيُّومُ بِرَحْمَتِكَ أَسْتَغِيثُ». وَقَالَ ﷺ: «أَلِظُّوا بِيَا ذَا الْجَلَالِ وَالْإِكْرَامِ» - أَيْ: أَكْثِرُوا مِنَ التَّلَفُّظِ بِيَا ذَا الْجَلَالِ وَالْإِكْرَامِ.

وَرَوَى الْبَيْهَقِيُّ عَنِ الضَّحَّاكِ قَالَ: دَعَا مُوسَى حِينَ تَوَجَّهَ إِلَى فِرْعَوْنَ، وَدَعَا رَسُولُ اللهِ ﷺ يَوْمَ حُنَيْنٍ:

---

(٣٩) رَوَاهُ ابْنُ مَاجَه.

Kunta wa takūn,[48] *wa anta Ḥayyun lā tamūt, tanāmu al-ʿuyūn, wa tankadiru al-nujūm, wa anta Ḥayyun Qayyūmun lā taʾkhudhuhū sinatun wa lā nawm; yā Ḥayyu yā Qayyūm.*

'You are and You were, and You are Ever Living and will never die. The eyes sleep, the stars go out, and You are Ever Living, Sustainer of all, never overtaken by sleep or enervation; Ever Living, Sustainer of all.'"

Ṭabarānī reports on the authority of Anas ﷠ that the Prophet ﷺ said: "If you ask for a thing wishing for success in its fulfilment, then say: *Lā ilāha illā Allāhu waḥdahū lā sharīka lahū al-ʿAliyyu al-ʿAẓīm, lā ilāha illā Allāhu waḥdahū lā sharīka lahū al-Ḥalīmu al-Karīm, bismillāhi alladhī lā ilāha illā huwa al-Ḥayyu al-Qayyūm al-Ḥakīm, subḥāna Rabbi al-ʿarshi al-ʿaẓīm. Al-ḥamdu lillāhi Rabbi al-ʿālamīn. Kaʾannahum yawma yarawna mā yūʿaduna lam yalbathū illā sāʿatan min nahārin balāgh, fa-hal yuhlahku illā al-qawmu al-fāsiqūn. Kaʾannahum yawma yarawnahā lam yalbathū illā ʿashiyyatan aw ḍuḥāhā. Allāhumma innī asʾaluka mūjibāti raḥmatik, wa azāʾima maghfiratik, wa al-ghanīmata min kulli birr, wa al-salāmata min kulli ithm, wa al-fawza bil-jannati wa al-najāta min al-nār. Allāhumma lā tadaʿ lī dhanban illā ghafartah, wa lā hamman illā fajartah, wa lā daynan illā qaḍaytah, wa lā ḥājatan min ḥawāʾiji al-dunyā wa al-ākhirati illā qaḍaytahā bi-raḥmatika yā Arḥama al-rāḥimīn.*

'There is no god but Allah, alone without associates, the Most High, the Sublime. There is no god but Allah, alone without associates, the Forbearing, the Most Generous. In the Name of Allah, other than whom there is no god but He, the Ever Living, the Sustainer, the All Wise. Glory be to Allah, the Lord of the Great Throne. "In the Name of Allah – the Most Compassionate, Most Merciful."[49] "On the Day they see what they have been threatened with, it will be as if they had only stayed [in this world] for an hour of a day. This is a [sufficient] warning! Then, will anyone be destroyed except the rebellious people?"[50] "On the Day they see it, it will be as if they had stayed [in the world] no more than one evening or its

---

48   Meaning, 'You, My Lord, are the Infinite, the Eternal.'

49   *al-Fātiḥah,* 1.

50   *al-Aḥqāf,* 35.

«كُنتَ وَتَكُونُ[٤٠]، وَأَنْتَ حَيٌّ لَا تَمُوتُ، تَنَامُ الْعُيُونُ، وَتَنْكَدِرُ النُّجُومُ، وَأَنْتَ حَيٌّ قَيُّومٌ لَا تَأْخُذُهُ سِنَةٌ وَلَا نَوْمٌ، يَا حَيُّ يَا قَيُّومُ».

وَفِي الطَّبَرَانِيِّ عَنْ أَنَسٍ رَضِيَ اللهُ عَنْهُ عَنِ النَّبِيِّ ﷺ: «إِذَا طَلَبْتَ حَاجَةً فَأَحْبَبْتَ أَنْ تَنْجَحَ قُلْ: لَا إِلَهَ إِلَّا اللهُ وَحْدَهُ لَا شَرِيكَ لَهُ الْعَلِيُّ الْعَظِيمُ، لَا إِلَهَ إِلَّا اللهُ وَحْدَهُ لَا شَرِيكَ لَهُ الْحَلِيمُ الْكَرِيمُ، بِسْمِ اللهِ الَّذِي لَا إِلَهَ إِلَّا هُوَ الْحَيُّ الْقَيُّومُ الْحَكِيمُ، سُبْحَانَ اللهِ رَبِّ الْعَرْشِ الْعَظِيمِ، ﴿ٱلْحَمْدُ لِلَّهِ رَبِّ ٱلْعَٰلَمِينَ﴾، ﴿كَأَنَّهُمْ يَوْمَ يَرَوْنَ مَا يُوعَدُونَ لَمْ يَلْبَثُوٓاْ إِلَّا سَاعَةً مِّن نَّهَارٍۭ بَلَٰغٌۚ فَهَلْ يُهْلَكُ إِلَّا ٱلْقَوْمُ ٱلْفَٰسِقُونَ﴾ ﴿كَأَنَّهُمْ يَوْمَ يَرَوْنَهَا لَمْ يَلْبَثُوٓاْ إِلَّا عَشِيَّةً أَوْ ضُحَىٰهَا﴾، اَللَّهُمَّ إِنِّي أَسْأَلُكَ مُوجِبَاتِ رَحْمَتِكَ، وَعَزَائِمَ مَغْفِرَتِكَ، وَالْغَنِيمَةَ مِنْ كُلِّ بِرٍّ، وَالسَّلَامَةَ مِنْ كُلِّ إِثْمٍ، وَالْفَوْزَ بِالْجَنَّةِ وَالنَّجَاةَ مِنَ النَّارِ، اَللَّهُمَّ لَا تَدَعْ لِي ذَنْبًا إِلَّا غَفَرْتَهُ، وَلَا هَمًّا إِلَّا فَرَّجْتَهُ، وَلَا دَيْنًا إِلَّا قَضَيْتَهُ، وَلَا حَاجَةً مِنْ حَوَائِجِ الدُّنْيَا وَالْآخِرَةِ إِلَّا قَضَيْتَهَا بِرَحْمَتِكَ يَا أَرْحَمَ الرَّاحِمِينَ».

---

(٤٠) وَالْمَعْنَى أَنْتَ يَا رَبِّيَ الْأَزَلِيُّ الْأَبَدِيُّ.

morning."[51] Allah, I ask You for that which obliges Your mercy, the means to Your forgiveness, the benefit of every good deed and safety from every sin, success in attaining the Garden, and deliverance from the Fire. Allah, leave not for us a sin but that You have forgiven it, nor worry but that you relieve it, nor a debt but that you fulfil on our behalf, nor a need of this world or the next but that you fulfil for us, by Your mercy, Most Merciful of those who show mercy.'

Ḥākim authenticated a narration on the authority of ʿAlī ﵁ that he said to a man: "Shall I not teach you some words taught to me by the Messenger of Allah ﷺ that would incite Allah to relieve your debts even if they were like a *ṣīr*[52]? Say:

Allāhumma ikfinī bi-ḥalālika ʿan ḥarāmika wa aghninī bi-faḍlika ʿan man siwāk.

'Allah, suffice me by what is lawful from the unlawful, and enrich me through Your favour from all other than You.'"

On the authority of Ibrāhīm ibn Khallād: "Jibrīl descended upon Yaʿqūb ﵇. The latter complained of his state to the former, so he said: 'Shall I teach you a supplication that if you make, Allah will relieve your troubles? Say:

Yā man lā yaʿlamu kayfa huwa illā hū, wa yā man lā yablughu qudratahū ghayruh, farrij ʿannī.

"There is no one who knows how You are but You, and there are none who may reach Your power other than You; give me relief."' – the bringer of glad-tidings came to him thereupon."[53]

---

51 *al-Nāziʿāt*, 46.

52 Referring to the mountain of *Ṭay'*, as found in *al-Nihāyah*.

53 Ibn Abī al-Dunyā.

وَصَحَّحَ الْحَاكِمُ عَنْ عَلِيٍّ رَضِيَ اللهُ تَعَالَى عَنْهُ أَنَّهُ قَالَ لِرَجُلٍ:

أَلَا أُعَلِّمُكَ كَلِمَاتٍ عَلَّمَنِيهِنَّ رَسُولُ اللهِ ﷺ وَلَوْ كَانَ عَلَيْكَ مِثْلُ صِيرٍ[٤١] دَيْنًا لَأَدَّاهُ اللهُ عَنْكَ، قُلْ:

«اَللّٰهُمَّ اكْفِنِي بِحَلَالِكَ عَنْ حَرَامِكَ، وَأَغْنِنِي بِفَضْلِكَ عَمَّنْ سِوَاكَ».

وَعَنْ إِبْرَاهِيمَ بْنِ خَلَّادٍ:

(نَزَلَ جِبْرِيلُ عَلَى يَعْقُوبَ عَلَيْهِمَا الصَّلَاةُ وَالسَّلَامُ فَشَكَا إِلَيْهِ مَا هُوَ فِيهِ فَقَالَ: أَلَا أُعَلِّمُكَ دُعَاءً إِذَا دَعَوتَ بِهِ فَرَّجَ اللهُ عَنْكَ؟، قُلْ: يَا مَنْ لَا يَعْلَمُ كَيْفَ هُوَ إِلَّا هُوَ، وَيَا مَنْ لَا يَبْلُغُ قُدْرَتَهُ غَيْرُهُ، فَرِّجْ عَنِّي) - فَأَتَاهُ الْبَشِيرُ[٤٢].

---

(٤١) جَبَلُ طَيِّءٍ، كَمَا فِي النِّهَايَةِ.

(٤٢) رَوَاهُ ابْنُ أَبِي الدُّنيا.

Ibn ʿAsākir narrated on the authority of Saʿīd ibn al-Musayyib that he said: "A matter afflicted me, causing me anguish, so I went out in the night towards the Mosque of the Prophet ﷺ. I entered it, then heard some moving pebbles. I looked but found no one in the direction of the sound, but I heard someone say: 'Supplicate Allah regarding your affliction and say:

Allāhumma innī as'aluka fa-innaka lanā Mālik, wa innaka ʿalā kulli shay'in Qadīrun Muqtadir, wa innaka mā tashā'u min amrin yakūn.

"Allah, I ask You as You are our Owner, and You are over all things Most Capable and Powerful. Whatever You will is exacted."' I never supplicated Allah with these words but it was realized."

In *al-Musnad* and elsewhere, on the authority of Ibn Masʿūd ﷺ the Messenger of Allah ﷺ said: "No worry nor grief afflicts a person who then says:

Allāhumma innī ʿabduk, ibnu ʿabdik, ibnu amatik, nāṣiyatī bi-yadik, māḍin fiyya ḥukmuk, ʿadlun fiyya qaḍā'uk, as'aluka bi-kulli ismin huwa lak: sammayta bihī nafsak, aw anzaltahu fī kitābik, aw ʿallamtahu aḥadan min khalqik, aw ista'tharta bihī fī ʿilmi al-ghaybi ʿindak, an tajʿala al-Qur'āna al-ʿaẓīma rabīʿa qalbī, wa nūra baṣarī, wa jalā'a ḥuznī wa dhahāba hammī.

'Allah, I am your slave, the offspring of your male and female slaves. My forelock is in Your Hand. Your judgement does pass over me. Your decree is just for me. I ask you with every name that is Yours: that you have called Yourself, or revealed in Your Book, or taught one of Your slaves, or favoured for Yourself in the realm of the unseen, that You make the Glorious Qur'an the spring of my heart, the light of my sight, the leave of my sadness, and the removal of my worry' but that Allah does away with his grief and worry, replacing them with joy."

On the authority of Abū Bakr ﷺ: "Allah's Messenger ﷺ said: 'The supplication of the troubled is:

Allāhumma raḥmataka arjū falā takilnī ilā nafsī ṭarfata ʿayn, wa aṣliḥ lī sha'nī kullahū lā ilāha illā ant.

"Allah, I beg for Your mercy, so do not entrust me to myself for a blink of an eye, and set right all my affairs; there is no god but You."'"

وَرَوَى ابْنُ عَسَاكِرٍ عَنْ سَعِيدِ بْنِ الْمُسَيَّبِ قَالَ: نَزَلَ بِي أَمْرٌ أَهَمَّنِي فَخَرَجْتُ مِنَ اللَّيْلِ إِلَى مَسْجِدِ النَّبِيِّ ﷺ فَدَخلتُ الْمَسْجِدَ فَسَمِعْتُ حَرَكَةَ الْحَصَى فَالتَفَتُّ فَلَمْ أَرَ أَحَدًا، وَسَمِعْتُ قَائِلًا يَقُولُ: أُدْعُ اللهَ فِيْ هَذَا الْأَمْرِ الَّذِيْ يَهُمُّكَ وَقُلْ: اَللّٰهُمَّ إِنِّي أَسْأَلُكَ فَإِنَّكَ لَنَا مَالِكٌ، وَإِنَّكَ عَلَى كُلِّ شَيْءٍ قَدِيرٌ مُقْتَدِرٌ، وَإِنَّكَ مَا تَشَاءُ مِنْ أَمْرٍ يَكُونُ - قَالَ: فَمَا دَعَوتُ اللهَ بِهِ فِيْ شَيْءٍ إِلَّا وَقَدْ رَأَيتُهُ. وَفِي الْمُسْنَدِ وَغَيْرِهِ عَنِ ابْنِ مَسْعُودٍ رَضِيَ اللهُ تَعَالَى عَنْهُ عَنِ النَّبِيِّ ﷺ قَالَ: «مَا أَصَابَ عَبْدًا هَمٌّ أَوْ حُزْنٌ فَقَالَ: اَللّٰهُمَّ إِنِّي عَبْدُكَ، وَابْنُ عَبْدِكَ، وَابْنُ أَمَتِكَ، نَاصِيَتِيْ بِيَدِكَ، مَاضٍ فِيَّ حُكْمُكَ، عَدْلٌ فِيَّ قَضَاؤُكَ، أَسْأَلُكَ بِكُلِّ اسْمٍ هُوَ لَكَ: سَمَّيتَ بِهِ نَفْسَكَ، أَوْ أَنْزَلْتَهُ فِي كِتَابِكَ، أَوْ عَلَّمْتَهُ أَحَدًا مِنْ خَلْقِكَ، أَوِ اسْتَأْثَرْتَ بِهِ فِي عِلْمِ الْغَيْبِ عِنْدَكَ، أَنْ تَجْعَلَ الْقُرْآنَ الْعَظِيمَ رَبِيعَ قَلْبِيْ، وَنُورَ بَصَرِيْ، وَجِلَاءَ حُزْنِيْ وَذَهَابَ هَمِّيْ - إِلَّا أَذْهَبَ اللهُ حُزْنَهُ وَهَمَّهُ وَأَبْدَلَ مَكَانَهُ فَرَحًا».

وَعَنْ أَبِي بَكْرٍ رَضِيَ اللهُ عَنْهُ قَالَ: قَالَ رَسُولُ اللهِ ﷺ: «دَعَوَاتُ الْمَكْرُوْبِ: اَللّٰهُمَّ رَحْمَتَكَ أَرْجُوْ فَلَا تَكِلْنِيْ إِلَى نَفْسِي طَرْفَةَ عَيْنٍ، وَأَصْلِحْ لِي شَأْنِي كُلَّهُ لَا إِلٰهَ إِلَّا أَنْتَ»(٤٣).

(٤٣) رواهُ ابْنُ حِبَّان وَغَيْرُه.

On the authority of Ibn ʿAbbās 🌸, the Prophet 🌼 said: "Whoever says:
Lā ilāha illā Allāhu qabla kulli shay', wa lā ilāha illā Allāhu baʿda kulli shay', wa lā ilāha illā Allāhu yabqā rabbunā wa yafnā kullu shay'.
'There is no god but Allah before everything. There is no god but Allah after everything. There is no god but Allah, our Lord remains and all else perishes' will be safe from worry and grief."[54]

On the authority of Ibn Masʿūd 🌸, Allah's Messenger 🌼 said: "Shall I teach you the words that Mūsā 🌼 said once he had passed through the sea with the Children of Israel?" I said: "Yes, Messenger of Allah." He said: "Say:
Allāhumma laka al-ḥamd, wa ilayka al-mushtakā, wa anta al-mustaʿān, wa lā ḥawla wa lā quwwata illā billāhi al-ʿAliyyi al-ʿAẓīm.
'Allah, to You belongs all praise, complaints are raised to You, and You are the One we seek for help. There is no might nor strength but through Allah, the Most High, the Sublime.'"

On the authority of Ibn ʿAbbās 🌸, the Prophet 🌼 said: "Jibrīl 🌼 came to me with some supplications, saying: 'If a worldly matter troubles you, say these words first, then ask for your need:
Yā Badīʿa al-samāwāti wa al-arḍ, yā Dhā al-jalāli wa al-ikrām, yā Ṣarīkha al-mustaṣrikhīn, ya Ghiyātha al-mustaghīthīn, ya kāshifa al-sūʾi yā Arḥama al-rāḥimīn, yā Mujība daʿwati al-muḍṭarrīn, ya Ilāha al-ʿalamīn, bika unzilu ḥājatī wa anta Aʿlamu bihā, fa-iqḍihā.
"Innovator of the heavens and Earth, Possessor of majesty and generosity, Object of those who cry out, Rescuer of those pleading for deliverance, Remover of evil, Most Merciful of those who show mercy, Answer of the desperate's call, God of all worlds, I express my need to You and You know it best, so fulfil it.'"[55]

---

54 Ṭabarānī.
55 Mundhirī said: "Aṣbahānī reported it, and it has many testifying pieces of evidence."

وَعَنِ ابْنِ عَبَّاسٍ رَضِيَ اللهُ عَنْهُمَا عَنِ النَّبِيِّ ﷺ أَنَّهُ قَالَ: «مَنْ قَالَ لَا إِلٰهَ إِلَّا اللهُ قَبْلَ كُلِّ شَيْءٍ، وَلَا إِلٰهَ إِلَّا اللهُ بَعْدَ كُلِّ شَيْءٍ، وَلَا إِلٰهَ إِلَّا اللهُ يَبْقَى رَبُّنَا وَيَفْنَى كُلُّ شَيْءٍ- عُوفِيَ مِنَ الْهَمِّ وَالْحَزَنِ»(٤٤). وَعَنِ ابْنِ مَسْعُودٍ رَضِيَ اللهُ عَنْهُ قَالَ: قَالَ رَسُولُ اللهِ ﷺ: «أَلَا أُعَلِّمُكَ الْكَلِمَاتِ الَّتِي تَكَلَّمَ بِهَا مُوسَى عَلَيْهِ السَّلَامُ حِينَ جَاوَزَ الْبَحْرَ بِبَنِي إِسْرَائِيلَ»؟ فَقُلْتُ: بَلَى يَا رَسُولَ اللهِ، قَالَ: قُلْ: «اَللّٰهُمَّ لَكَ الْحَمْدُ، وَإِلَيْكَ الْمُشْتَكَى، وَأَنْتَ الْمُسْتَعَانُ، وَلَا حَوْلَ وَلَا قُوَّةَ إِلَّا بِاللهِ الْعَلِيِّ الْعَظِيمِ». وَعَنِ ابْنِ عَبَّاسٍ رَضِيَ اللهُ عَنْهُمَا قَالَ: قَالَ رَسُولُ اللهِ ﷺ: «جَاءَنِي جِبْرِيلُ عَلَيْهِ السَّلَامُ بِدَعَوَاتٍ فَقَالَ: إِذَا نَزَلَ بِكَ أَمْرٌ مِنْ أَمْرِ دُنْيَاكَ فَقَدِّمْهُنَّ ثُمَّ سَلْ حَاجَتَكَ: يَا بَدِيعَ السَّمٰوَاتِ وَالْأَرْضِ، يَا ذَا الْجَلَالِ وَالْإِكْرَامِ، يَا صَرِيخَ الْمُسْتَصْرِخِينَ، يَا غِيَاثَ الْمُسْتَغِيثِينَ، يَا كَاشِفَ السُّوءِ يَا أَرْحَمَ الرَّاحِمِينَ، يَا مُجِيبَ دَعْوَةِ الْمُضْطَرِّينَ، يَا إِلٰهَ الْعَالَمِينَ، بِكَ أُنْزِلُ حَاجَتِي وَأَنْتَ أَعْلَمُ بِهَا، فَاقْضِهَا»(٤٥).

---

(٤٤) رَوَاهُ الطَّبَرَانِيُّ.

(٤٥) قَالَ الْمُنْذِرِيُّ: رَوَاهُ الْأَصْبَهَانِيُّ، وَلَهُ شَوَاهِدُ كَثِيرَةٌ.

Anas said: "I was at the Mother of the Believer's house, ʿĀ'ishah. I was there to grant her the good news of her divinely revealed innocence. She was crying, saying: 'By Allah, the near and the far deserted me, even cats! No food nor drink would be presented to me, so I would sleep hungry and thirsty. I saw in my dream someone who said to me: "Supplicate with these words, your trouble will be eased." I said: "What words?" He said: "Say:

Yā Sābigha al-niʿam, yā Dāfiʿa al-niqam, yā Fārija al-ghumam, yā Kāshifa al-ẓulam, yā Aʿdala man ḥakam, yā Ḥasība man ẓalam, yā Waliyya man ẓulim, yā Awwalun bilā bidāyah, yā Akhirun bilā nihāyah, yā man lahū ismun bilā kunyah, Allāhumma ijʿal lī min amri farajan wa makhrajā.

'Bestower of blessings, Reliever of stress, Remover of darkness, Most Just in judgement, Reckoner of the oppressor, Ally to the oppressed; First without beginning and Last without end, Known by His Name without alias; Allah, make for me a way out of my troubles.'" I then woke up satisfied from hunger and quenched from thirst, and relief from Allah the Exalted had come down.'"[56]

On the authority of ʿAbdullāh ibn Jaʿfar the Messenger of Allah said: *Allāhumma innī ashkū ilayka ḍaʿfa quwwatī, wa qillata ḥīlatī, wa hawānī ʿalā al-nās. Yā Arḥama al-rāḥimīn, ilā man takilunī? Ilā ʿaduwwin yatajahhamunī, am ilā qarībin mallaktahu amrī? In lam takun sākhiṭan ʿalayya falā ubālī, ghayra anna ʿāfiyataka awsaʿu lī. Aʿūdhu bi-nūri wajhika al-karīmi alladhī aḍā'at lahū al-samāwatu wa al-arḍ, wa ashraqat lahū al-ẓulumāt, wa ṣaluḥa ʿalayhi amru al-dunyā wa al-ākhirah: an tuḥilla ʿalayya ghaḍabak, aw tunzila ʿalayya sakhaṭak, wa laka al-ʿutbā ḥattā tarḍā, wa lā ḥawla wa lā quwwata illā bik.*

"Allah, I complain to You of my weakness, the scarcity of my resources, and the humiliation I have been subjected to by the people. Most Merciful of those who are merciful, You are Lord of the weak, and my Lord, too. To whom have you entrusted me? To a distant person who receives me with hostility? Or to an enemy to whom you have granted authority over my affair? So long as You are not angry with me, I do not mind, but Your

56 Ibn al-Najjār.

وَعَنْ أَنَسٍ رَضِيَ اللهُ عَنْهُ قَالَ: (كُنتُ جَالِسًا عِنْدَ أُمِّ الْمُؤْمِنِينَ عَائِشَةَ رَضِيَ اللهُ تَعَالَى عَنْهَا لِأُقِرَّ عَيْنَهَا بِالْبَرَاءَةِ وَهِيَ تَبْكِي فَقَالَت: وَاللهِ لَقَدْ هَجَرَنِي الْقَرِيبُ وَالْبَعِيدُ حَتَّى هَجَرَتْنِي الْهِرَّةُ، وَمَا عُرِضَ عَلَيَّ طَعَامٌ وَلَا شَرَابٌ، فَكُنْتُ أَرْقُدُ وَأَنَا جَائِعَةٌ ظَامِئَةٌ، فَرَأَيْتُ فِي مَنَامِي قَائِلًا قَالَ لِي: مَا لَكِ ؟ فَقُلْتُ: حَزِينَةٌ مِمَّا ذَكَرَ النَّاسُ، فَقَالَ: أُدْعِي بِهَذِهِ يُفَرِّجُ عَنْكِ، فَقُلْتُ: وَمَا هِيَ الدَّعَوَاتُ؟ فَقَالَ: قُولِي:

يَا سَابِغَ النِّعَمِ، يَا دَافِعَ النِّقَمِ، يَا فَارِجَ الْغُمَمِ، يَا كَاشِفَ الظُّلَمِ، يَا أَعْدَلَ مَنْ حَكَمَ، يَا حَسِيبَ مَنْ ظَلَمَ، يَا وَلِيَّ مَنْ ظُلِمَ، يَا أَوَّلَ بِلَا بِدَايَةٍ، يَا آخِرَ بِلَا نِهَايَةٍ، يَا مَنْ لَهُ اسْمٌ بِلَا كُنِيَّةٍ، اَللَّهُمَّ اجْعَلْ لِي مِنْ أَمْرِي فَرَجًا وَمَخْرَجًا، قَالَتْ: فَانْتَبَهْتُ وَأَنَا رَيَّانَةٌ شَبْعَانَةٌ، وَقَدْ أَنْزَلَ اللهُ تَعَالَىٰ مِنْهُ فَرَجاً)[٤٦]. وَعَنْ عَبْدِ اللهِ بْنِ جَعْفَرٍ رَضِيَ اللهُ تَعَالَىٰ عَنهُ قَالَ: إِنَّ رَسُولَ اللهِ ﷺ قَالَ: «اَللَّهُمَّ إِنِّي أَشْكُو إِلَيْكَ ضُعْفَ قُوَّتِي، وَقِلَّةَ حِيلَتِي، وَهَوَانِي عَلَى النَّاسِ، يَا أَرْحَمَ الرَّاحِمِينَ: إِلَى مَنْ تَكِلُنِي، إِلَى عَدُوٍّ يَتَجَهَّمُنِي، أَمْ إِلَى قَرِيبٍ مَلَّكْتَهُ أَمْرِي ؟ إِنْ لَمْ تَكُنْ سَاخِطًا عَلَيَّ فَلَا أُبَالِي، غَيْرَ أَنَّ عَافِيَتَكَ أَوْسَعُ لِي، أَعُوذُ بِنُورِ وَجْهِكَ الْكَرِيمِ الَّذِي أَضَاءَتْ لَهُ السَّمٰوَاتُ وَالْأَرْضُ، وَأَشْرَقَتْ لَهُ الظُّلُمَاتُ، وَصَلُحَ عَلَيْهِ أَمْرُ الدُّنْيَا وَالْآخِرَةِ: أَنْ

---

(٤٦) رَوَاهُ ابنُ النَّجَّارِ.

favour is of a more expansive relief to me. I seek refuge in the light of Your Face by which all darkness is dispelled and every affair of this world and the next is set right, lest Your anger or Your displeasure descend upon me. Appeasement is exclusively Yours until You are pleased. There is no power nor might except through You."[57]

It is narrated from the authority of Jaʿfar al-Ṣādiq that he said: "My father, Muḥammad al-Bāqir, narrated to me from ʿAlī Zayn al-ʿĀbidīn the son of al-Ḥusayn the son of ʿAlī ibn Abī Ṭālib ﷺ that the Prophet ﷺ used to make the following supplication when a troubling matter brought him anguish:

Allāhumma uḥrusnī bi-ʿaynika allatī lā tanām, wa uknufnī bi-ruknika alladhī lā yurām, wa irhamnī bi-qudratika ʿalayya fa-lā ahliku wa anta rajāʾī, fa-kam min niʿmatin anʿamta bihā ʿalayya qalla laka bihā ʿindahā shukrī? Wa kam min baliyyatin ibtalaytanī bihā qalla laka bihā ṣabrī? Fa-yā man qalla ʿinda niʿmatihī shukrī fa-lam yaḥrimnī, wa yā man qalla ʿinda baliyyatihī ṣabrī fa-lam yakhdhulnī, wa yā man ra'ānī ʿalā al-khaṭāyā fa-lam yafdaḥni, ya Dhā al-maʿrūfi alladhī la yanqaḍī abadā, wa ya Dhā al-niʿmati allatī lā tuḥṣā ʿadadā; as'aluka an tuṣalliya ʿalā Muḥammadin wa ʿalā āli Muḥammad, wa bika adra'u fī nuḥuri al-aʿdā'i wa al-jabbārin.

'Allah, guard me with Your eye that never sleeps, shield me with Your unyielding protection, and have mercy upon me by Your power over me, for I cannot be destroyed whilst You are my hope. Many a blessing You have bestowed upon me I showed little gratitude for. Many a trial You have tested me with I showed little patience in enduring. I showed little gratitude for Your blessings, yet You did not deprive me. I showed little patience over Your trials, yet You did not let me down. You saw me upon sin, and You did not expose me. Your goodness is never cut off, and Your blessings can never be enumerated. I ask You to confer exaltations upon Muhammad and the family of Muhammad, and I repel enemies and tyrants through You.'"

57 Ṭabarānī and others, and it is known as the Supplication of Ṭā'if.

تَحِلَّ عَلَيَّ غَضَبَكَ، أَوْ تُنْزِلَ عَلَيَّ سَخَطَكَ، وَلَكَ الْعُتْبَىٰ حَتَّىٰ تَرْضَى، وَ لَا حَوْلَ وَ لَا قُوَّةَ إِلَّا بِكَ»(٤٧).

وَعَنْ جَعْفَرٍ الصَّادِقِ قَالَ: حَدَّثَنِي أَبِي مُحَمَّدٌ الْبَاقِرُ عَنْ عَلِيٍّ زَيْنِ الْعَابِدِينَ بْنِ الْحُسَيْنِ بْنِ عَلِيِّ بْنِ أَبِي طَالِبٍ رَضِيَ اللهُ عَنْهُمْ أَنَّ النَّبِيَّ ﷺ كَانَ إِذَا حَزَبَهُ - أَيْ: أَهَمَّهُ - أَمْرٌ دَعَا بِهَذَا الدُّعَاءِ:

«اَللّٰهُمَّ احْرُسْنِي بِعَيْنِكَ الَّتِي لَا تَنَامُ، وَاكْنُفْنِي بِرُكْنِكَ الَّذِي لَا يُرَامُ، وَارْحَمْنِي بِقُدْرَتِكَ عَلَيَّ فَلَا أَهْلِكُ وَأَنْتَ رَجَائِي، فَكَمْ مِنْ نِعْمَةٍ أَنْعَمْتَ بِهَا عَلَيَّ قَلَّ لَكَ بِهَا عِنْدَهَا شُكْرِي ؟ وَكَمْ مِنْ بَلِيَّةٍ ابْتَلَيْتَنِي بِهَا قَلَّ لَكَ بِهَا صَبْرِي ؟ فَيَا مَنْ قَلَّ عِنْدَ نِعْمَتِهِ شُكْرِي فَلَمْ يَحْرِمْنِي، وَيَا مَنْ قَلَّ عِنْدَ بَلِيَّتِهِ صَبْرِي فَلَمْ يَخْذُلْنِي، وَيَا مَنْ رَآنِي عَلَى الْخَطَايَا فَلَمْ يَفْضَحْنِي، يَا ذَا الْمَعْرُوفِ الَّذِي لَا يَنْقَضِي أَبَدًا، وَيَا ذَا النِّعْمَةِ الَّتِي لَا تُحْصَى عَدَدًا؛ أَسْأَلُكَ أَنْ تُصَلِّيَ عَلَى مُحَمَّدٍ وَعَلَى آلِ مُحَمَّدٍ، وَبِكَ أَدْرَأُ - أَيْ: أَدْفَعُ - فِي نُحُورِ الْأَعْدَاءِ وَالْجَبَّارِينَ.

---

(٤٧) رَوَاهُ الطَّبَرَانِيُّ وَغَيْرُهُ وَيُسَمَّى دُعَاءُ الطَّائِفِ.

Allāhumma aʿinnī ʿalā dīnī bil-dunyā, wa ʿalā ākhiratī bil-taqwā, wa iḥfaẓnī fīmā ghibtu anh, wa lā takilnī ilā nafsī fīmā haẓartahū ʿalayy, yā man lā taḍurruhū al-dhunūbu wa lā yunqiṣuhū al-ʿafw, hab lī mā lā yunqiṣuk, wa ighfir lī mā lā yadurruk, innaka anta al-Wahhāb.

Allah, aid me in my religion through the worldly life, and in my afterlife through piety. Protect for me that which I am absent from, and do not entrust me to myself in that which You have forbidden me from. One Who is neither harmed by sin nor decreased by showing pardon, bestow upon me that which does not decrease You, and absolve me of what does not harm You, You are the Bestower.

As'aluka farajan qarībā, wa ṣabran jamīlā, wa rizqan wāsiʿā, wa al-ʿāfiyata min al-balāyā, wa as'aluka tamāma al-ʿāfiyah, wa as'aluka al-shukra ʿalā al-ʿāfiyah, wa as'aluka al-ghinā ʿan al-nās, wa lā ḥawla wa lā quwwata illā billāhi al-ʿAliyyi al-ʿAẓīm.

I ask You for imminent relief, beautiful patience, expansive provision, and protection from calamities. I ask You for complete and continuous wellness, and gratitude for being given it. I ask You for independence from the people. There is no might nor power but through Allah, the Most High, the Sublime.[58]

58 al-Daylamī and others, and this is his wording.

اَللّٰهُمَّ أَعِنِّيْ عَلَى دِينِيْ بِالدُّنْيَا، وَعَلَى آخِرَتِيْ بِالتَّقْوَىٰ، وَاحْفَظْنِيْ فِيمَا غِبْتُ عَنْهُ، وَلَا تَكِلْنِيْ إِلَى نَفْسِيْ فِيمَا حَظَرْتَهُ عَلَيَّ، يَا مَنْ لَا تَضُرُّهُ الذُّنُوبُ وَلَا يَنْقُصُهُ الْعَفْوُ، هَبْ لِيْ مَا لَا يُنْقِصُكَ، وَاغْفِرْ لِيْ مَا لَا يَضُرُّكَ، إِنَّكَ أَنْتَ الْوَهَّابُ.

أَسْأَلُكَ فَرَجًا قَرِيبًا، وَصَبْرًا جَمِيلًا، وَرِزْقًا وَاسِعًا وَالْعَافِيَةَ مِنَ الْبَلَايَا، وَأَسْأَلُكَ تَمَامَ الْعَافِيَةِ، وَأَسْأَلُكَ دَوَامَ الْعَافِيَةِ، وَأَسْأَلُكَ الشُّكْرَ عَلَى الْعَافِيَةِ، وَأَسْأَلُكَ الْغِنَى عَنِ النَّاسِ، وَلَا حَوْلَ وَلَا قُوَّةَ إِلَّا بِاللّٰهِ الْعَلِيِّ الْعَظِيمِ»(٤٨).

---

(٤٨) رَوَاهُ الدَّيْلَمِيُّ وَهَذَا لَفْظُهُ وَغَيْرُ الدَّيْلَمِيِّ أَيْضًا.

Say *Lā Ilāha Illā Allāh* Often

It is a statement that renews one's faith, shields from the unlawful, opens up the doors of heaven, and does away with estrangement.

On the authority of Abū Hurayrah ﷺ, the Messenger of Allah ﷺ said: "Renew your faith." It was said: "How do we do that, Allah's Messenger?"

He said: "Say:
Lā ilāha illā Allāh.
'There is no god but Allah' often."[59]

On the authority of Zayd ibn Arqam ﷺ, Allah's Messenger ﷺ said: "Whoever says *Lā ilāha illā Allāh* sincerely will be admitted into the Garden." It was said: "What makes it sincere?" He said: "Preventing its possessor from violating the sanctities of Allah, Exalted."[60]

On the authority of Anas ﷺ, Allah's Messenger ﷺ said: "A slave does not say *Lā ilāha illā Allāh* sincerely but the doors of the heavens are opened to him one after the other until the Throne – so long as major sins are avoided."[61] In another narration from him: "*Lā ilāha illā Allāh* has no barrier between it and Allah until it goes to Him purely."

On the authority of Ibn ʿUmar ﷺ, Allah's Messenger ﷺ said: "There is no alienation for the people of *Lā ilāha illā Allāh* in their graves and when they are resurrected. I can almost see the people of *Lā ilāha illā Allāh* wiping the dust from their heads, saying: 'Praise be to Allah, Who has kept away from us all [causes of] sorrow.'[62]"

---

59 Imam Aḥmad.

60 Ṭabarānī.

61 Tirmidhī.

62 *Fāṭir*, 34

أَكْثِرْ مِنْ قَوْلِ لَا إِلٰهَ إِلَّا اللهُ

فَإِنَّهَا تُجَدِّدُ الْإِيمَانَ، وَتَحْجُزُ عَنِ الْمَحَارِمِ، وَتُفْتَحُ لَهَا أَبْوَابُ السَّمَاءِ، وَتُذْهِبُ الْوَحْشَةَ. عَنْ أَبِي هُرَيْرَةَ رَضِيَ اللهُ عَنْهُ قَالَ: قَالَ رَسُولُ اللهِ ﷺ: «جَدِّدُوا إِيمَانَكُم»، قِيلَ: يَا رَسُولَ اللهِ وَكَيْفَ نُجَدِّدُ إِيمَانَنَا ؟ قَالَ: «أَكْثِرُوا مِنْ قَوْلِ لَا إِلٰهَ إِلَّا اللهُ» - رَوَاهُ الْإِمَامُ أَحْمَدُ. وَعَنْ زَيْدِ بْنِ أَرْقَمَ رَضِيَ اللهُ تَعَالَىٰ عَنْهُ قَالَ: قَالَ رَسُولُ اللهِ ﷺ: «مَنْ قَالَ لَا إِلٰهَ إِلَّا اللهُ مُخْلِصًا دَخَلَ الْجَنَّةَ» قِيلَ: وَمَا إِخْلَاصُهَا؟ قَالَ: «أَنْ تَحْجُزَهُ عَنْ مَحَارِمِ اللهِ تَعَالَىٰ» رَوَاهُ الطَّبَرَانِيُّ. وَعَنْ أَبِي هُرَيْرَةَ رَضِيَ اللهُ تَعَالَىٰ عَنْهُ قَالَ: قَالَ رَسُولُ اللهِ ﷺ: «مَا قَالَ عَبْدٌ لَا إِلٰهَ إِلَّا اللهُ قَطُّ مُخْلِصًا إِلَّا فُتِحَتْ لَهُ أَبْوَابُ السَّمَاءِ حَتَّى يُفْضِيَ إِلَى الْعَرْشِ مَا اجْتُنِبَتِ الْكَبَائِرُ» رَوَاهُ التِّرْمِذِيُّ. وَفِي رِوَايَةٍ لَهُ: «وَ لَا إِلٰهَ إِلَّا اللهُ لَيْسَ لَهَا دُونَ اللهِ حِجَابٌ حَتَّى تَخْلُصَ إِلَيْهِ». وَعَنِ ابْنِ عُمَرَ رَضِيَ اللهُ عَنْهُمَا قَالَ: قَالَ رَسُولُ اللهِ ﷺ: «لَيْسَ عَلَى أَهْلِ لَا إِلٰهَ إِلَّا اللهُ وَحْشَةٌ فِي قُبُورِهِمْ وَلَا مَنْشَرِهِمْ، وَكَأَنِّي أَنْظُرُ إِلَى أَهْلِ لَا إِلٰهَ إِلَّا اللهُ وَهُمْ يَنْفُضُونَ التُّرَابَ عَنْ رُؤُوسِهِمْ وَيَقُولُونَ: ﴿ٱلْحَمْدُ لِلَّهِ ٱلَّذِىٓ أَذْهَبَ عَنَّا ٱلْحَزَنَ﴾ رَوَاهُ الطَّبَرَانِيُّ.

Nasā'ī narrates with his chain of transmission to the Prophet ﷺ that he said:

"A slave does not say:
Lā ilāha illā Allāhu waḥdahū lā sharīka lah, lahū al-mulku wa lahū al-ḥamdu wa huwa ʿalā kulli shay'in Qadīr.

'There is no god but Allah, alone without associates. To Him belongs dominion and praise, and He is Most Capable over all things' with sincerity in his soul, truthfulness in his heart, uttering it with his tongue, except that Allah breaks up the heavens just so that He may look upon the one who uttered it. A slave whom Allah has looked upon is most deserving of Allah giving him what he asks for."[63]

63 This is found in the *Targhīb* of Mundhirī. Its meaning is that Allah, Exalted, looks fondly upon the one who says it, with a special eye of mercy. He opens up the heavens so that His mercy may descend therefrom, reaching that person. Allah is not held back by barriers.

وَرَوَى النَّسَائِيُّ بِإِسْنَادِهِ عَنِ النَّبِيِّ ﷺ أَنَّهُ قَالَ: «مَا قَالَ عَبْدٌ قَطُّ: لَا إِلٰهَ إِلَّا اللهُ وَحْدَهُ لَا شَرِيكَ لَهُ، لَهُ الْمُلْكُ؛ وَلَهُ الْحَمْدُ؛ وَهُوَ عَلَى كُلِّ شَيْءٍ قَدِيرٌ؛ مُخْلِصًا بِهَا رُوحُهُ، مُصَدِّقًا بِهَا قَلْبُهُ، نَاطِقًا بِهَا لِسَانُهُ؛ إِلَّا فَتَقَ اللهُ عَزَّ وَجَلَّ لَهُ السَّمَاءَ فَتْقًا حَتَّى يَنْظُرَ إِلَى قَائِلِهَا مِنَ الْأَرْضِ، وَحُقَّ لِعَبْدٍ نَظَرَ اللهُ إِلَيهِ أَنْ يُعْطِيَهِ سُؤْلَهُ»[٤٩].

(٤٩) كَمَا فِي تَرْغِيبِ الْمُنْذِرِيِّ، وَالْمَعْنَى: أَنَّ اللهَ تَعَالَىٰ يَنْظُرُ إِلَى قَائِلِهَا نَظَرَ رَحْمَةٍ خَاصَّةٍ، فَيَفْتَحُ السَّمَاءَ، وَيُنْزِلُ عَلَيْهِ الرَّحْمَةَ، وَيُوصِلُهَا إِلَيْهِ، لِأَنَّ اللهَ تَعَالَىٰ لَا يَحْجُبُهُ شَيْءٌ عَنْ شَيْءٍ.

Be Abundant with the Lasting Good Deeds

On the authority of Abū Saʿīd al-Khudrī ﵁, Allah's Messenger ﷺ said: "Do plenty of lasting good deeds." It was said: "What are those, Messenger of Allah?" He said: "*Takbīr* (*Allāhu Akbar*), *tahlīl* (*lā ilāha illā Allāh*), *tasbīḥ* (*subḥān Allāh*), *al-ḥamdu lillāh*, and *lā ḥawla wa lā quwwata illā billāhi al-ʿAliyyi al-ʿAẓīm*."[64], [65] These words are:

Subḥān Allāh, al-ḥamdu lillāh, lā ilāha illā Allāh, Allāhu Akbar, wa lā ḥawla wa lā quwwata illā billāhi al-ʿAliyyi al-ʿAẓīm.

Glorified is Allah in sanctity, praise is to Allah, there is no god but Allah, Allah is Greatest, and there is no might nor strength but through Allah the Most High, the Sublime.

On the authority of Ibn Masʿūd ﵁, Allah's Messenger ﷺ said: "I met Ibrāhīm ﵇ on the night I was taken on the Journey (*Isrā'*). He said to me: 'Muhammad, confer my greetings to your nation, and tell them that the Garden has pure soil, sweet water, full of plains (qīʿān)[66]; and that its cultivation is through: *Subḥān Allāh, al-ḥamdu lillāh, lā ilāha illā Allāh,* and *Allāhu Akbar*.'"[67] The latter added: *Lā ḥawla wa lā quwwata illā billāhi al-ʿAliyyi al-ʿAẓīm.*

Ḥākim narrated with his chain of transmission to the Prophet ﷺ that he said: "Whoever says: '*Subḥān Allāh, al-ḥamdu lillāh, lā ilāha illā Allāh, Allāhu Akbar*, and *lā ḥawla wa lā quwwata illā billāhi al-ʿAliyyi al-ʿAẓīm*', Allah the Exalted says: 'My slave has submitted and surrendered.'"

---

64 These are among the most important verbal good deeds which remain with the believer in the realms following the worldly life.

65 Nasā'ī, Aḥmad, and others.

66 Vast land that is ready for seeds to be placed therein.

67 Tirmidhī and Ṭabarānī.

اِسْتَكْثِرْ مِنَ الْبَاقِيَاتِ الصَّالِحَاتِ

عَنْ أَبِي سَعِيدٍ رَضِيَ اللّٰهُ عَنْهُ أَنَّ رَسُولَ اللّٰهِ ﷺ قَالَ: «اِسْتَكْثِرُوا مِنَ الْبَاقِيَاتِ الصَّالِحَاتِ»، قِيلَ: وَمَا هُنَّ يَا رَسُولَ اللّٰهِ ؟ قَالَ: «التَّكْبِيرُ، وَالتَّهْلِيلُ، وَالتَّسْبِيحُ، وَالْحَمْدُ لِلّٰهِ، وَلَا حَولَ وَلَا قُوَّةَ إِلَّا بِاللّٰهِ»[٥٠] رَوَاهُ النَّسَائِيُّ وَأَحْمَدُ وَغَيْرُهُمَا. وَيَجْمَعُ ذَلِكَ كُلَّهُ: سُبْحَانَ اللّٰهِ، وَالْحَمْدُ لِلّٰهِ، وَلَا إِلٰهَ إِلَّا اللّٰهُ، وَاللّٰهُ أَكْبَرُ، وَلَا حَوْلَ وَلَا قُوَّةَ إِلَّا بِاللّٰهِ الْعَلِيِّ الْعَظِيمِ.

وَعَنِ ابْنِ مَسْعُودٍ رَضِيَ اللّٰهُ عَنْهُ قَالَ: قَالَ رَسُولُ اللّٰهِ ﷺ: «لَقِيتُ إِبْرَاهِيمَ عَلَيْهِ السَّلَامُ لَيْلَةَ أُسْرِيَ بِي فَقَالَ: يَا مُحَمَّدُ [ﷺ]، أَقْرِئْ أُمَّتَكَ مِنِّي السَّلَامَ، وَأَخْبِرْهُمْ أَنَّ الْجَنَّةَ طَيِّبَةُ التُّرْبَةِ، عَذْبَةُ الْمَاءِ، وَأَنَّهَا قِيعَانٌ[٥١]، وَأَنَّ غِرَاسَهَا: سُبْحَانَ اللّٰهِ، وَالْحَمْدُ لِلّٰهِ، وَلَا إِلٰهَ إِلَّا اللّٰهُ، وَاللّٰهُ أَكْبَرُ» رَوَاهُ التِّرْمِذِيُّ، وَالطَّبَرَانِيُّ بِزِيَادَةِ: «وَلَا حَولَ وَلَا قُوَّةَ إِلَّا بِاللّٰهِ الْعَلِيِّ الْعَظِيمِ». وَرَوَى الْحَاكِمُ بِإِسْنَادِهِ عَنِ النَّبِيِّ ﷺ أَنَّهُ قَالَ: «مَنْ قَالَ: سُبْحَانَ اللّٰهِ، وَالْحَمْدُ لِلّٰهِ، وَلَا إِلٰهَ إِلَّا اللّٰهُ، وَاللّٰهُ أَكْبَرُ، وَلَا حَوْلَ وَلَا قُوَّةَ إِلَّا بِاللّٰهِ الْعَلِيِّ الْعَظِيمِ؛ قَالَ اللّٰهُ تَعَالَىٰ: أَسْلَمَ عَبْدِي وَاسْتَسْلَمَ».

---

(٥٠) فَهَذِهِ مِنْ أَهَمِّ الصَّالِحَاتِ الْقَوْلِيَّةِ الَّتِي تَبْقَى مَعَ الْمُؤْمِنِ فِي سَائِرِ الْعَوَالِمِ الْآتِيَةِ.

(٥١) أَيْ: أَمَاكِنُ مُسْتَوِيَةٌ وَاسِعَةٌ مُسْتَعِدَّةٌ لِلْغَرْسِ.

Pithy Words of Glorification and Praise

On the authority of Juwayriyah 🕊, the Prophet 🕊 left from her house then came back at the forenoon, and she was still sitting at the same spot. He said: "You are still in the same state I left you in?" meaning, of glorification and praise. She replied: "Yes." The Prophet 🕊 said: "I said four statements after I left you thrice; if they were weighed against what you said today, they would outbalance them:

Subḥān Allāhi wa bi-ḥamdihī ʿadada khalqihī wa riḍāʾa nafsihī wa zinata ʿarshihī wa midāda kalimātih.

'Glory be to Allah and praise, equal to the number of His creatures, the satisfaction of His Self, the weight of His Throne, and the ink-worth of all His words.'"[68]

On the authority of Abū Umāmah 🕊, "The Prophet 🕊 saw me moving my lips, so he asked: 'What are you moving your lips to say, Abū Umāmah?' I replied: 'In remembrance of Allah, Allah's Messenger.' He said: 'Shall I tell you of that which is more and better than your words of remembrance in the day and night?' I said: 'Yes, Messenger of Allah.' He said:

Subḥān Allāhi ʿadada mā khalaq, subḥān Allāhi milʾa mā khalaq. Subḥān Allāhi ʿadada mā fī al-arḍ, subḥān Allāhi milʾa mā fī al-arḍ. Subḥān Allāhi ʿadada mā aḥṣā kitābuh, subḥān Allāhi milʾa mā aḥṣā kitābuh. Subḥān Allāhi ʿadada kulli shayʾ, subḥān Allāhi milʾa kulli shayʾ. Al-ḥamdu lillāhi ʿadada mā khalaq, al-ḥamdu lillāhi milʾa mā khalaq. Al-ḥamdu lillāhi ʿadada mā fī al-arḍi wa al-samāʾ, al-ḥamdu lillāhi milʾa mā fī al-arḍi wa al-samāʾ. Al-ḥamdu lillāhi ʿadada mā aḥṣā kitābuh, al-ḥamdu lillāhi milʾa mā aḥṣā kitābuh. Al-ḥamdu lillāhi ʿadada kulli shayʾ, al-ḥamdu lillāhi milʾa kulli shayʾ.

'Glory be to Allah equal to the number of things He created; glory be to Allah filling everything He created. Glory be to Allah equal to the number

---

68 Muslim and others.

مِنْ جَوَامِعِ التَّسْبِيحِ وَالْحَمْدِ

عَنْ جُوَيْرِيَةَ رَضِيَ اللهُ عَنْهَا أَنَّ النَّبِيَّ ﷺ خَرَجَ مِنْ عِنْدِهَا ثُمَّ رَجَعَ بَعْدَ أَنْ أَضْحَى وَهِيَ جَالِسَةٌ، فَقَالَ: «مَا زِلْتِ عَلَى الْحَالِ الَّتِي فَارَقْتُكِ عَلَيْهَا»؟ ‐ أَيْ: مِنَ التَّسْبِيحِ وَالْحَمْدِ ‐ فَقَالَتْ: نَعَمْ، فَقَالَ النَّبِيُّ ﷺ: «لَقَدْ قُلْتُ بَعْدَكِ أَرْبَعَ كَلِمَاتٍ ثَلَاثَ مَرَّاتٍ، لَوْ وُزِنَتْ بِمَا قُلْتِ مُنْذُ الْيَوْمَ لَوَزَنَتْهُنَّ: سُبْحَانَ اللهِ وَبِحَمْدِهِ عَدَدَ خَلْقِهِ، وَرِضَاءَ نَفْسِهِ، وَزِنَةَ عَرْشِهِ، وَمِدَادَ كَلِمَاتِهِ» رَوَاهُ مُسْلِمٌ وَغَيْرُهُ.

وَعَنْ أَبِي أُمَامَةَ رَضِيَ اللهُ عَنْهُ أَنَّهُ قَالَ: رَآنِي النَّبِيُّ ﷺ وَأَنَا أُحَرِّكُ شَفَتَيَّ، فَقَالَ لِي: «بِأَيِّ شَيْءٍ تُحَرِّكُ شَفَتَيْكَ يَا أَبَا أُمَامَةَ»؟. فَقُلْتُ: أَذْكُرُ اللهَ يَا رَسُولَ اللهِ فَقَالَ: «أَلَا أُخْبِرُكَ بِأَكْثَرَ وَأَفْضَلَ مِنْ ذِكْرِكَ بِاللَّيْلِ وَالنَّهَارِ»؟ قُلْتُ: بَلَى يَا رَسُولَ اللهِ، فَقَالَ:

«سُبْحَانَ اللهِ عَدَدَ مَا خَلَقَ، سُبْحَانَ اللهِ مِلْءَ مَا خَلَقَ، سُبْحَانَ اللهِ عَدَدَ مَا فِي الْأَرْضِ، سُبْحَانَ اللهِ مِلْءَ مَا فِي الْأَرْضِ، سُبْحَانَ اللهِ عَدَدَ مَا أَحْصَى كِتَابُهُ، سُبْحَانَ اللهِ مِلْءَ مَا أَحْصَى كِتَابُهُ، سُبْحَانَ اللهِ عَدَدَ كُلِّ شَيْءٍ، سُبْحَانَ اللهِ مِلْءَ كُلِّ شَيْءٍ، وَالْحَمْدُ لِلهِ عَدَدَ مَا خَلَقَ، وَالْحَمْدُ لِلهِ مِلْءَ

of things on Earth; glory be to Allah filling the whole Earth. Glory be to Allah equal to what His Book encompasses; glory be to Allah filling what His Book encompasses. Glory be to Allah equal to the number of all things; glory be to Allah filling everything. Praise be to Allah equal to the number of things He created; praise be to Allah filling everything He created. Praise be to Allah equal to the number of things in heaven and Earth; praise be to Allah filling heaven and Earth. Praise be to Allah equal to what His Book encompasses; praise be to Allah filling what His Book encompasses. Praise be to Allah equal to the number of all things; praise be to Allah filling everything.'"[69]

69 Nasā'ī, Aḥmad, and others.

مَا خَلَقَ، وَالْحَمْدُ لِلّٰهِ عَدَدَ مَا فِي الْأَرْضِ وَالسَّمَاءِ، وَالْحَمْدُ لِلّٰهِ مِلْءَ مَا فِي الْأَرْضِ وَالسَّمَاءِ، وَالْحَمْدُ لِلّٰهِ عَدَدَ مَا أَحْصَى كِتَابُهُ، وَالْحَمْدُ لِلّٰهِ مِلْءَ مَا أَحْصَى كِتَابُهُ، وَالْحَمْدُ لِلّٰهِ عَدَدَ كُلِّ شَيْءٍ، وَالْحَمْدُ لِلّٰهِ مِلْءَ كُلِّ شَيْءٍ»

رَوَاهُ النَّسَائِيُّ وَأَحْمَدُ وَغَيْرُهُمَا.

Pithy Words of Praise

On the authority of Ibn ʿUmar ﵄, the Prophet ﷺ narrated to them that a slave of Allah said:

Yā Rabbi laka al-ḥamdu kamā yanbaghī li-jalāli wajhika wa ʿaẓīmi sulṭānik.

"My Lord, praise be to You as it ought to be for the majesty of Your Face and the greatness of Your kingdom." This posed a problem for the two angels, as they did not know what to record. They therefore ascended to the heavens and said: "Our Lord, your slave has said a statement that we do not know how to record." He asked – though He best knows what he said: "What did My slave say?" They said: "He said: 'My Lord, praise be to You as it ought to be for the majesty of Your Face and the greatness of Your kingdom.'" Allah, Exalted, said to them: "Record it as my slave has said it until he meets Me and I reward him for it."[70]

On the authority of Ibn ʿUmar ﵄, the Messenger of Allah ﷺ said: "Whoever says:

Al-ḥamdu lillāhi Rabbi al-ʿālamīn ḥamdan ṭayyiban mubārakan fīh, ḥamdan yuwāfī niʿamahū wa yukāfi'u mazīdah.

'Praise be to Allah, the Lord of the worlds: a pure, blessed praise, proclaimed in all states. Praise that befits His bounties and that is equal to His surplus' three times, the recording angelic scribes say: 'Our Lord, we do not fully fathom what Your slave has sanctified and praised You with, and we do not know how to record it.' Allah inspires them that they should write it as he said it."[71]

---

70 Aḥmad and Ibn Mājah.

71 Bukhārī reports this in *al-Ḍuʿafāʾ*.

مِنْ جَوَامِعِ الْمَحَامِدِ

عَنِ ابْنِ عُمَرَ رَضِيَ اللهُ عَنْهُمَا أَنَّ رَسُولَ اللهِ ﷺ حَدَّثَهُمْ: «أَنَّ عَبْدًا مِنْ عِبَادِ اللهِ تَعَالَىٰ قَالَ: يَا رَبِّ لَكَ الْحَمْدُ كَمَا يَنْبَغِي لِجَلَالِ وَجْهِكَ، وَلِعَظِيمِ سُلْطَانِكَ – فَعَضَّلَتْ بِالْمَلَكَيْنِ فَلَمْ يَدْرِيَا كَيْفَ يَكْتُبَانِهَا فَصَعِدَا إِلَى السَّمَاءِ فَقَالَا: يَا رَبَّنَا إِنَّ عَبْدَكَ قَدْ قَالَ مَقَالَةً لَا نَدْرِي كَيْفَ نَكْتُبُهَا، قَالَ اللهُ تَعَالَىٰ – وَهُوَ أَعْلَمُ بِمَا قَالَ عَبْدُهُ – مَا ذَا قَالَ عَبْدِي؟ فَقَالَا: يَا رَبِّ إِنَّهُ قَدْ قَالَ: يَا رَبِّ لَكَ الْحَمْدُ كَمَا يَنْبَغِي لِجَلَالِ وَجْهِكَ، وَلِعَظِيمِ سُلْطَانِكَ، فَقَالَ اللهُ تَعَالَىٰ لَهُمَا: اُكْتُبَاهَا كَمَا قَالَ عَبْدِي حَتَّى يَلْقَانِي فَأَجْزِيَهُ بِهَا» رَوَاهُ أَحْمَدُ وَابْنُ مَاجَه.

وَعَنِ ابْنِ عُمَرَ رَضِيَ اللهُ عَنْهُمَا عَنْ رَسُولِ اللهِ ﷺ قَالَ: «مَنْ قَالَ: اَلْحَمْدُ لِلهِ رَبِّ الْعَالَمِينَ حَمْدًا طَيِّبًا مُبَارَكًا فِيهِ عَلَىٰ كُلِّ حَالٍ، حَمْدًا يُوَافِي نِعَمَهُ، وَيُكَافِئُ مَزِيدَهُ – ثَلَاثَ مَرَّاتٍ – فَتَقُولُ الْحَفَظَةُ: رَبَّنَا لَا نُحْسِنُ كُنْهَ مَا قَدَّسَكَ عَبْدُكَ هَذَا وَحَمِدَكَ، وَمَا نَدْرِي كَيْفَ نَكْتُبُهُ؟ فَيُوحِي اللهُ تَعَالَىٰ إِلَيْهِمْ أَنِ اكْتُبُوهُ كَمَا قَالَ عَبْدِي» رَوَاهُ الْبُخَارِيُّ فِي الضُّعَفَاءِ.

Be Abundant with Pithy Praises and Extolments

Allāhumma laka al-ḥamdu anta Qayyūmu al-samāwāti wal-arḍi wa man fīhinn, wa laka al-ḥamdu anta Nūru al-samāwāti wal-arḍi wa man fīhinn, wa laka al-ḥamdu anta Rabbu al-samāwāti wal-arḍi wa man fīhinn, wa laka al-ḥamdu anta Maliku al-samāwāti wal-arḍi wa man fīhinn, wa laka al-ḥamdu anta al-Ḥaqq, wa waʿduka al-ḥaqq, wa liqā'uka ḥaqq, wa qawluka ḥaqq, wa al-jannatu ḥaqq, wa al-nāru ḥaqq, wa al-nabiyyūna ḥaqq, wa Muḥammadun ṣallā Allāhu ʿalayhi wa sallama ḥaqq, wa al-sāʿatu ḥaqq.

Allah, to You belongs all praise, You are the Sustainer of the heavens and the Earth and all that is in them. To You belongs all praise, You are the Light of the heavens and the Earth and all that is in them. To You belongs all praise, You are the Lord of the heavens and the Earth and all that is in them. To You belongs all praise, You are the King of the heavens and the Earth and all that is in them. To You belongs all praise, You are the True. Your promise is the truth. Meeting You is true. Your word is true. The Garden is true. The Fire is true. The Prophets are true. Muhammad ﷺ is true. The Hour is true.

Allāhumma laka aslamtu wa bika āmant, wa ʿalayka tawakkaltu wa ilayka anabt, wa bika khāṣamtu wa ilayka ḥākamt, fa-ighfir lī mā qaddamtu wa mā akhkhart, wa mā asrartu wa mā aʿlant, wa mā anta aʿlamu bihī minnī, anta al-Muqaddimu wa anta al-Mu'akhkhir, lā ilāha illā anta wa lā ilāha ghayruk, lā ilāha illā anta wa lā ḥawla wa lā quwwata illā billāhi al-ʿAliyyi al-ʿAẓīm.

Allah, I submit to You and have faith in You. I rely upon You and return to You. I forsake for You and seek You as a judge. Forgive my first and last misdeeds, the private of them and the public, You are the One Who advances and postpones. There is no god but You, and no god other than You. There is no god but You, no might nor power save through the Most High, the Sublime.

أَكْثِرْ مِنْ جَوَامِعِ الْحَمْدِ وَالثَّنَاءِ

اَللّٰهُمَّ لَكَ الْحَمْدُ أَنْتَ قَيُّومُ السَّمٰوَاتِ وَالْأَرْضِ وَمَنْ فِيهِنَّ، وَلَكَ الْحَمْدُ أَنْتَ نُورُ السَّمٰوَاتِ وَالْأَرْضِ وَمَنْ فِيهِنَّ، وَلَكَ الْحَمْدُ أَنْتَ رَبُّ السَّمٰوَاتِ وَالْأَرْضِ وَمَنْ فِيهِنَّ، وَلَكَ الْحَمْدُ أَنْتَ مَلِكُ السَّمٰوَاتِ وَالْأَرْضِ وَمَنْ فِيهِنَّ، وَلَكَ الْحَمْدُ أَنْتَ الْحَقُّ، وَوَعْدُكَ الْحَقُّ، وَلِقَاؤُكَ حَقٌّ، وَقَوْلُكَ حَقٌّ، وَالْجَنَّةُ حَقٌّ، وَالنَّارُ حَقٌّ، وَالنَّبِيُّونَ حَقٌّ، وَمُحَمَّدٌ ﷺ حَقٌّ، وَالسَّاعَةُ حَقٌّ.

اَللّٰهُمَّ لَكَ أَسْلَمْتُ وَبِكَ آمَنْتُ، وَعَلَيْكَ تَوَكَّلْتُ وَإِلَيْكَ أَنَبْتُ، وَبِكَ خَاصَمْتُ، وَإِلَيْكَ حَاكَمْتُ، فَاغْفِرْ لِي مَا قَدَّمْتُ وَمَا أَخَّرْتُ، وَمَا أَسْرَرْتُ وَمَا أَعْلَنْتُ؛ وَمَا أَنْتَ أَعْلَمُ بِهِ مِنِّي، أَنْتَ الْمُقَدِّمُ، وَأَنْتَ الْمُؤَخِّرُ، لَا إِلٰهَ إِلَّا أَنْتَ، وَلَا إِلٰهَ غَيْرُكَ، لَا إِلٰهَ إِلَّا أَنْتَ، وَلَا حَوْلَ وَلَا قُوَّةَ إِلَّا بِاللّٰهِ الْعَلِيِّ الْعَظِيمِ(٥٢).

(٥٢) رَوَاهُ الْبُخَارِيُّ وَمُسْلِمٌ وَالتِّرْمِذِيُّ وَالْإِمَامُ مَالِكٌ عَنِ ابْنِ عَبَّاسٍ رَضِيَ اللّٰهُ عَنْهُمَا أَنَّهُ قَالَ: كَانَ النَّبِيُّ ﷺ إِذَا قَامَ يَتَهَجَّدُ فِي اللَّيْلِ قَالَ: «اللّٰهُمَّ..» إِلَى تَمَامِهِ.

Tamma nūruka fa-hadayta fa-laka al-ḥamd, ʿaẓuma ḥilmuka fa-ghafarta fa-laka al-ḥamd, basaṭta yadaka fa-aʿṭayta fa-laka al-ḥamd. Rabbanā wajhuka akramu al-wujūh, wa jāhuka aʿzamu al-jāh, wa aṭiyyatuka afḍalu al-ʿaṭiyyati wa ahnāhā, tuṭāʿu Rabbanā fa-tashkur, wa tuʿṣā Rabbanā fa-taghfir, wa tujību al-muḍṭarr, wa takshifu al-ḍurr, wa tashfī al-saqīm, wa taghfiru al-dhanb, wa taqbalu al-tawbah, wa lā yajzī bi-ālā'ika aḥad, wa lā yablughu midḥataka[72] qawlu qā'il.[73]

You guide as Your light is perfected, so praise be to You. You forgive as Your forbearance is immense, so praise be to You. You give as You extend Your Hand, so praise be to You. Our Lord, Your Face is the most noble, Your eminence is the most great, and Your bestowal is the best and most satisfying. You are Thankful when obeyed and Forgiving when disobeyed, Our Lord. You answer the desperate, uplift harm, cure the sick, forgive sins, and accept repentance. None can gift Your favours, nor can anyone do justice to Your praise.

Al-Ḥamdu lillāhi alladhī tawāḍaʿa kullu shay'in li-ʿaẓamatih, wa al-ḥamdu lillāhi alladhī dhalla kullu shay'in li-ʿizzatih, wa al-ḥamdu lillāhi alladhī istaslama kullu shay'in li-qudratih.[74]

Praise be to Allah to Whose greatness everything humbles. Praise be to Allah to Whose honour everything is abjected. Praise be to Allah to Whose power everything submits.

---

72   Meaning, no one can truly show gratitude for Your blessings, nor can anyone satisfactorily praise and extol You.

73   Abū Yaʿlā from ʿAlī 🙵: "The one of you ought to stand and pray four units and say what the Prophet 🙵 used to say: 'You guide as Your light is perfected...'"

74   Ṭabarānī as *marfūʿ* from Ibn ʿUmar 🙵, as found in *al-Targhīb* of Mundhirī.

تَمَّ نُورُكَ فَهَدَيْتَ فَلَكَ الْحَمْدُ، عَظُمَ حِلْمُكَ فَغَفَرْتَ فَلَكَ الْحَمْدُ، بَسَطْتَ يَدَكَ فَأَعْطَيْتَ فَلَكَ الْحَمْدُ، رَبَّنَا وَجْهُكَ أَكْرَمُ الْوُجُوهِ، وَجَاهُكَ أَعْظَمُ الْجَاهِ، وَعَطِيَّتُكَ أَفْضَلُ الْعَطِيَّةِ وَأَهْنَاهَا، تُطَاعُ رَبَّنَا فَتَشْكُرُ، وَتُعْصَى رَبَّنَا فَتَغْفِرُ، وَتُجِيبُ الْمُضْطَرَّ وَتَكْشِفُ الضُّرَّ، وَتَشْفِي السَّقِيمَ، وَتَغْفِرُ الذَّنْبَ، وَتَقْبَلُ التَّوْبَةَ، وَلَا يَجْزِي بِآلَائِكَ أَحَدٌ، وَلَا يَبْلُغُ مِدْحَتَكَ(٥٣) قَوْلُ قَائِلٍ(٥٤).

اَلْحَمْدُ لِلّٰهِ الَّذِي تَوَاضَعَ كُلُّ شَيْءٍ لِعَظَمَتِهِ، وَالْحَمْدُ لِلّٰهِ الَّذِي ذَلَّ كُلُّ شَيْءٍ لِعِزَّتِهِ، وَالْحَمْدُ لِلّٰهِ الَّذِي اسْتَسْلَمَ كُلُّ شَيْءٍ لِقُدْرَتِهِ(٥٥).

---

(٥٣) أَيْ: لَا أَحَدٌ يُحْصِي شُكْرًا عَلَى نِعْمَتِكَ، وَلَا أَحَدٌ يُحْصِي مَدْحًا وَثَنَاءً عَلَيْكَ.

(٥٤) رَوَاهُ أَبُو يَعْلَى عَنْ عَلِيٍّ رَضِيَ اللهُ عَنْهُ أَنَّهُ قَالَ: أَلَا يَقُومُ أَحَدُكُمْ فَيُصَلِّي أَرْبَعَ رَكَعَاتٍ وَيَقُولُ مَا كَانَ رَسُولُ اللهِ ﷺ يَقُولُ: «تَمَّ نُورُكَ فَهَدَيْتَ...».

(٥٥) رَوَاهُ الطَّبَرَانِيُّ عَنِ ابْنِ عُمَرَ رَضِيَ اللهُ عَنْهُمَا مَرْفُوعًا كَمَا فِي (التَّرْغِيبِ) لِلْمُنْذِرِيِّ.

Allāhumma laka al-ḥamdu ḥamdan khālidan maʿa khulūdik, wa laka al-ḥamdu ḥamdan lā muntahā lahū dūna ʿilmik, wa laka al-ḥamdu ḥamdan lā muntahā lahū dūna mashīʾatik, wa laka al-ḥamdu ḥamdan lā ākhira li-qāʾilihī illā riḍāk.[75]

Allah, abundant, eternal praise be to You, eternal as You are. Praise be to You that has no limit but Your knowledge. Praise be to You that has no limit but Your will. Praise be to You that results in naught but Your pleasure for the one who says it.

---

75 Bayhaqī as *marfūʿ* from ʿAlī ☸, though it has *inqiṭāʿ* (breaking in the narration).

اَللّٰهُمَّ لَكَ الْحَمْدُ حَمْدًا كَثِيرًا خَالِدًا مَعَ خُلُودِكَ، وَلَكَ الْحَمْدُ حَمْدًا لَا مُنْتَهَى لَهُ دُونَ عِلْمِكَ، وَلَكَ الْحَمْدُ حَمْدًا لَا مُنْتَهَى لَهُ دُونَ مَشِيئَتِكَ، وَلَكَ الْحَمْدُ حَمْدًا لَا آخِرَ لِقَائِلِهِ إِلَّا رِضَاكَ[٥٦].

(٥٦) رَوَاهُ الْبَيْهَقِيُّ عَنْ عَلِيٍّ رَضِيَ اللهُ عَنْهُ مَرْفُوعًا وَفِيهِ انْقِطَاعٌ.

Be Abundant in Seeking Forgiveness and its Pithy Supplications

Seeking forgiveness fulfils the directive of the Prophet ﷺ when he said: "Glad tidings for the one who finds plenty of supplications of forgiveness in his book of deeds."[76] It is also narrated that he ﷺ said: "Whoever likes that his book of deeds brings him joy should supplicate for forgiveness often."[77]

Among the Pithy Supplications of Forgiveness is the Master of Atonement (*Sayyid al-Istighfār*)

Allāhumma anta Rabbī lā ilāha illā anta khalaqtanī wa ana ʿabduk, wa ana ʿalā ʿahdika wa waʿdika mā istaṭaʿt, Aʿūdhu bika min sharri mā ṣanaʿt, abū'u laka bi-niʿmatika ʿalayya wa abū'u bi-dhanbī, fa-ighfir lī fa-innahū lā yaghfiru al-dhunūba illā ant.

Allah, You are my Lord, there is none worthy of worship but You. You created me and I am Your slave. I keep Your covenant and my pledge to You so far as I am able. I seek refuge in You from the evil of what I have done. I admit to Your blessings upon me, and I admit to my misdeeds. Forgive me, for there is none who may forgive sins but You.

---

76 Ibn Mājah with an authentic chain of transmission, as well as by Bayhaqī.

77 Bayhaqī with a fine chain of transmission.

أَكْثِرْ مِنَ الْاِسْتِغْفَارِ وَمِنْ جَوَامِعِهِ

عَمَلًا بِمَا وَرَدَ عَنِ النَّبِيِّ ﷺ أَنَّهُ قَالَ: «طُوبَىٰ لِمَنْ وُجِدَ فِي صَحِيفَتِهِ اسْتِغْفَارٌ كَثِيرٌ»(٥٧).

وَبِمَا رُوِيَ عَنْهُ ﷺ أَنَّهُ قَالَ: «مَنْ أَحَبَّ أَنْ تَسُرَّهُ صَحِيفَتُهُ فَلْيُكْثِرْ فِيهَا مِنَ الْاِسْتِغْفَارِ»(٥٨).

وَمِنْ جَوَامِعِ الْاِسْتِغْفَارِ: سَيِّدُ الْاِسْتِغْفَارِ

اَللّٰهُمَّ أَنْتَ رَبِّي لَا إِلٰهَ إِلَّا أَنْتَ خَلَقْتَنِي وَأَنَا عَبْدُكَ، وَأَنَا عَلَى عَهْدِكَ وَوَعْدِكَ مَا اسْتَطَعْتُ، أَعُوذُ بِكَ مِنْ شَرِّ مَا صَنَعْتُ، أَبُوءُ لَكَ بِنِعْمَتِكَ عَلَيَّ، وَأَبُوءُ بِذَنْبِي، فَاغْفِرْ لِي فَإِنَّهُ لَا يَغْفِرُ الذُّنُوبَ إِلَّا أَنْتَ.

---

(٥٧) رَوَاهُ ابْنُ مَاجَه بِإِسْنَادٍ صَحِيحٍ، وَالْبَيْهَقِيُّ.

(٥٨) رَوَاهُ الْبَيْهَقِيُّ بِإِسْنَادٍ لَا بَأْسَ بِهِ.

Among them also:

Astaghfirullāha alladhī lā ilāha illā huwa al-Ḥayya al-Qayyūma wa atūbu ilayh[78] *- three times.*

I seek Allah's forgiveness. There is none worthy of worship other than Him, the Ever Living Sustainer of all, and I repent to Him.

Also:

Subḥānaka Allāhumma wa bi-ḥamdik, ʿamiltu sū'an, wa ẓalamtu nafsī, fa-ighfir lī innaka Khayru al-ghāfirīn, lā ilāha illā anta subḥānaka wa bi-ḥamdik; ʿamiltu sū'an wa ẓalamtu nafsī, fa-irḥamnī innaka Arḥamu al-raḥimīn, lā ilāha illā anta subḥānaka wa bi-ḥamdik, ʿamiltu sū'an wa ẓalamtu nafsī, fa-tub ʿalayya innaka anta al-Tawwābu al-Raḥīm.[79]

Glory be to You, Allah, as well as praise. I have done evil and wronged myself. Forgive me, for You are the Best of those who forgive. There is no god but You, glory and praise are Yours. I have done evil and wronged myself. Have mercy upon me, for You are the Most Merciful of those who show mercy. There is no god but You, glory and praise are Yours. I have done evil and wronged myself. Accept my repentance, for You are the Ever Relenting, the Most Merciful.

Also:

Allāhumma maghfiratuka awsaʿu min dhunūbī, wa raḥmatuka arjā ʿindī min ʿamalī.[80]

Allah, Your forgiveness is more expansive than my sins, and Your mercy inspires more hope within me than my deeds.

---

78 Abū Dāwūd and Tirmidhī from the Prophet ﷺ.

79 Bayhaqī on the authority of Anas ibn Mālik ؓ in the exegesis of the Qur'anic verse: "Then Adam was inspired with words [of prayer] by his Lord, so He accepted his repentance" (*al-Baqarah*, 37).

80 Ḥākim from him ﷺ when he taught the man who came to him saying: "Oh my sins! Oh my sins!" He ﷺ told him to repeat these words, and then said to him: "Get up, for Allah has forgiven you."

وَمِنْ ذَلِكَ: أَسْتَغْفِرُ اللهَ الَّذِي لَا إِلَهَ إِلَّا هُوَ الْحَيُّ الْقَيُّومُ وَأَتُوبُ إِلَيْهِ(٥٩) – يَقُولُهَا ثَلَاثًا.

وَمِنْ ذَلِكَ: سُبْحَانَكَ اللَّهُمَّ وَبِحَمْدِكَ، عَمِلْتُ سُوءاً، وَظَلَمْتُ نَفْسِي، فَاغْفِرْ لِي إِنَّكَ خَيْرُ الْغَافِرِينَ، لَا إِلَهَ إِلَّا أَنْتَ سُبْحَانَكَ وَبِحَمْدِكَ، عَمِلْتُ سُوءاً وَظَلَمْتُ نَفْسِي، فَارْحَمْنِي إِنَّكَ أَرْحَمُ الرَّاحِمِينَ، لَا إِلَهَ إِلَّا أَنْتَ سُبْحَانَكَ وَبِحَمْدِكَ، عَمِلْتُ سُوءاً وَظَلَمْتُ نَفْسِي، فَتُبْ عَلَيَّ إِنَّكَ أَنْتَ التَّوَّابُ الرَّحِيمُ(٦٠).

وَمِنْ ذَلِكَ: اَللَّهُمَّ مَغْفِرَتُكَ أَوْسَعُ مِنْ ذُنُوبِي، وَرَحْمَتُكَ أَرْجَى عِنْدِي مِنْ عَمَلِي(٦١).

(٥٩) رَوَاهُ أَبُو دَاوُدَ وَالتِّرْمِذِيُّ عَنِ النَّبِيِّ ﷺ.

(٦٠) رَوَاهُ الْبَيْهَقِيُّ عَنْ أَنَسِ بْنِ مَالِكٍ رَضِيَ اللهُ عَنْهُ فِي تَفْسِيرِ الْكَلِمَاتِ فِي قَوْلِهِ تَعَالَى: ﴿فَتَلَقَّىٰٓ ءَادَمُ مِن رَّبِّهِۦ كَلِمَٰتٍ فَتَابَ عَلَيْهِ﴾ الْآيَةَ.

(٦١) رَوَاهُ الْحَاكِمُ عَنْهُ ﷺ فِي تَعْلِيمِهِ الرَّجُلَ لَمَّا جَاءَهُ فَقَالَ: وَاذُنُوبَاهُ وَاذُنُوبَاهُ فَأَمَرَهُ ﷺ أَنْ يَقُولَ ذَلِكَ وَيُكَرِّرُهُ ثُمَّ قَالَ لَهُ: «قُمْ فَقَدْ غَفَرَ اللهُ لَكَ».

Recite the Verses of Protection from Evil

Bismillāhi al-Raḥmāni al-Raḥīm. Allāhu lā ilāha illā huwa al-Ḥayyu al-Qayyūm. Lā ta'khudhuhū sinatun wa lā nawm. Lahū mā fī al-samawāti wa mā fī al-arḍ. Man dhā alladhī yashfaʿu ʿindahū illā bi'idhnih. Yaʿlamu mā bayna aydīhim wa mā khalfahum wa lā yuḥīṭūna bi-shay'in min ʿilmihī illā bimā shā'. Wasiʿa kursiyyuhū al-samāwāti wal-arḍa wa lā ya'ūduhū ḥifẓuhumā, wa huwa al-ʿAliyyu al-ʿAẓīm.

"In the Name of Allah, the Most Compassionate, Most Merciful. Allah! There is no god [worthy of worship] except Him, the Ever-Living, All-Sustaining. Neither drowsiness nor sleep overtakes Him. To Him belongs whatever is in the heavens and whatever is on the earth. Who could possibly intercede with Him without His permission? He [fully] knows what is ahead of them and what is behind them, but no one can grasp any of His knowledge – except what He wills [to reveal]. His Seat encompasses the heavens and the earth, and the preservation of both does not tire Him. For He is the Most High, the Greatest."[81]

Fallāhu khayrun ḥāfiẓā, wa huwa Arḥamu al-rāḥimīn.

"[Only] Allah is the best Protector, and He is the Most Merciful of the merciful."[82]

Lahū muʿaqqibātun min bayni yadayhi wa min khalfihī yaḥfaẓūnahū min amri Allāh.

"For each one there are successive angels before and behind, protecting them by Allah's command."[83]

Innā naḥnu nazzalnā al-dhikra wa innā lahū la-ḥāfiẓūn.

---

81 *al-Baqarah*, 255.

82 *Yūsuf*, 64.

83 *al-Raʿd*, 11.

اِقْرَأْ آيَاتِ الحِفْظِ مِنَ الْمَكَارِهِ وَالشُّرُورِ

١ - ﴿بِسْمِ ٱللَّهِ ٱلرَّحْمَٰنِ ٱلرَّحِيمِ: ٱللَّهُ لَآ إِلَٰهَ إِلَّا هُوَ ٱلْحَىُّ ٱلْقَيُّومُ ۚ لَا تَأْخُذُهُۥ سِنَةٌ وَلَا نَوْمٌ ۚ لَّهُۥ مَا فِى ٱلسَّمَٰوَٰتِ وَمَا فِى ٱلْأَرْضِ ۗ مَن ذَا ٱلَّذِى يَشْفَعُ عِندَهُۥٓ إِلَّا بِإِذْنِهِۦ ۚ يَعْلَمُ مَا بَيْنَ أَيْدِيهِمْ وَمَا خَلْفَهُمْ ۖ وَلَا يُحِيطُونَ بِشَىْءٍ مِّنْ عِلْمِهِۦٓ إِلَّا بِمَا شَآءَ ۚ وَسِعَ كُرْسِيُّهُ ٱلسَّمَٰوَٰتِ وَٱلْأَرْضَ ۖ وَلَا يَـُٔودُهُۥ حِفْظُهُمَا ۚ وَهُوَ ٱلْعَلِىُّ ٱلْعَظِيمُ﴾.

٢ - ﴿فَٱللَّهُ خَيْرٌ حَٰفِظًا ۖ وَهُوَ أَرْحَمُ ٱلرَّٰحِمِينَ﴾.

٣ - ﴿لَهُۥ مُعَقِّبَٰتٌ مِّنۢ بَيْنِ يَدَيْهِ وَمِنْ خَلْفِهِۦ يَحْفَظُونَهُۥ مِنْ أَمْرِ ٱللَّهِ﴾.

"It is certainly We Who have revealed the Reminder, and it is certainly We Who will preserve it."[84]

Wa ḥāfiẓnāhā min kulli shayṭānin rajīm.

"And We protected it from every accursed devil."[85]

Wa ḥifẓan min kulli shayṭānin mārid.

"And [for] protection from every rebellious devil."[86]

Wa ḥifẓā, dhālika taqdīru al-ʿAzīzu al-ʿAlīm.

"And for protection. That is the design of the Almighty, All-Knowing."[87]

In kullu nafsin lammā ʿalayhā ḥāfiẓ.

"There is no soul without a vigilant angel [recording everything]."[88]

Inna baṭsha Rabbika la-shadīd. Innahū huwa yubdi'u wa yuʿīd. Wa huwa al-Ghafūru al-Wadūd. Dhū al-ʿarshi al-Majīd. Faʿʿālun limā yurīd. Hal atāka ḥadīthu al-junūd. Firʿawna wa Thamūd. Bali alladhīna kafarū fī takdhīb, wa Allāhu min warā'ihim Muḥīṭ. Bal huwa Qur'ānun majīd. Fī lawḥin maḥfūẓ.

"Indeed, the [crushing] grip of your Lord is severe. [For] He is certainly the One Who originates and resurrects [all]. And He is the All-Forgiving, All-Loving – Lord of the Throne, the All-Glorious, Doer of whatever He wills. Has the story of the [destroyed] forces reached you [O Prophet] – [the forces of] Pharaoh and Thamūd? Yet the disbelievers [still] persist in denial. But Allah encompasses them from all sides. In fact, this is a glorious Qur'an, [recorded] in a Preserved Tablet."[89]

---

84 *al-Ḥijr*, 9.

85 *al-Ḥijr*, 17.

86 *al-Ṣāffāt*, 7.

87 *Fuṣṣilat*, 12.

88 *al-Ṭāriq*, 4.

89 *al-Burūj*, 12-22.

٤ - ﴿إِنَّا نَحۡنُ نَزَّلۡنَا ٱلذِّكۡرَ وَإِنَّا لَهُۥ لَحَٰفِظُونَ﴾.

٥ - ﴿وَحَفِظۡنَٰهَا مِن كُلِّ شَيۡطَٰنٖ رَّجِيمٍ﴾.

٦ - ﴿وَحِفۡظٗا مِّن كُلِّ شَيۡطَٰنٖ مَّارِدٖ﴾.

٧ - ﴿وَحِفۡظٗاۚ ذَٰلِكَ تَقۡدِيرُ ٱلۡعَزِيزِ ٱلۡعَلِيمِ﴾.

٨ - ﴿إِن كُلُّ نَفۡسٖ لَّمَّا عَلَيۡهَا حَافِظٞ﴾.

٩ - ﴿إِنَّ بَطۡشَ رَبِّكَ لَشَدِيدٌ ١٢ إِنَّهُۥ هُوَ يُبۡدِئُ وَيُعِيدُ ١٣ وَهُوَ
ٱلۡغَفُورُ ٱلۡوَدُودُ ١٤ ذُو ٱلۡعَرۡشِ ٱلۡمَجِيدُ ١٥ فَعَّالٞ لِّمَا يُرِيدُ ١٦ هَلۡ
أَتَىٰكَ حَدِيثُ ٱلۡجُنُودِ ١٧ فِرۡعَوۡنَ وَثَمُودَ ١٨ بَلِ ٱلَّذِينَ كَفَرُواْ فِي
تَكۡذِيبٖ ١٩ وَٱللَّهُ مِن وَرَآئِهِم مُّحِيطُۢ ٢٠ بَلۡ هُوَ قُرۡءَانٞ مَّجِيدٞ ٢١
فِي لَوۡحٖ مَّحۡفُوظِۭ ٢٢﴾.

Recite the Curing Verses or Drink from Their Water

The erudite scholar al-Qasṭalānī said in *al-Mawāhib*: "It has been transmitted from the esteemed Sheikh Abū al-Qāsim al-Qushayrī, may Allah the Exalted have mercy upon him, that his son was severely sick such that he seemed close to death. This was very difficult for his father to go through. He said: 'I saw the Prophet ﷺ in my sleep, and he said to me: "Where are you with the Curing Verses?" I woke up then contemplated upon this, then found cure to be in six places in the Book of Allah:

Wa yashfi ṣudūra qawmin mu'minīn.

"And soothe the hearts of the believers."[90]

Wa shifā'un limā fī al-ṣudūr.

"A cure for what is in the hearts."[91]

Yakhruju min buṭūnihā sharābun mukhtalifun alwānuhū fīhi shifā'un lil-nās.

"From their bellies comes forth liquid of varying colours, in which there is healing for people."[92]

Wa nunazzilu min al-Qur'āni mā huwa shifā'un wa raḥmatun lil-mu'minīn.

"We send down the Qur'an as a healing and mercy for the believers."[93]

Wa idhā mariḍtu fa-huwa yashfīn.

"And He [alone] heals me when I am sick."[94]

---

90 *al-Tawbah*, 14.

91 *Yūnus*, 57.

92 *al-Naḥl*, 69.

93 *al-Isrā'*, 82.

94 *al-Shu'arā'*, 80.

اِقْرَأْ آيَاتِ الشِّفَاءِ أَوِ اشْرَبْ مِنْ مَائِهَا

قَالَ الْعَلَّامَةُ الْقَسْطَلَّانِيُّ فِي الْمَوَاهِبِ: نُقِلَ عَنِ الشَّيْخِ أَبِي الْقَاسِمِ الْقُشَيْرِيِّ رَحِمَهُ اللهُ تَعَالَىٰ أَنَّ وَلَدَهُ مَرِضَ مَرَضًا شَدِيدًا حَتَّى أَشْرَفَ مِنْهُ عَلَى الْمَوْتِ، وَاشْتَدَّ عَلَيْهِ الْأَمْرُ قَالَ: فَرَأَيْتُ النَّبِيَّ ﷺ فِي الْمَنَامِ فَشَكَوْتُ إِلَيْهِ مَا بِوَلَدِي، فَقَالَ ﷺ: «أَيْنَ أَنْتَ مِنْ آيَاتِ الشِّفَاءِ»؟ فَانْتَبَهْتُ فَفَكَّرْتُ فِيهَا فَإِذَا هِيَ فِي سِتَّةِ مَوَاضِعَ مِنْ كِتَابِ اللهِ تَعَالَىٰ وَهِيَ قَوْلُهُ:

﴿وَيَشۡفِ صُدُورَ قَوۡمٖ مُّؤۡمِنِينَ﴾ ، ﴿وَشِفَآءٞ لِّمَا فِي ٱلصُّدُورِ﴾ ، ﴿يَخۡرُجُ مِنۢ بُطُونِهَا شَرَابٞ مُّخۡتَلِفٌ أَلۡوَٰنُهُۥ فِيهِ شِفَآءٞ لِّلنَّاسِ﴾ ، ﴿وَنُنَزِّلُ مِنَ ٱلۡقُرۡءَانِ مَا هُوَ شِفَآءٞ وَرَحۡمَةٞ لِّلۡمُؤۡمِنِينَ﴾ ، ﴿وَإِذَا مَرِضۡتُ فَهُوَ يَشۡفِينِ﴾ ،

Qul huwa lilladhīna āmanu hudan wa shifā'.

"Say [O Prophet], 'It is a guide and a healing to the believers.'"[95]

I wrote them down, then dissolved the writing in water and gave it to my son to drink. When he did, it was as if he was reinvigorated after severe cramping.'"

The erudite scholar al-Zurqānī said: "It is found in *al-Kawākib al-Durriyyah* in al-Qushayrī›s biography that a son of his got severely ill such that he despaired of his case. He then saw the True, Exalted be He, in his sleep. He told him to recite the Curing Verses or write them down and dissolute them in water for him to drink. He did so, and the boy was cured."

Al-Zurqānī further states: "Perhaps the same incident occurred twice to the same boy, or maybe it was two of his sons who were afflicted. He informed of both incidents as to proclaim Allah's favour upon him that he saw Him, Exalted, in his sleep, as well as the Messenger ﷺ."

---

95 *Fuṣṣilat*, 44.

﴿قُلۡ هُوَ لِلَّذِينَ ءَامَنُواْ هُدٗى وَشِفَآءٞۚ﴾ .

قَالَ: فَكَتَبْتُهَا ثُمَّ حَلَلْتُهَا بِالْمَاءِ وَسَقَيْتُهُ إِيَّاهَا فَكَأَنَّمَا نَشِطَ مِنْ عُقَالٍ.

قَالَ الْعَلَّامَةُ الزُّرْقَانِيُّ: وَفِي (الْكَوَاكِبِ الدُّرِّيَّةِ) فِي تَرْجَمَةِ الْقُشَيْرِيِّ: أَنَّهُ مَرِضَ لَهُ وَلَدٌ بِحَيْثُ أَيِسَ مِنْهُ، فَرَأَى الْحَقَّ تَعَالَىٰ فِي النَّوْمِ فَقَالَ لَهُ اجْمَعْ آيَاتِ الشِّفَاءِ وَاقْرَأْهَا أَوِ اكْتُبْهَا فِي إِنَاءٍ وَاسْقِهِ إِيَّاهُ فَفَعَلَ ذَلِكَ فَعُوفِيَ.

قَالَ الزُّرْقَانِيُّ: فَلَعَلَّ الْوَاقِعَةَ تَعَدَّدَتْ فِي الْوَلَدِ نَفْسِهِ أَوْ فِي غَيْرِهِ، فَأَخْبَرَ بِهِمَا جَمِيعًا تَحَدُّثًا بِنِعْمَةِ رُؤْيَةِ اللهِ تَعَالَىٰ فِي الْمَنَامِ، وَرُؤْيَةِ رَسُولِهِ ﷺ.

Say *Lā Ḥawla Wa Lā Quwwata Illā Billāh* Often

Tirmidhī narrates on the authority of Abū Hurayrah ﵁ that: "Allah's Messenger ﷺ said to me: 'Say:

Lā ḥawla wa lā quwwata illā billāh,

"There is no might nor strength except through Allah" often, for it is one of the treasures of the Garden.'"

Makḥūl said: "Whoever says it and then adds after it:

Lā malja'a wa lā manjā min Allāhi illā ilayh,

'There is no refuge nor escape from Allah except to Him' Allah will alleviate seventy doors of harm from him, the lowest of which is poverty."

In the narration of Ḥākim, he ﷺ says: "Shall I tell you of a statement from underneath the Throne that is from the treasures of the Garden?" In the narration of Aḥmad from Muʿādh ﵁, he ﷺ says: "Shall I not inform you of one of the doors to the Garden?" He replied: "What is it?" He said: "*Lā ḥawla wa lā quwwata illā billāh.*"

أَكْثِرْ مِنْ قَوْلِ لَا حَوْلَ وَلَا قُوَّةَ إِلَّا بِاللهِ الْعَلِيِّ الْعَظِيمِ

رَوَى التِّرْمِذِيُّ عَنْ أَبِي هُرَيْرَةَ رَضِيَ اللهُ عَنْهُ قَالَ: قَالَ لِي رَسُولُ اللهِ ﷺ: «أَكْثِرْ مِنْ قَوْلِ لَا حَوْلَ وَلَا قُوَّةَ إِلَّا بِاللهِ الْعَلِيِّ الْعَظِيمِ؛ فَإِنَّهَا مِنْ كَنْزِ الْجَنَّةِ».

قَالَ مَكْحُولٌ: فَمَنْ قَالَهَا ثُمَّ قَالَ - بَعْدَهَا -: لَا مَلْجَأَ وَلَا مَنْجَا مِنَ اللهِ إِلَّا إِلَيْهِ - كَشَفَ اللهُ عَنْهُ سَبْعِينَ بَابًا مِنَ الضُّرِّ أَدْنَاهُنَّ الْفَقْرُ.

وَفِي رِوَايَةِ الْحَاكِمِ أَنَّهُ ﷺ قَالَ: «أَلَا أَدُلُّكَ عَلَى كَلِمَةٍ مِنْ تَحْتِ الْعَرْشِ مِنْ كَنْزِ الْجَنَّةِ»، وَفِي حَدِيثِ أَحْمَدَ عَنْ مُعَاذٍ رَضِيَ اللهُ عَنْهُ أَنَّهُ ﷺ قَالَ لَهُ: «أَلَا أَدُلُّكَ عَلَى بَابٍ مِنْ أَبْوَابِ الْجَنَّةِ»؟ قَالَ: وَمَا هُوَ؟ قَالَ: «لَا حَوْلَ وَلَا قُوَّةَ إِلَّا بِاللهِ».

Pray for the Prophet ﷺ at All Times Generally and on the Night and Day of Friday Especially

He ﷺ said: "Those who have the best claim to me are the ones who pray for me most."96 It is also narrated that he ﷺ said: "Pray for me plentifully on the night that is the Honourable Night (*al-laylah al-gharrā'*) and the Blossoming Day (*al-yawm al-azhar*),[97] for your prayers are presented before me."[98] Furthermore, it is narrated that he ﷺ said: "Pray for me plentifully on the day and night of Friday. I will be a witness and an intercessor on the Day of Resurrection for whoever does this."[99] Additionally, he ﷺ said: "Pray for me plentifully on Friday, for it is a day that is witnessed by the angels. None of you pray for me but that their prayer is displayed before me until he concludes it."[100]

The esteemed Sheikh Abū Ṭālib al-Makkī, may Allah the Exalted have mercy upon him, said: "The fewest number considered to satisfy plenitude is three-hundred times."

If you are able to do so one-thousand times, this is better for you. This is due to what is narrated from his saying ﷺ: "Whoever prays upon me one-thousand times will not die until he sees his seat in the Garden."[101]

---

96 Tirmidhī and Ibn Ḥibbān.

97 Referring to the morn and eve of Friday.

98 Bayhaqī and others.

99 Bayhaqī.

100 Ibn Mājah.

101 Abū Ḥafṣ ibn Shāhīn, as found in *al-Targhīb* by Mundhirī.

أَكْثِرْ مِنَ الصَّلَاةِ عَلَى النَّبِيِّ ﷺ فِي سَائِرِ الْأَوْقَاتِ عَامَّةً وَلَيْلَةِ الْجُمُعَةِ وَيَوْمِ الْجُمُعَةِ خَاصَّةً

قَالَ ﷺ: «إِنَّ أَوْلَى النَّاسِ بِي يَوْمَ الْقِيَامَةِ أَكْثَرُهُمْ عَلَيَّ صَلَاةً»(٦٢). وَعَنْهُ ﷺ أَنَّهُ قَالَ: «أَكْثِرُوا الصَّلَاةَ عَلَيَّ فِي اللَّيْلَةِ الْغَرَّاءِ وَالْيَوْمِ الْأَزْهَرِ؛ فَإِنَّ صَلَاتَكُمْ تُعْرَضُ عَلَيَّ»(٦٣). وَعَنْهُ ﷺ أَنَّهُ قَالَ: «أَكْثِرُوا مِنَ الصَّلَاةِ عَلَيَّ فِي يَوْمِ الْجُمُعَةِ وَلَيْلَةِ الْجُمُعَةِ، فَمَنْ فَعَلَ ذَلِكَ كُنْتُ لَهُ شَهِيدًا وَشَافِعًا يَوْمَ الْقِيَامَةِ»(٦٤). وَعَنْهُ ﷺ أَنَّهُ قَالَ: «أَكْثِرُوا مِنَ الصَّلَاةِ عَلَيَّ فِي يَوْمِ الْجُمُعَةِ، فَإِنَّهُ يَوْمٌ مَشْهُودٌ تَشْهَدُهُ الْمَلَائِكَةُ، وَإِنَّ أَحَدًا لَنْ يُصَلِّيَ عَلَيَّ إِلَّا عُرِضَتْ عَلَيَّ صَلَاتُهُ حَتَّى يَفْرُغَ مِنْهَا».

وَذَكَرَ الشَّيْخُ أَبُو طَالِبٍ الْمَكِّيُّ رَحِمَهُ اللهُ تَعَالَى: أَنَّ أَقَلَّ الْأَكْثَرِيَّةِ: ثَلَاثُمِائَةِ مَرَّةٍ. اهـ أَقُولُ وَإِذَا أَوْصَلْتَهَا إِلَى أَلْفِ مَرَّةٍ فَذَاكَ خَيْرٌ لَكَ لِمَا رُوِيَ عَنْهُ ﷺ أَنَّهُ قَالَ: «مَنْ صَلَّى عَلَيَّ فِي يَوْمٍ أَلْفَ مَرَّةٍ - لَمْ يَمُتْ حَتَّى يَرَى مَقْعَدَهُ مِنَ الْجَنَّةِ».

---

(٦٢) رَوَاهُ التِّرْمِذِيُّ وَابْنُ حِبَّانَ.

(٦٣) رَوَاهُ الْبَيْهَقِيُّ وَغَيْرُهُ.

(٦٤) رَوَاهُ الْبَيْهَقِيُّ.

Recite Pithy Prayers upon the Prophet ﷺ

Bismillāhi al-Raḥmāni al-Raḥīm. Inna Allāha wa malā'ikatahū yuṣallūna ʿala al-nabiyy; yā ayyuha alladhīna āmanū ṣallū ʿalayhi wa sallimū taslīmā.

"Indeed, Allah showers His blessings upon the Prophet, and His angels pray for him. O believers! Invoke Allah's blessings upon him, and salute him with worthy greetings of peace."[102]

Allāhumma ṣalli ʿalā sayyidinā Muḥammadin wa ʿalā āli sayyidinā Muḥammadin kamā ṣallayta ʿalā sayyidinā Ibrāhīm wa ʿalā āli sayyidinā Ibrāhīm, innaka Ḥamīdun Majīd; wa bārik ʿalā sayyidinā Muḥammadin wa ʿalā āli sayyidinā Muḥammadin kamā bārakta ʿalā sayyidinā Ibrāhīm wa ʿalā āli sayyidinā Ibrāhīm, fī al-ʿālamīna innaka Ḥamīdun Majīd.

Allah, confer Your exaltations upon our Master Muhammad and the family of our Master Muhammad as you have conferred upon our Master Ibrāhīm and the family of our Master Ibrāhīm. Truly, You are Praiseworthy and Glorious. Allah, confer Your blessings in all worlds upon our Master Muhammad and the family of our Master Muhammad, as You have blessed our Master Ibrāhīm and the family of our Master Ibrāhīm. Truly, You are Praiseworthy and Glorious.

Allāhumma wa taḥannan ʿalā sayyidinā Muḥammadin wa ʿalā āli sayyidinā Muḥammadin kamā ṣallayta ʿalā sayyidinā Ibrāhīm wa ʿalā āli sayyidinā Ibrāhīm, innaka Ḥamīdun Majīd.

Allah, confer tender kindness upon our Master Muhammad and the family of our Master Muhammad as you have conferred upon our Master Ibrāhīm and the family of our Master Ibrāhīm. Truly, You are Praiseworthy and Glorious.

---

102 *al-Aḥzāb*, 56.

اِقْرَأْ جَوامِعَ الصَّلَوَاتِ عَلَى النَّبِيِّ ﷺ

﴿بِسْمِ ٱللَّهِ ٱلرَّحْمَٰنِ ٱلرَّحِيمِ: إِنَّ ٱللَّهَ وَمَلَٰٓئِكَتَهُۥ يُصَلُّونَ عَلَى ٱلنَّبِيِّۚ يَٰٓأَيُّهَا ٱلَّذِينَ ءَامَنُواْ صَلُّواْ عَلَيْهِ وَسَلِّمُواْ تَسْلِيمًا﴾.

اَللّٰهُمَّ صَلِّ عَلَى سَيِّدِنَا مُحَمَّدٍ وَعَلَى آلِ سَيِّدِنَا مُحَمَّدٍ، كَمَا صَلَّيْتَ عَلَى سَيِّدِنَا إِبْرَاهِيمَ وَعَلَى آلِ سَيِّدِنَا إِبْرَاهِيمَ؛ إِنَّكَ حَمِيدٌ مَجِيدٌ، وَبَارِكْ عَلَى سَيِّدِنَا مُحَمَّدٍ وَعَلَى آلِ سَيِّدِنَا مُحَمَّدٍ، كَمَا بَارَكْتَ عَلَى سَيِّدِنَا إِبْرَاهِيمَ وَعَلَى آلِ سَيِّدِنَا إِبْرَاهِيمَ فِي الْعَالَمِينَ إِنَّكَ حَمِيدٌ مَجِيدٌ.

اَللّٰهُمَّ وَتَرَحَّمْ عَلَى سَيِّدِنَا مُحَمَّدٍ وَعَلَى آلِ سَيِّدِنَا مُحَمَّدٍ، كَمَا تَرَحَّمْتَ عَلَى سَيِّدِنَا إِبْرَاهِيمَ وَعَلَى آلِ سَيِّدِنَا إِبْرَاهِيمَ؛ إِنَّكَ حَمِيدٌ مَجِيدٌ.

اَللّٰهُمَّ وَتَحَنَّنْ عَلَى سَيِّدِنَا مُحَمَّدٍ وَعَلَى آلِ سَيِّدِنَا مُحَمَّدٍ، كَمَا تَحَنَّنْتَ عَلَى سَيِّدِنَا إِبْرَاهِيمَ وَعَلَى آلِ سَيِّدِنَا إِبْرَاهِيمَ؛ إِنَّكَ حَمِيدٌ مَجِيدٌ.

Allāhumma wa sallim ʿalā sayyidinā Muḥammadin wa ʿalā āli sayyidinā Muḥammadin kamā ṣallayta ʿalā sayyidinā Ibrāhīm wa ʿalā āli sayyidinā Ibrāhīm, innaka Ḥamīdun Majīd – ʿadada khalqika wa riḍā'a nafsika wa zinata ʿarshika wa midāda kalimātika kullamā dhakaraka al-dhākirūna wa ghafala ʿan dhikrika al-ghāfilūn.

Allah, confer greetings of peace upon our Master Muhammad and the family of our Master Muhammad as you have conferred upon our Master Ibrāhīm and the family of our Master Ibrāhīm. Truly, You are Praiseworthy and Glorious. This, as many times as is equal to: the number of Your creatures, the satisfaction of Your Self, the weight of Your Throne, and the ink-worth of all Your words – whenever the mindful remember You and the heedless forget You.

Allāhumma ijʿal ṣalawātika wa raḥmatika wa barakātika ʿalā sayyidi al-mursalīn, wa imām al-muttaqīn, wa khātima al-nabiyyīna Muḥammadin ʿabdika wa rasūlika imām al-khayri wa qā'ida al-khayri wa rasūli al-raḥmah.

Allah, make Your exaltations, mercy, and blessings be upon the Master of Messengers, the Leader of the Pious, the Seal of the Prophets, Muhammad – Your slave and Messenger, the lead and guide to goodness, and the Messenger of Mercy.

Allāhumma ibʿathhu maqāman maḥmūdan yaghbiṭuhū bihī al-awwalūna wa al-ākhirūn.

Allah, prepare for him such a praiseworthy station that the foremost and last would jealously admire him for.

Allāhumma ṣalli ʿalā sayyidinā Muḥammadin wa ʿalā āli sayyidinā Muḥammadin kamā ṣallayta ʿalā sayyidinā Ibrāhīm wa ʿalā āli sayyidinā Ibrāhīm, innaka Ḥamīdun Majīd. Allāhumma bārik ʿalā sayyidinā Muḥammadin wa ʿalā āli sayyidinā Muḥammadin kamā bārakta ʿalā sayyidinā Ibrāhīm wa ʿalā āli sayyidinā Ibrāhīm, innaka Ḥamīdun Majīd.[103]

---

103 This version is narrated by Ibn Mājah with a sound (*ḥasan*) chain of transmission from the words of Ibn Masʿūd ﷺ.

اللّٰهمَّ وَسَلِّمْ عَلَى سَيِّدِنَا مُحَمَّدٍ وَعَلَى آلِ سَيِّدِنَا مُحَمَّدٍ، كَمَا سَلَّمْتَ عَلَى سَيِّدِنَا إِبْرَاهِيمَ وَعَلَى آلِ سَيِّدِنَا إِبْرَاهِيمَ؛ إِنَّكَ حَمِيدٌ مَجِيدٌ(٦٥) - عَدَدَ خَلْقِكَ، وَرِضَاءَ نَفْسِكَ، وَزِنَةَ عَرْشِكَ، وَمِدَادَ كَلِمَاتِكَ، كُلَّمَا ذَكَرَكَ الذَّاكِرُونَ وَغَفَلَ عَنْ ذِكْرِكَ الْغَافِلُونَ.

اَللّٰهُمَّ اجْعَلْ صَلَوَاتِكَ وَرَحْمَتَكَ وَبَرَكَاتِكَ عَلَى سَيِّدِ الْمُرْسَلِيْنَ وَإِمَامِ الْمُتَّقِينَ، وَخَاتَمِ النَّبِيِّيْنَ مُحَمَّدٍ عَبْدِكَ وَرَسُولِكَ؛ إِمَامِ الْخَيْرِ، وَقَائِدِ الْخَيْرِ، وَرَسُولِ الرَّحْمَةِ.

اَللّٰهُمَّ ابْعَثْهُ مَقَامًا مَحْمُودًا يَغْبِطُهُ بِهِ الْأَوَّلُوْنَ وَالْآخِرُوْنَ.
اَللّٰهُمَّ صَلِّ عَلَى سَيِّدِنَا مُحَمَّدٍ وَعَلَى آلِ سَيِّدِنَا مُحَمَّدٍ، كَمَا صَلَّيْتَ عَلَى سَيِّدِنَا إِبْرَاهِيمَ وَعَلَى آلِ سَيِّدِنَا إِبْرَاهِيمَ؛ إِنَّكَ حَمِيدٌ مَجِيدٌ.

اَللّٰهُمَّ بَارِكْ عَلَى سَيِّدِنَا مُحَمَّدٍ وَعَلَى آلِ سَيِّدِنَا مُحَمَّدٍ، كَمَا بَارَكْتَ عَلَى سَيِّدِنَا إِبْرَاهِيمَ وَعَلَى آلِ سَيِّدِنَا إِبْرَاهِيمَ؛ إِنَّكَ حَمِيدٌ مَجِيدٌ(٦٦).

(٦٥) هَذِهِ الصِّيغَةُ رُوِيَتْ فِي الْمَرْفُوعَاتِ الْمُسَلْسَلَةِ.

(٦٦) هَذِهِ الصِّيَغَةُ كُلُّهَا رَوَاهَا ابْنُ مَاجَه بِإِسْنَادٍ حَسَنٍ عَنِ ابْنِ مَسْعُودٍ رَضِيَ اللهُ عَنْهُ مِنْ كَلَامِهِ.

Allah, confer Your exaltations upon our Master Muhammad and the family of our Master Muhammad as you have conferred upon our Master Ibrāhīm and the family of our Master Ibrāhīm. Truly, You are Praiseworthy and Glorious. Allah, confer Your blessings upon our Master Muhammad and the family of our Master Muhammad, as You have blessed our Master Ibrāhīm and the family of our Master Ibrāhīm. Truly, You are Praiseworthy and Glorious.

Allāhumma innī as'aluka bi-nūri wajh Allāhi al-ʿAẓīm, alladhī mala'a arkāna ʿarsh Allāhi al-ʿAẓīm, wa qāmat bihī ʿawālimu Allāhi al-ʿAẓīm, an tuṣalliya ʿalā mawlānā Muḥammadin dhī al-qadr al-ʿaẓīm, wa ʿalā āli nabiyyi Allāhi al-ʿaẓīm, bi-qadri ʿaẓamati dhāti Allāhi al-ʿAẓīm, fī kulli lamḥatin wa nafasin ʿadada mā fī ʿilmi Allāhi al-ʿAẓīm, ṣalātan dā'imatan bi-dawāmi Allahi al-ʿAẓīm, taʿẓīman li-ḥaqqika yā mawlānā yā Muḥammadu yā dhā al-khuluqi al-ʿaẓīm, wa sallim ʿalayhi wa ʿalā ālihī mithla dhālik, wa ijmaʿ baynī wa baynahū kamā jamaʿta bayna al-rūḥi wa al-nafs, ẓāhiran wa bāṭinā, yaqaẓatan wa manāmā, wa ijʿalhu yā Rabbi rūḥan li-dhātī min jamīʿi al-wujūhi fī al-dunyā wa al-ākhirah.

Allah, I ask you by the Light of Allah's Face, the Great, which has filled the corners of the Throne of Allah the Great, and through which the realms of Allah the Great are established, that you confer exaltations upon our Master Muhmmad, possessor of great status, and upon the family of the Great Prophet of Allah. I ask You to do this in a way that is befitting of Allah's mighty essence, the Great. That You do so at every moment and with every breath, in an amount equal to the knowledge of Allah the Great – an eternal exaltation that is as eternal as Allah the Great. This is an extolment of your right, our Master Muhammad, possessor of great character. Confer greetings upon him and his family in the same way, and gather us together as You have gathered between the spirit and the self, manifestly and inwardly, in wakefulness and sleep. Allah, Most Great, make him the spirit to my essence in every way, in this life before the next.

اَللّٰهُمَّ إِنِّي أَسأَلُكَ بِنُورِ وَجْهِ اللّٰهِ الْعَظِيمِ، الَّذِي مَلأَ أَرْكَانَ عَرْشِ اللّٰهِ الْعَظِيمِ، وَقَامَتْ بِهٖ عَوَالِمُ اللّٰهِ الْعَظِيمِ،

أَنْ تُصَلِّيَ عَلَى مَوْلَانَا مُحَمَّدٍ ذِي الْقَدْرِ الْعَظِيمِ، وَعَلَى آلِ نَبِيِّ اللّٰهِ الْعَظِيمِ، بِقَدْرِ عَظَمَةِ ذَاتِ اللّٰهِ الْعَظِيمِ، فِي كُلِّ لَمْحَةٍ وَنَفَسٍ عَدَدَ مَا فِي عِلْمِ اللّٰهِ الْعَظِيمِ؛

صَلَاةً دَائِمَةً بِدَوَامِ اللّٰهِ الْعَظِيمِ، تَعْظِيمًا لِحَقِّكَ يَا مَوْلَانَا يَا مُحَمَّدُ يَا ذَا الْخُلُقِ الْعَظِيمِ،

وَسَلِّمْ عَلَيْهِ وَعَلَى آلِهِ مِثْلَ ذَلِكَ، وَاجْمَعْ بَيْنِي وَبَيْنَهُ كَمَا جَمَعْتَ بَيْنَ الرُّوحِ وَالنَّفْسِ، ظَاهِرًا وَّ بَاطِنًا يَقْظَةً وَّمَنَامًا، وَاجْعَلْهُ يَا رَبِّ رُوحًا لِذَاتِيْ مِنْ جَمِيعِ الْوُجُوهِ فِي الدُّنْيَا قَبْلَ الْآخِرَةِ يَا عَظِيمُ.

Allāhumma ṣalli ṣalātan kāmilatan, wa sallim salāman tāmman ʿalā sayyidinā Muḥammadin alladhī tanḥallu bihī al-ʿuqad, wa tanfariju bihī al-kurab, wa tuqḍā bihī al-ḥawā'ij, wa tunālu bihī al-raghā'ib, wa ḥusnu al-khawātim, wa yustasqā al-ghamāmu bi-wajhihī al-karīm, wa ʿalā ālihī wa ṣaḥbihī fī kulli lamḥatin wa nafasin bi-ʿadadi kulli maʿlūmin lak.

Allah, confer perfect exaltations and complete greetings of peace upon our Master Muhammad through whom knots are undone, calamities are uplifted, needs are fulfilled, and wants as well as good endings are realized. Through his noble face the release of rain clouds is sought. Likewise upon his family and Companions at every moment and with every breath, in accordance with all that is known to You.

Allāhumma ṣalli ʿalā sayyidinā Muḥammadin miftaḥi khazā'inik. Allāhumma iftaḥ lanā bi-sayyidinā Muḥammadin ṣallā Allāhu ʿalayhi wa sallama mā ughliqa ʿalaynā.

Allah, confer Your exaltations upon our Master Muhammad, the key to Your stores. Allah, open for us through our Master Muhammad that which has been locked.

Allāhumma ṣalli ʿalā sayyidinā Muḥammadin al-nabiyyi al-ummiyyi al-qurashiyyi baḥri anwārik, wa maʿdini asrārik, wa lisāni ḥujjatik, wa khayri khalqika, wa aḥabbi al-khalqi ilayk, ʿabdika wa nabiyyika alladhī khatamta bihī al-anbiya'i wa al-mursalīn, wa ʿalā ālihī wa ṣaḥbihī wa sallim, Subḥān Rabbika Rabbi al-ʿizzati ʿammā yaṣifūn, wa salāmun ʿalā al-mursalīn, wa al-ḥamdu lillāhi Rabbi al-ʿālamīn.

Allah, confer Your exaltations and greetings upon our Master Muhammad the Unlettered Qurashī Prophet; the ocean of Your light, the reservoir of Your secrets, the eye of Your care, the tongue of Your proof, the best of Your creation, the most beloved of Your creation to You, Your slave and prophet with whom You concluded all Prophets and Messengers. Likewise upon his family and Companions. "Glorified is your Lord – the Lord of Honour and Power – above what they claim! Peace be upon the

اَللّٰهُمَّ صَلِّ صَلَاةً كَامِلَةً، وَسَلِّمْ سَلَامًا تَامًّا عَلَى سَيِّدِنَا مُحَمَّدٍ الَّذِي تَنْحَلُّ بِهِ الْعُقَدُ، وَتَنْفَرِجُ بِهِ الْكُرَبُ، وَتُقْضَى بِهِ الْحَوَائِجُ، وَتُنَالُ بِهِ الرَّغَائِبُ، وَحُسْنُ الْخَوَاتِمِ، وَيُسْتَسْقَى الْغَمَامُ بِوَجْهِهِ الْكَرِيمِ، وَعَلَى آلِهِ وَصَحْبِهِ فِي كُلِّ لَمْحَةٍ وَنَفَسٍ بِعَدَدِ كُلِّ مَعْلُومٍ لَكَ.

اَللّٰهُمَّ صَلِّ عَلَى سَيِّدِنَا مُحَمَّدٍ مِفْتَاحِ خَزَائِنِكَ، اَللّٰهُمَّ افْتَحْ لَنَا بِسَيِّدِنَا مُحَمَّدٍ ﷺ مَا أُغْلِقَ عَلَيْنَا.

اَللّٰهُمَّ صَلِّ عَلَى سَيِّدِنَا مُحَمَّدٍ النَّبِيِّ الْأُمِّيِّ الْقُرَشِيِّ بَحْرِ أَنْوَارِكَ، وَمَعْدِنِ أَسْرَارِكَ، وَعَيْنِ عِنَايَتِكَ، وَلِسَانِ حُجَّتِكَ، وَخَيْرِ خَلْقِكَ، وَأَحَبِّ الْخَلْقِ إِلَيْكَ، عَبْدِكَ وَنَبِيِّكَ الَّذِي خَتَمْتَ بِهِ الْأَنْبِيَاءَ وَالْمُرْسَلِينَ، وَعَلَى آلِهِ وَصَحْبِهِ وَسَلِّمْ؛

﴿سُبْحَٰنَ رَبِّكَ رَبِّ ٱلْعِزَّةِ عَمَّا يَصِفُونَ ﴿١٨٠﴾ وَسَلَٰمٌ عَلَى ٱلْمُرْسَلِينَ ﴿١٨١﴾ وَٱلْحَمْدُ لِلَّهِ رَبِّ ٱلْعَٰلَمِينَ ﴿١٨٢﴾﴾.

messengers. And praise be to Allah – Lord of all worlds."[104]

Allāhumma ṣalli ʿalā al-nūri al-lāmiʿ, wa al-qamari al-sāṭiʿ, wa al-badri al-ṭāliʿ, wa al-fayḍi al-hāmiʿ, wa al-madadi al-wāsiʿ, wa al-ḥabībi al-shāfiʿ, wa al-nabiyyi al-shāriʿ, wa al-rasūli al-ṣādiʿ, wa al-mamūri al-ṭāʾiʿ, wa al-mukhāṭabi al-sāmiʿ, wa al-sayfi al-qāṭiʿ, wa al-qalbi al-jāmiʿ, wa al-ṭarfi al-dāmiʿ – sayyidinā Muḥammadin wa ʿalā ālihī wa awlādihī al-kirām, wa aṣḥābihī al-ʿiẓām, wa atbāʿihim min ahli al-sunnati wa al-islām.

Allah, confer Your exaltations upon the shining light, the splendid moon, the manifest full moon, the flooding stream, the expansive aid, the beloved intercessor, the law-giving Prophet, the unwavering Messenger, the one to whom Allah spoke and he hears Him, the cutting sword, the uniting heart, the tearing eye – our Master Muhammad and his family, noble progeny, great Companions, and his Muslim followers who hold fast to his way.

Allāhumma ṣalli ʿalā sayyidinā Muḥammadin ṣalātan tuktabu bihā al-suṭūr, wa tashrahu bihā al-ṣudūr, wa tuhawwanu bihā jamīʿu al-umūr, bi-raḥmatin minka yā ʿAzīzu yā Ghafūr, wa ʿalā ālihī wa ṣaḥbihī wa sallim.

Allah, confer Your exaltations upon our Master Muhammad, such exaltations that fill the scribes' lines, expand our chests, lighten upon us the load of all things, by a mercy from You, Most Merciful, Most Forgiving. Likewise upon his family and Companions.

Allāhumma ṣalli wa sallim wa bārik ʿalā al-dhāti al-mukammalah, wa al-raḥmati al-munazzalah: ʿabdika wa rasūlika wa ḥabībika wa ṣafiyyika sayyidinā Muḥammad, wa ʿalā ālihī wa azwājihī wa awlādihī wa jīrānih, ʿadada mā dhakaraka al-dhākirūna wa ghafala ʿan dhikrika al-ghāfilūn.

Allah, confer Your exaltations, greetings, and blessings upon the perfected essence and the descended mercy: Your slave, Messenger, beloved, and chosen one, our Master Muhammad. Likewise upon his family, wives,

104 *al-Ṣāffāt*, 180-182.

اَللّٰهُمَّ صَلِّ عَلَى النُّورِ اللاَّمِعِ، وَالْقَمَرِ السَّاطِعِ، وَالْبَدْرِ الطَّالِعِ، وَالْفَيْضِ الْهَامِعِ، وَالْمَدَدِ الْوَاسِعِ، وَالْحَبِيبِ الشَّافِعِ، وَالنَّبِيِّ الشَّارِعِ، وَالرَّسُولِ الصَّادِعِ، وَالْمَأْمُورِ الطَّائِعِ، وَالْمُخَاطَبِ السَّامِعِ، وَالسَّيْفِ الْقَاطِعِ، وَالْقَلْبِ الْجَامِعِ، وَالطَّرْفِ الدَّامِعِ - سَيِّدِنَا مُحَمَّدٍ وَعَلَى آلِهِ وَأَوْلَادِهِ الْكِرَامِ، وَأَصْحَابِهِ الْعِظَامِ، وَأَتْبَاعِهِمْ مِنْ أَهْلِ السُّنَّةِ وَالْإِسْلَامِ.

اَللّٰهُمَّ صَلِّ عَلَى سَيِّدِنَا مُحَمَّدٍ صَلَاةً تُكْتَبُ بِهَا السُّطُورُ، وَتَشْرَحُ بِهَا الصُّدُورُ، وَتُهَوَّنُ بِهَا جَمِيعُ الأُمُورِ، بِرَحْمَةٍ مِنْكَ يَا عَزِيزُ يَا غَفُورُ، وَعَلَى آلِهِ وَصَحْبِهِ وَسَلِّمْ.

اَللّٰهُمَّ صَلِّ وَسَلِّمْ وَبَارِكْ عَلَى الذَّاتِ الْمُكَمَّلَةِ، وَالرَّحْمَةِ الْمُنَزَّلَةِ: عَبْدِكَ وَرَسُولِكَ وَحَبِيبِكَ وَصَفِيِّكَ سَيِّدِنَا مُحَمَّدٍ، وَعَلَى آلِهِ وَأَزْوَاجِهِ وَأَوْلَادِهِ وَجِيرَانِهِ، عَدَدَ مَا ذَكَرَكَ الذَّاكِرُونَ وَغَفَلَ عَنْ ذِكْرِكَ الْغَافِلُونَ.

children, and neighbours. This, as many times as the mindful remember You and the heedless forget You.

Allāhumma ṣalli ʿalā sayyidinā Muḥammadin sayyidi al-sādāt, wa manbaʿi al-kamālāt, wa bābi al-hidāyāt, wa kanzi al-ʿinayāt, wa baḥri al-ifādāt, wa maẓhari al-saʿādāt, wa sullami al-raqāyāt, wa ʿayni al-khayrāt, wa ʿalā ālihī wa aṣḥābihī wa al-tābiʿīna lahum fī kulli al-ḥālāt, wa ijʿalnā yā Rabbi min al-maqbūlīna ʿindah, wa al-muqarrabīna ladayh, wa al-ʿārifīna bih, innaka Samīʿun Qarībun Mujību al-daʿawāt.

Allah, confer Your exaltations upon our Master Muhammad, the lord of all masters, the source of perfection, the door of guidance, the treasure of divine care, the ocean of benefit, the manifestation of happiness, the ladder to lofty stations, the stream of goodness, and upon his family, Companions, and their followers in all states. Make us, Allah, of those who are accepted by him, made close to him, and those who have true knowledge of him. You are All Hearing, Most Close, Answering of supplications.

Allāhumma ṣalli wa sallim wa bārik ʿalā sayyidinā Muḥammadin al-nabiyyi al-malīḥ, ṣāḥibi al-maqāmi al-aʿlā wa al-lisani al-faṣīḥ, wa ʿalā ālihī wa aṣḥābihī - aṣḥābi al-madadi al-ʿālī wa al-qadami al-ṣaḥīḥ - Āmīn.

Allah, confer Your exaltations, greetings, and blessings upon our Master Muhammad the handsome prophet, owner of the lofty station and the eloquent tongue, and upon his family and Companions, those given lofty aid and firm foothold. Āmīn.

Allāhumma yā Allāh ṣalli ʿalā sayyidinā Muḥammadin wa man wālāh ʿadada mā taʿlamuhū min bad'i al-amri wa muntahāh, wa sallim ʿalayh wa ʿalayhim kathīrā.

Allah, O Allah, confer Your exaltations upon our Master Muhammad and those who ally themselves to him, as many times equal to Your knowledge of the start and end of events. Confer plentiful greetings upon them.

اَللّٰهُمَّ صَلِّ عَلَى سَيِّدِنَا مُحَمَّدٍ سَيِّدِ السَّادَاتِ، وَمَنْبَعِ الْكَمَالَاتِ، وَبَابِ الْهِدَايَاتِ، وَكَنْزِ الْعِنَايَاتِ، وَبَحْرِ الْإِفَادَاتِ، وَمَظْهَرِ السَّعَادَاتِ، وَسُلَّمِ الرِّقَايَاتِ، وَعَيْنِ الْخَيْرَاتِ، وَعَلَى آلِهِ وَأَصْحَابِهِ وَالتَّابِعِينَ لَهُمْ فِي كُلِّ الْحَالَاتِ، وَاجْعَلْنَا يَا رَبِّ مِنَ الْمَقْبُولِينَ عِنْدَهُ، وَالْمُقَرَّبِينَ لَدَيْهِ، وَالْعَارِفِينَ بِهِ، إِنَّكَ سَمِيعٌ قَرِيبٌ مُّجِيبُ الدَّعَوَاتِ.

اَللّٰهُمَّ صَلِّ وَسَلِّمْ وَبَارِكْ عَلَى سَيِّدِنَا مُحَمَّدٍ النَّبِيِّ الْمَلِيحِ، صَاحِبِ الْمَقَامِ الْأَعْلَى وَاللِّسَانِ الْفَصِيحِ، وَعَلَى آلِهِ وَأَصْحَابِهِ - أَصْحَابِ الْمَدَدِ الْعَالِيِّ وَالْقَدَمِ الصَّحِيحِ - آمِين.

اَللّٰهُمَّ يَا اَللّٰهُ صَلِّ عَلَى سَيِّدِنَا مُحَمَّدٍ وَّمَنْ وَّالَاهُ، عَدَدَ مَا تَعْلَمُهُ مِنْ بَدْءِ الْأَمْرِ وَمُنْتَهَاهُ، وَسَلِّمْ عَلَيْهِ وَعَلَيْهِمْ كَثِيرًا.

Allāhumma yā Allāh ṣalli ʿalā sayyidinā Muḥammadin ʿadada mā kān, wa ʿadada mā huwa kāʾinun fī ʿilmi Allāh, wa ʿalā ālihī wa ṣaḥbihī wa sallim.

Allah, confer Your exaltations and greetings upon our Master Muhammad as many times equal to what was and what is in the knowledge of Allah. Likewise upon his family and Companions.

Allāhumma ṣalli ʿalā sayyidinā Muḥammadin al-nabiyyi al-ummiyyi al-ṭāhiri al-zakiyy, ṣalātan tuḥallu bihā al-ʿuqad, wa tufakku bihā al-kurab, wa ʿalā ālihī wa ṣaḥbihī wa sallim.[105]

Allah, confer Your exaltations and greetings upon our Master Muhammad the pure, good Unlettered Prophet, such exaltations that undo complications and uplift calamities; likewise upon his family and Companions.

Allāhumma ṣalli wa sallim ʿalā sayyidinā wa mawlānā Muḥammad: baḥri anwārik, wa maʿdini asrārik, wa lisāni ḥujjatik, wa ʿarūsi mamlakatik, wa imāmi ḥaḍratik, wa ṭirāzi mulkik, wa khazāʾini raḥmatik, wa ṭarīqi sharīʿatik, al-mutaladhdhidhi bi-mushāhadatik, insāni ʿayni al-wujūd, wa al-sababi fī kulli mawjūd, ʿayni aʿyāni khalqik, al-mutaqaddimi min nūri ḍiyāʿik, ṣalātan taḥullu bihā ʿuqdatī, wa tufarriju bihā kurbatī, ṣalātan turḍīka wa turḍīhi wa tarḍā bihā ʿannā yā Rabba al-ʿālamīn, ʿadada mā aḥāṭa bihī ʿilmuk, wa aḥṣāhu kitābuk, wa jarā bihī qalamuk, wa ʿadada al-amṭāri wa al-aḥjāri wa al-ashjār, wa malāʾikati al-biḥār, wa jamīʿi mā khalaqa Mawlānā min awwali al-zamāni ilā ākhirih, wa al-ḥamdu lillāhi waḥdah.[106]

Allah, confer Your exaltations and greetings upon our Master and Chief Muhammad: the ocean of Your light, the reservoir of Your secrets, the tongue of Your proof, the adornment of Your kingdom, the leader of those in Your presence, the embellishment of what You own, the store of Your mercy, the way of Your law; the one who is relishing witnessing You, the pupil of the eye to existence, the reason of all that exists, the

---

105   All these prayers are attributed to the grand Imam, the esteemed Sheikh, Aḥmad al-Rifāʿī.

106   This supplication is attributed to the grand Imam, the esteemed Sheikh, ʿAbd al-Qādir al-Jīlānī

اَللّٰهُمَّ صَلِّ عَلَى سَيِّدِنَا مُحَمَّدٍ عَدَدَ مَا كَانَ، وَعَدَدَ مَا هُوَ كَائِنٌ فِي عِلْمِ اللّٰهِ، وَعَلَى آلِهِ وَصَحْبِهِ وَسَلِّمْ.

اَللّٰهُمَّ صَلِّ عَلَى سَيِّدِنَا مُحَمَّدٍ النَّبِيِّ الْأُمِّيِّ الطَّاهِرِ الزَّكِيِّ، صَلَاةً تُحَلُّ بِهَا الْعُقَدُ، وَتُفَكُّ بِهَا الْكُرَبُ، وَعَلَى آلِهِ وَصَحْبِهِ وَسَلِّمْ(٦٧).

اَللّٰهُمَّ صَلِّ وَسَلِّمْ عَلَى سَيِّدِنَا وَمَوْلَانَا مُحَمَّدٍ: بَحْرِ أَنْوَارِكَ، وَمَعْدِنِ أَسْرَارِكَ، وَلِسَانِ حُجَّتِكَ، وَعَرُوسِ مَمْلَكَتِكَ، وَإِمَامِ حَضْرَتِكَ، وَطِرَازِ مُلْكِكَ، وَخَزَائِنِ رَحْمَتِكَ، وَطَرِيقِ شَرِيعَتِكَ، اَلْمُتَلَذِّذِ بِمُشَاهَدَتِكَ، إِنْسَانِ عَيْنِ الْوُجُودِ، وَالسَّبَبِ فِي كُلِّ مَوْجُودٍ، عَيْنِ أَعْيَانِ خَلْقِكَ، اَلْمُتَقَدِّمِ مِنْ نُورِ ضِيَائِكَ، صَلَاةً تُحَلُّ بِهَا عُقْدَتِي، وَتُفَرِّجُ بِهَا كُرْبَتِي، صَلَاةً تُرْضِيكَ وَتُرْضِيهِ وَتَرْضَى بِهَا عَنَّا يَا رَبَّ الْعَالَمِينَ، عَدَدَ مَا أَحَاطَ بِهِ عِلْمُكَ، وَأَحْصَاهُ كِتَابُكَ، وَجَرَى بِهِ قَلَمُكَ، وَعَدَدَ الْأَمْطَارِ وَالْأَحْجَارِ وَالْأَشْجَارِ، وَمَلَائِكَةِ الْبِحَارِ، وَجَمِيعِ مَا خَلَقَ مَوْلَانَا مِنْ أَوَّلِ الزَّمَانِ إِلَى آخِرِهِ، وَالْحَمْدُ لِلّٰهِ وَحْدَهُ(٦٨).

---

(٦٧) هَذِهِ الصَّلَوَاتُ كُلُّهَا مَنْسُوبَةٌ إِلَى الْإِمَامِ الْكَبِيرِ السَّيِّدِ الشَّيْخِ أَحْمَدَ الرِّفَاعِيِّ رَضِيَ اللّٰهُ تَعَالَى عَنْهُ وَنَفَعَنَا بِهِ.

(٦٨) هَذِهِ الصَّلَاةُ مَنْسُوبَةٌ إِلَى الْإِمَامِ الْكَبِيرِ السَّيِّدِ الشَّيْخِ عَبْدِ الْقَادِرِ الْجِيلَانِيِّ رَضِيَ اللّٰهُ تَعَالَى عَنْهُ وَنَفَعَنَا بِهِ.

most worthy of Your creation, the resultant of the light of Your radiance, such exaltations that undo my affliction, relieve my troubles. Exaltations which please You and him – so that You are pleased with us, Lord of all worlds. This, as many times as is equal to what Your knowledge engulfs, Your Book encompasses, and Your Pen writes. As many times as there are raindrops, pebbles, and trees. As many times as the angels of the ocean, and as many times as all our Lord created since the beginning of time to its end. Praise is to Allah alone.

Allāhumma ṣalli wa sallim wa bārik ʿalā sayyidinā wa mawlānā Muḥammadin shajarati al-aṣli al-nūrāniyyah, wa lamʿati al-qabḍati al-raḥmāniyyah, wa afḍali al-khalīqati al-insāniyyah, wa ashrafi al-ṣūrati al-jismāniyyah, wa maʿdini al-asrāri al-rabbāniyyah, wa khazāʾini al-ʿulūmi al-iṣṭifāʾiyyah, ṣāḥibi al-qabḍati al-aṣliyyah, wa al-bahjati al-saniyyah, wa al-rutbati al-ʿaliyyah, man indarajati al-nabiyyūna taḥta liwāʾih fa-hum minhu wa ilayh, wa ṣalli wa sallim wa bārik ʿalayhi wa ʿalā ālihi wa ṣaḥbihī ʿadada: mā khalaqt, wa razaqt, wa amatt, wa aḥyayt – ilā yawmi tabʿathu man afnayt, wa sallim taslīman kathīrā, wa al-ḥamdu lillāhi Rabbi al-ʿālamīn.[107]

Allah, confer Your exaltations, greetings, and blessings upon our Master and Chief Muhammad: the original tree of light, the glow of the merciful grasp, the best of human beings, the noblest of bodily forms, the reservoir of divine secrets, the store of the chosen knowledge, possesssor of the original grasp, magnificent splendor, and lofty station. The one whose flag the Prophets follow, so that they are from him and belong to him. Allah, confer Your exaltations, greetings, and blessings upon him, his family, and his Companions; as many times as is equal to what You have created and provided, and what You have given death to and what You have given life, until the day You resurrect those You have caused to perish. Confer also abundant greetings upon them. Praise be to Allah, the Lord of all worlds.

---

107   This supplication belongs to the grand Imam, the esteemed Sheikh, Aḥmad al-Badawī
🌸.

اَللّٰهُمَّ صَلِّ وَسَلِّمْ وَبَارِكْ عَلَى سَيِّدِنَا وَمَوْلَانَا مُحَمَّدٍ شَجَرَةِ الْأَصْلِ النُّوْرَانِيَّةِ، وَلَمْعَةِ الْقَبْضَةِ الرَّحْمَانِيَّةِ، وَأَفْضَلِ الْخَلِيقَةِ الْإِنْسَانِيَّةِ، وَأَشْرَفِ الصُّوْرَةِ الْجِسْمَانِيَّةِ، وَمَعْدِنِ الْأَسْرَارِ الرَّبَّانِيَّةِ، وَخَزَائِنِ الْعُلُومِ الْاِصْطِفَائِيَّةِ، صَاحِبِ الْقَبْضَةِ الْأَصْلِيَّةِ، وَالْبَهْجَةِ السَّنِيَّةِ، وَالرُّتْبَةِ الْعَلِيَّةِ، مَنِ انْدَرَجَتِ النَّبِيُّوْنَ تَحْتَ لِوَائِهِ فَهُم مِنْهُ وَإِلَيْهِ، وَصَلِّ وَسَلِّمْ وَبَارِكْ عَلَيْهِ وَعَلَى آلِهِ وَصَحْبِهِ عَدَدَ: مَا خَلَقْتَ، وَرَزَقْتَ، وَأَمَتَّ، وَأَحْيَيْتَ - إِلَى يَوْمِ تَبْعَثُ مَنْ أَفْنَيْتَ، وَسَلِّمْ تَسْلِيمًا كَثِيرًا، وَالْحَمْدُ لِلّٰهِ رَبِّ الْعَالَمِينَ(٦٩).

(٦٩) هَذِهِ الصَّلَاةُ لِلإِمَامِ الْكَبِيرِ السَّيِّدِ الشَّيْخِ أَحْمَدَ الْبَدْوِيِّ رَضِيَ اللّٰهُ تَعَالَى عَنْهُ وَنَفَعَنَا بِهِ.

Allāhumma ṣalli ʿalā al-dhāti al-muḥammadiyyah, al-laṭīfati al-aḥadiyyah, shamsi samā'i al-asrār, wa maẓhari al-anwāri wa markazi madāri al-jalāl, wa quṭbi falaki al-jamāl.

Allah, confer Your exaltations upon the kind, unique Muhammadan essence, the Sun of the sky of secrets, the manifestation of lights, the center to majesty's circulation, and the pole of beauty's orbit.

Allāhumma bi-sirrihī ladayk, wa bi-sayrihī ilayk: āmin khawfī, wa aqil ʿathratī, wa adhhib ḥuznī wa ḥirsī, wa kun lī, wa khudh bī ilayka minnī, wa urzuqnī al-ghanā'a ʿannī, wa lā tajʿalnī maftunan bi-nafsī, maḥjūban bi-ḥissī, wa ikshif lī ʿan kulli sirrin maktūmin yā Ḥayyu yā Qayyūm.[108]

Allah, by his secret with You, and his traversing towards You: calm my fear, lessen my stumbling, do away with my grief and mistrust. Be on my side, and take me from my own self towards You. Grant me independence from my own self, and make me not trialled by it, nor veiled off by it. Uncover for me all concealed secrets, Ever Living, Sustainer of all.

Allāhumma ṣalli ʿalā man minhu inshaqqati al-asrār, wa infalaqati al-anwār, wa fīhi irtaqat al-ḥaqā'iq, wa tanazzalat ʿulūmu Ādam fa-aʿjaza al-khalā'iq, wa lahū taḍā'alat al-fuhūmu fa-lam yudrikhu minnā sābiqun wa lā lāḥiq; fa-riyāḍu al-malakūti bi-zuhri jamālihī mūnaqah, wa ḥiyāḍu al-jabarūti bi-fayḍi anwārihī mutadaffiqah, wa lā shay'a illā wa huwa bihī manūṭ, idh lawlā al-wāsiṭata la-dhahaba – kamā qīla – al-mawsūṭ, ṣalātan talīqu bika minka ilayh, kamā huwa ahluh.

Allah, confer Your exaltations upon the one from whom secrets emerge and lights emanate. In him truths arise. The sciences of Adam descended upon him, thus he incapacitated all other creatures. Understanding succumbed to him that nor the first nor last among us perceive. The meadows of the kingdom are made exquisite by his brilliant beauty. The fountains of the dominion flood forth with his overflowing light. There is not a thing but that it goes back to him, for with the means – as they say – there

108 This supplication belongs to the grand Imam, the esteemed Sheikh, Ibrāhīm al-Dusūqī ﷺ.

اَللّٰهُمَّ صَلِّ عَلَى الذَّاتِ الْمُحَمَّدِيَّةِ، اللَّطِيفَةِ الْأَحَدِيَّةِ، شَمْسِ سَمَاءِ الْأَسْرَارِ، وَمَظْهَرِ الْأَنْوَارِ وَمَرْكَزِ مَدَارِ الْجَلَالِ، وَقُطْبِ فَلَكِ الْجَمَالِ.

اَللّٰهُمَّ بِسِرِّهِ لَدَيْكَ، وَبِسَيْرِهِ إِلَيْكَ: آمِنْ خَوْفِي، وَأَقِلْ عَثْرَتِي، وَأَذْهِبْ حُزْنِي وَحِرْصِي، وَكُنْ لِي، وَخُذْ بِي إِلَيْكَ مِنِّي، وَارْزُقْنِي الْغَنَاءَ عَنِّي، وَلَا تَجْعَلْنِي مَفْتُونًا بِنَفْسِي، مَحْجُوبًا بِحِسِّي، وَاكْشِفْ لِيَ عَنْ كُلِّ سِرٍّ مَكْتُومٍ يَا حَيُّ يَا قَيُّومُ(٧٠).

اَللّٰهُمَّ صَلِّ عَلَى مَنْ مِنْهُ انْشَقَّتِ الْأَسْرَارُ، وَانْفَلَقَتِ الْأَنْوَارُ، وَفِيهِ ارْتَقَتِ الْحَقَائِقُ، وَتَنَزَّلَتْ عُلُومُ آدَمَ فَأَعْجَزَ الْخَلَائِقَ، وَلَهُ تَضَاءَلَتِ الْفُهُومُ فَلَمْ يُدْرِكْهُ مِنَّا سَابِقٌ وَلَا لَاحِقٌ؛ فَرِيَاضُ الْمَلَكُوتِ بِزَهْرِ جَمَالِهِ مُونِقَةٌ، وَحِيَاضُ الْجَبَرُوتِ بِفَيْضِ أَنْوَارِهِ مُتَدَفِّقَةٌ، وَلَا شَيْءَ إِلَّا وَهُوَ بِهِ مَنُوطٌ، إِذْ لَوْلَا الْوَاسِطَةُ لَذَهَبَ -كَمَا قِيلَ - الْمَوْسُوطُ، صَلَاةً تَلِيقُ بِكَ مِنْكَ إِلَيْهِ، كَمَا هُوَ أَهْلُهُ.

(٧٠) هَذِهِ الصَّلَاةُ لِلْإِمَامِ الْكَبِيرِ السَّيِّدِ الشَّيْخِ إِبْرَاهِيمَ الدَّسُوقِيِّ رَضِيَ اللّٰهُ تَعَالَىٰ عَنْهُ وَنَفَعَنَا بِهِ.

would be no ends. Make it such exaltation that is befitting of You, from You to him, as he is worthy of.

Allāhumma innahū sirruka al-jāmiʿu al-dāllu ʿalayk, wa ḥijābuka al-aʿẓamu al-qā'imu laka bayna yadayk.

Allah, he is Your all-encompassing secret that points to You, and Your greatest veil that stands for You in front of You.

Allāhumma alḥiqnī bi-nasabih, wa ḥaqqiqnī bi-ḥasabih, wa ʿarrifnī iyyāhu maʿrifatan aslamu bihā min mawāridi al-jahl, wa akraʿu bihā min mawāridi al-faḍl, wa iḥmilnī ʿalā sabīlihī ilā ḥaḍratika ḥamlan maḥfūẓan bi-nuṣratik, wa iqdhif bī ʿalā al-bāṭili fa-admaghuh, wa zujja bī fī biḥāri al-aḥadiyyah, wa unshulnī min awḥāli al-tawḥīd, wa aghriqnī fī ʿayni baḥri al-wiḥdah, ḥattā lā arā wa lā asmāʿ, wa lā ajida wa lā uḥissa illā bihā, wa ijʿal al-ḥijāba al-aʿẓama ḥayāta rūḥī, wa rūḥahū sirra ḥaqīqatī, wa ḥaqīqatahū jamīʿa ʿawālimī, bi-taḥqīqi al-ḥaqqi al-awwal, yā Awwal, yā Ākhir, yā Ẓāhiru yā Bāṭin – ismaʿ nidā'ī bimā samiʿta bihī nidā'a ʿabdika Zakariyyā, wa unṣurnī bika lak, wa ayyidnī bika lak, wa ijmaʿ baynī wa baynak, ḥul baynī wa bayna ghayrik, Allāh, Allāh, Allāh, inna alladhī faraḍa ʿalayka al-Qur'āna la-rādduka ilā maʿād, Rabbanā ātinā min ladunka raḥmatan wa hayyi' lanā min amrinā rashadā.[109]

Allah, allow me to reach his lineage, make me true through his ancestry, and make me know him to a degree that keeps me safe from ignorance and allows me to quaff from the sources of virtue. Carry me upon his way towards Your presence a carrying that is preserved by Your support. Hurl me against falsehood so that I break it. Throw me in the oceans of divine uniqueness. Save me from falling[110] away from divine unity, and drown me in the pupil of the eye of divine oneness[111] until I do not see, hear,

---

109 This supplication belongs to the grand Imam, the esteemed Sheikh, Abd al-Salām ibn Mashīsh ﷺ. It is good to recite them after the prayers wherein the Qur'an is recited out loud – three by three.

110 Meaning minor forms of polytheism in all its types.

111 Meaning pure monotheism.

اَللّٰهُمَّ إِنَّهُ سِرُّكَ الْجَامِعُ الدَّالُّ عَلَيْكَ، وَحِجَابُكَ الْأَعْظَمُ الْقَائِمُ لَكَ بَيْنَ يَدَيْكَ.

اَللّٰهُمَّ أَلْحِقْنِي بِنَسَبِهِ، وَحَقِّقْنِي بِحَسَبِهِ، وَعَرِّفْنِي إِيَّاهُ مَعْرِفَةً أَسْلَمُ بِهَا مِنْ مَوَارِدِ الْجَهْلِ، وَأَكْرَعُ بِهَا مِنْ مَوَارِدِ الْفَضْلِ، وَاحْمِلْنِي عَلَى سَبِيلِهِ إِلَى حَضْرَتِكَ حَمْلًا مَحْفُوظًا بِنُصْرَتِكَ، وَاقْذِفْ بِي عَلَى الْبَاطِلِ فَأَدْمَغَهُ، وَزُجَّ بِي فِي بِحَارِ الْأَحَدِيَّةِ، وَانْشُلْنِي مِنْ أَوْحَالِ(٧١) التَّوْحِيدِ، وَأَغْرِقْنِي فِي عَيْنِ بَحْرِ الْوَحْدَةِ(٧٢)، حَتَّى لَا أَرَى وَلَا أَسْمَعَ، وَلَا أَجِدَ وَلَا أُحِسَّ إِلَّا بِهَا، وَاجْعَلِ الْحِجَابَ(٧٣) الْأَعْظَمَ حَيَاةَ رُوحِي، وَرُوحَهُ سِرَّ حَقِيقَتِي، وَحَقِيقَتَهُ جَامِعَ عَوَالِمِي، بِتَحْقِيقِ الْحَقِّ الْأَوَّلِ، يَا أَوَّلُ، يَا آخِرُ، يَا ظَاهِرُ يَا بَاطِنُ - اِسْمَعْ نِدَائِي بِمَا سَمِعْتَ بِهِ نِدَاءَ عَبْدِكَ زَكَرِيَّا، وَانْصُرْنِي بِكَ لَكَ، وَأَيِّدْنِي بِكَ لَكَ، وَاجْمَعْ بَيْنِي وَبَيْنَكَ، وَحُلْ بَيْنِي وَبَيْنَ غَيْرِكَ، اَللّٰهُ، اَللّٰهُ، اَللّٰهُ، ﴿إِنَّ ٱلَّذِى فَرَضَ عَلَيْكَ ٱلْقُرْءَانَ لَرَآدُّكَ إِلَىٰ مَعَادٍ﴾، ﴿رَبَّنَآ ءَاتِنَا مِن لَّدُنكَ رَحْمَةً وَهَيِّئْ لَنَا مِنْ أَمْرِنَا رَشَدًا﴾(٧٤).

(٧١) يَعْنِي: الشِّرْكَ الْأَصْغَرَ بِأَنْوَاعِهِ.

(٧٢) أَيْ: اَلتَّوْحِيد الْخَالِص.

(٧٣) رَمْزٌ إِلَى بَابِ اللهِ الْأَعْظَمِ، الَّذِي هُوَ الْوَاسِطَةُ الْكُبْرَى، وَالْوَسِيلَةُ الْعُظْمَى سَيِّدُنَا مُحَمَّدٌ رَسُولُ اللهِ صَلَّى اللهُ عَلَيْهِ وَآلِهِ وَسَلَّمَ.

(٧٤) هَذِهِ الصَّلَاةُ لِلْإِمَامِ الشَّيْخِ السَّيِّدِ عَبْدِ السَّلَامِ بْنِ مَشِيشٍ رَضِيَ اللهُ تَعَالَى عَنْهُ وَنَفَعَنَا بِهِ، وَيُحْسِنُ قِرَاءَتَهَا

sense, nor feel except through it. Make the Sublime Veil[112] the life of my soul, and his soul the secret to my truth, and his truth the amalgamation of my worlds, by realizing the first truth. You are First, Last, Manifest, and Hidden – Hear my call as You have heard that of Zakariyyā. Support me through You to You, and give me help by You towards You. Gather between me and You, and separate between me and all other than You. Allah, Allah, Allah, "Most certainly, the One Who has ordained the Qur'an for you will bring you back home"[113], "Our Lord! Grant us mercy from Yourself and guide us rightly through our ordeal."[114]

Inna Allāha wa malā'ikatahū yuṣallūna ʿala al-nabiyy; yā ayyuha alladhīna āmanū ṣallū ʿalayhi wa sallimū taslīmā.

"Indeed, Allah showers His blessings upon the Prophet, and His angels pray for him. O believers! Invoke Allah's blessings upon him, and salute him with worthy greetings of peace."[115]

Allāhumma bika tawassaltu, wa ilayka tawajjaht, wa fīka lā fī aḥadin siwāk raghibt, lā as'alu siwāk, wa lā aṭlubu minka illā iyyāk.

Allah, I seek closeness to You to You, and I face myself towards You, I desire naught but You and none other than You. I ask none either but You, and request from You naught but You.

Allāhumma wa atawassalu ilayka fī qabūli dhālika bil-wasīlati al-ʿuẓmā, wa al-faḍīlati al-kubrā wa al-ḥabībi al-adnā wa al-waliyyi al-mawlā, Muḥammadin al-muṣṭafā, wa al-ṣafiyyi al-murtaḍā, wa al-nabiyyi al-mujtabā ṣallā Allāhu ʿalayhi wa sallam, wa bihī as'aluka an tuṣalliya ʿalayhi ṣalātan abadiyyatan daymūmiyyatan qayyūmiyyatan ilāhiyyatan rabbāniyyah, bi-ḥaythu tushhidunī fī dhālika ʿayna kamālih, wa tastahlikunī fī ʿayni maʿārifi dhātih, wa ʿalā ālihī wa

---

112 This is referring to Allah's greatest door, the mightiest and greatest means to Him, our Master Muhammad, the Messenger of Allah ﷺ.

113 *al-Qaṣaṣ*, 85.

114 *al-Kahf*, 10.

115 *al-Aḥzāb*, 56.

﴿إِنَّ ٱللَّهَ وَمَلَٰٓئِكَتَهُۥ يُصَلُّونَ عَلَى ٱلنَّبِيِّۚ يَٰٓأَيُّهَا ٱلَّذِينَ ءَامَنُواْ صَلُّواْ عَلَيۡهِ وَسَلِّمُواْ تَسۡلِيمًا﴾.

اَللّٰهُمَّ بِكَ تَوَسَّلْتُ، وَإِلَيْكَ تَوَجَّهْتُ، وَفِيكَ لَا فِي أَحَدٍ سِوَاكَ رَغِبْتُ، لَا أَسْأَلُ سِوَاكَ، وَلَا أَطْلُبُ مِنْكَ إِلَّا إِيَّاكَ.

اَللّٰهُمَّ وَأَتَوَسَّلُ إِلَيْكَ فِي قَبُولِ ذَلِكَ بِالْوَسِيلَةِ الْعُظْمَى، وَالْفَضِيلَةِ الْكُبْرَى وَالْحَبِيبِ الْأَدْنَى - أَيِ: الْأَقْرَبِ - وَالْوَلِيِّ الْمَوْلَى، مُحَمَّدٍ الْمُصْطَفَى، وَالصَّفِيِّ الْمُرْتَضَى، وَالنَّبِيِّ الْمُجْتَبَى ﷺ، وَبِهِ أَسْأَلُكَ أَن تُصَلِّيَ عَلَيْهِ صَلَاةً أَبَدِيَّةً دَيْمُومِيَّةً، قَيُّومِيَّةً، إِلٰهِيَّةً، رَبَّانِيَّةً، بِحَيْثُ تُشْهِدُنِي فِي ذَلِكَ عَيْنَ كَمَالِهِ، وَتَسْتَهْلِكُنِي فِي عَيْنِ مَعَارِفِ ذَاتِهِ، وَعَلَى آلِهِ وَصَحْبِهِ كَذَلِكَ، فَأَنْتَ وَلِيُّ ذَلِكَ، وَلَا حَوْلَ وَلَا قُوَّةَ إِلَّا بِاللّٰهِ الْعَلِيِّ الْعَظِيمِ، وَالْحَمْدُ لِلّٰهِ رَبِّ الْعَالَمِينَ(٧٥).

بَعْدَ الصَّلَوَاتِ الْجَهْرِيَّةِ - ثَلَاثًا ثَلَاثًا.

(٧٥) هَذِهِ الصَّلَاةُ لِلْإِمَامِ الْأَزْهَرِ وَالشَّيْخِ الْأَكْبَرِ السَّيِّدِ مُحِيِّ الدِّينِ بْنِ عَرَبِيٍّ رَضِيَ اللّٰهُ تَعَالَىٰ عَنْهُ وَنَفَعَنَا بِهِ.

ṣaḥbihī kadhālik, fa-anta waliyyu dhālik, wa lā ḥawla wa lā quwwata illā billāhi al-ʿAliyyi al-ʿAẓīm, wa al-ḥamdu lillāhi Rabbi al-ʿālamīn.

Allah, I seek closeness to You in accepting this through the great means and the great virtue, the most beloved ally and Master Muhammad, the Chosen One. He is the purified, accepted one, and the preferred prophet ﷺ. I ask You by him that You confer exaltations upon him – eternal, continual, sustaining, godly, divine exaltations; such that You allow me to witness through this his exact perfection, and exert me in knowing the precise sciences of his essence. Likewise confer them upon his family and Companions, for You are the Safekeeper to do so. There is no might nor strength save through Allah the Most High, the Sublime, and praise belongs to Allah, the Lord of all worlds.

Allāhumma yā dā'ima al-faḍli ʿalā al-bariyyah, yā Bāsiṭa al-yadayni bil-ʿaṭiyyah, yā Ṣāḥiba al-mawāhibi al-saniyyah: ṣalli wa sallim ʿalā sayyidinā Muḥammadin khayri al-warā sajiyyah, wa ʿalā ālihī wa aṣḥābihī al-bararati al-naqiyyah, wa ighfir lanā yā Rabbanā fī hādhihī al-ʿashiyyah.

Allah, Consistent in Your favour upon creation, Extending Your Hands in giving, Owner of exquisite gifts, confer Your exaltations and greetings upon our Master Muhammad, the best of creation in his demeanour. Likewise upon his righteous and pure family and Companions. Forgive us, Allah, on this evening.

Allāhumma innī as'aluka bika an tuṣalliya ʿalā sayyidinā Muḥammad, wa ʿalā sā'iri al-anbiyā'i wa al-mursalīn, wa ʿalā ālihim wa ṣaḥbihim ajmaʿīn, wa an taghfira lī mā maḍā, wa taḥfaẓanī fīmā baqā, yā Khayra al-ghāfirīn, wa yā Arḥama al-rāḥimīn – Āmīn.

Allah, I ask You by You that You confer exaltations upon our Master Muhammad, and upon all Prophets and Messengers, their families and Companions, and that You forgive me for what has passed, protect me in what is to come, Best of those who forgive, Most Merciful of those who show mercy. Āmīn.

اَللّٰهُمَّ يَا دَائِمَ الْفَضْلِ عَلَى الْبَرِيَّةِ، يَا بَاسِطَ الْيَدَيْنِ بِالْعَطِيَّةِ، يَا صَاحِبَ الْمَوَاهِبِ السَّنِيَّةِ: صَلِّ وَسَلِّمْ عَلَى سَيِّدِنَا مُحَمَّدٍ خَيْرِ الْوَرَىٰ سَجِيَّةً، وَعَلَى آلِهِ وَأَصْحَابِهِ الْبَرَرَةِ النَّقِيَّةِ، وَاغْفِرْ لَنَا يَا رَبَّنَا فِي هَذِهِ الْعَشِيَّةِ(٧٦).

اَللّٰهُمَّ إِنِّي أَسْأَلُكَ بِكَ أَن تُصَلِّيَ عَلَى سَيِّدِنَا مُحَمَّدٍ، وَعَلَى سَائِرِ الْأَنْبِيَاءِ وَالْمُرْسَلِينَ، وَعَلَى آلِهِمْ وَصَحْبِهِمْ أَجْمَعِينَ، وَأَنْ تَغْفِرَ لِي مَا مَضَى، وَتَحْفَظَنِي فِيمَا بَقِيَ، يَا خَيْرَ الْغَافِرِينَ، وَيَا أَرْحَمَ الرَّاحِمِينَ - آمِين.

---

(٧٦) هَذِهِ الصَّلَاةُ مَنْسُوبَةٌ لِابْنِ عَبَّاسٍ رَضِيَ اللهُ تَعَالَىٰ عَنْهُمَا وَنَفَعَنَا بِهِمَا.

In the Name of Allah, the Lord of Mercy, the Giver of Mercy

❝ Allah, exalt the Chosen One of Muḍar,
The Prophets, and all the Messengers upon their mention.

Pray, my Lord, upon the Guide and his kin
And Companions – they tired for the expansion of religion;

They fought with him for Allah, exerted themselves,
Migrated, sheltered him, and they surely supported him.

They clarified the obligatory and the recommended,
Holding fast by Allah, uniting for Him, so were victorious.

The most pure, prolific, and prestigious of prayers
The fragrant spread of which perfumes the entire world.

Followed by the sweet scent of musk, distilled;
From its aroma does the attar of divine pleasure exude.

As many as the pebbles, earth, and then the sands,
The stars in the sky, plants in the Earth, and its loam.

As many as the trees may hold of their leaves,
And every letter that is found recited or inscribed.

As heavy as the weights of the mounts, and then
Followed by the droplets of all water as well as rain.

Also the birds, beasts, fish, along with livestock,
Followed by the jinnkind, the angels, and all of mankind.

Then seeds, bees, a collection of all types of grain,
Then hair, wool, as well as feathers, and even fur.

Then all that expansive knowledge engulfs, and all
That the trusted Pen writes forth, and all of decree.

بِسْمِ اللهِ الرَّحْمٰنِ الرَّحِيمِ

يَا رَبِّ صَلِّ عَلَى الْمُخْتَارِ مِنْ مُضَرٍ   وَالْأَنْبِيَا وَجَمِيعِ الرُّسْلِ مَا ذُكِرُو
وَصَلِّ رَبِّي عَلَى الْهَادِي وَشِيْعَتِهِ   وَصَحْبِهِ مَنْ لِطَيِّ الدِّينِ قَدْ نَشَرُو
وَجَاهَدُوا مَعَهُ فِي اللهِ وَاجْتَهَدُو   وَهَاجَرُوا وَلَهُ آوَوْا وَقَدْ نَصَرُو
وَبَيَّنُوا الْفَرْضَ وَالْمَسْنُونَ وَاعْتَصَمُو   بِاللهِ وَاعْتَصَبُوا لِلهِ فَانْتَصَرُو
أَزْكَى صَلَاةٍ وَأَنْمَاهَا وَأَشْرَفَهَا   يُعَطِّرُ الْكَوْنَ رَيًّا نَشْرِهَا الْعَطِرُ
مَعْبُوقَةً بِعَبِيقِ الْمِسْكِ زَكِيَّةً   مِنْ طِيبِهَا أَرَجُ الرِّضْوَانِ يَنْتَشِرُ
عَدَّ الْحَصَى وَالثَّرَى والرَّمْلِ يَتْبَعُهَا   نَجْمُ السَّمَاءِ وَنَبَاتُ الْأَرْضِ وَالْمَدَرُ
وَعَدَّ مَا حَوَتِ الْأَشْجَارُ مِنْ وَرَقٍ   وَكُلِّ حَرْفٍ غَدَا يُتْلَى وَيُسْتَطَرُ
وَعَدَّ وَزْنَ مَثَاقِيلِ الْجِبَالِ كَذَا   يَتْلُوهُ قَطْرُ جَمِيعِ الْمَاءِ وَالْمَطَرُ
وَالطَّيْرُ وَالْوَحْشُ وَالْأَسْمَاكُ مَعَ نَعَمٍ   يَتْلُونَهَا الْجِنُّ وَالْأَمْلَاكُ وَالْبَشَرُ
وَالذَّرُّ وَالنَّحْلُ مَعَ جَمْعِ الْحُبُوبِ كَذَا   وَالشَّعْرُ والصُّوفُ وَالْأَرْيَاشُ وَالْوَبَرُ
وَمَا أَحَاطَ بِهِ الْعِلْمُ الْمُحِيطُ وَمَا   جَرَىٰ بِهِ الْقَلَمُ الْمَأْمُونُ وَالْقَدَرُ

Then equal to his esteemed status which honours
All the other Prophets and angels – they boast of it.

Then as much as what is in all the worlds, my Liege,
And whatever be in existence until forms are resurrected.

With every blink of an eye they blink thereby –
The inhabitants of the heavens and earths – with every gaze.

As much as what fills the heavens, earths, and mountains,
Along with the Throne, the Floor, the Stool, and their worth.

So long as Allah brings into perishment the existent and
Brings forth into existence – a continuous prayer, unbound.

It outlasts its measurement throughout time as well as
Exceeds its bound – it lets not a thing be nor does it leave.

For in it there is no limit nor end, Sublime One,
Nor does its time run out, such that it concludes.

Add to this: peaceful greetings as much as before,
Then multiply them, Lord, their virtue is ever spreading.

As You love and as pleases You, Master, and as
You have commanded us to pray – You are Most Powerful.

All this multiplied by Your right which manifests
In every breath of a creature, be they few or many.

Many times over the number of atoms that exist,
And every which Verses and Chapters have come to reveal.

Many times over what has gone by of numbers,
And a few times over more, Owner of absolute ability.

Lord, forgive him he who recites or listens to it,
And all of the Muslims wherever they may reside.

وَعَدَّ مِقْدَارَهُ السَّامِي الَّذِي شَرُفَتْ　　　بِهِ النَّبِيُّونَ وَالْأَمْلَاكُ وافْتَخَرُو

وَعَدَّ مَا كَانَ فِي الْأَكْوَانِ يَا سَنَدِي　　　وَمَا يَكُونُ إِلَى أَنْ تُبْعَثَ الصُّوَرُ

فِي كُلِّ طَرْفَةِ عَيْنٍ يَطْرِفُونَ بِهَا　　　أَهْلُ السَّمٰوَاتِ وَالْأَرْضِينَ أَوْ يَذَرُو

مِلْءَ السَّمٰوَاتِ وَالْأَرْضِينَ مَعَ جَبَلٍ　　　وَالْعَرْشِ وَالْفَرْشِ وَالْكُرْسِيِّ وَمَا حَصَرُو

مَا أَعْدَمَ اللهُ مَوْجُوداً وَأَوْجَدَ مَعـ　　　ـدُوماً صَلَاةً دَوَاماً لَيْسَ تَنْحَصِرُ

تَسْتَغْرِقُ الْعَدَّ مَعَ جَمْعِ الدُّهُورِ كَمَا　　　تُحِيطُ بِالْحَدِّ لَا تُبْقِي وَلَا تَذَرُ

لَا غَايَةً وَانْتِهَاءَ يَا عَظِيمُ لَهَا　　　وَلَا لَهَا أَمَدٌ يُقْضَى فَيُعْتَبَرُ

مَعَ السَّلَامِ كَمَا قَدْ مَرَّ مِنْ عَدَدٍ　　　رَبِّ وَضَاعِفْهُمَا وَالْفَضْلُ مُنْتَشِرُ

كَمَا تُحِبُّ وَتَرْضَى سَيِّدِي وَكَمَا　　　أَمَرْتَنَا أَنْ نُصَلِّيَ أَنْتَ مُقْتَدِرُ

وَكُلُّ ذَلِكَ مَضْرُوبٌ بِحَقِّكَ فِي　　　أَنْفَاسِ خَلْقِكَ إِنْ قَلُّوا وَإِنْ كَثُرُو

وَعَدَّ أَضْعَافِ ذَرَّاتِ الْوُجُودِ وَمَا　　　جَاءَتْ بِتِبْيَانِهِ الْآيَاتُ وَالسُّوَرُ

وَعَدَّ أَضْعَافِ مَا قَدْ مَرَّ مِنْ عَدَدٍ　　　مَعَ ضَعْفِ أَضْعَافِهِ يَا مَنْ لَهُ الْقَدَرُ

يَا رَبِّ وَاغْفِرْ لِقَارِيهَا وَسَامِعِهَا　　　وَالْمُسْلِمِينَ جَمِيعاً أَيْنَمَا حَضَرُو

Also our parents, our families, and our neighbours,
All of us, my Lord, are most needy of pardon.

We commit sins that cannot be enumerated,
But Your pardon does not leave a thing behind.

We beg You, O Lord, to show us mercy in both abodes,
By the worth of him in whose hand the pebbles glorified You.

Be graciously kind to us, O Lord, in every calamity,
Such kindness that engulfs us, they undo all troubles.

Our Lord, magnify for us great reward and forgiveness,
Your munificence is surely an ocean without a shore.

Give a noble ending. We are Your bondsmen, we
Wish for only You – all good and harm come back to You.

Pleasure be upon Abū Bakr, his vicegerent,
The one who stood forth giving victory to the religion.

And upon Abū Ḥafṣ, the Differentiator, his friend,
Whose word was firm, exact in his judgement, ʿUmar.

Be kind to ʿUthmān, of Two Lights, the one for whom
The good of both abodes was perfected and prosperity.

Likewise ʿAlī, his two sons, and their mother,
Those of the Cloak, as has reached us through the report.

Saʿd, Saʿīd, Ibn ʿAwf, Ṭalḥah, and Abū Ubaydah,
As well as Zubayr – they are all magnanimous masters.

Ḥamzah also, and al-ʿAbbās is our master,
and his erudite son, through whom tribulations go.

The Family, Companions, and Followers exceedingly,
At the entering of every night and the appearing dawn. ”

وَوَالِدِيْنَا وَأَهْلِيْنَا وَجِيْرَتِنَا وَكُلُّنَا سَيِّدِي لِلْعَفْوِ مُفْتَقِرُ

وَقَدْ جَنَيْنَا ذُنُوباً لَا عَدَادَ لَهَا لٰكِنَّ عَفْوَكَ لَا يُبْقِي وَلَا يَذَرُ

نَرْجُوكَ يَا رَبِّ فِي الدَّارَيْنِ تَرْحَمُنَا بِجَاهِ مَنْ فِي يَدَيْهِ سَبَّحَ الْحَجَرُ

وَالْطُفْ بِنَا رَبَّنَا فِي كُلِّ نَازِلَةٍ لُطْفًا عَمِيمًا بِهِ الْأَهْوَالُ تَنْحَسِرُ

يَا رَبِّ وَأَعْظِمْ لَنَا أَجْراً وَمَغْفِرَةً لِأَنَّ جُوْدَكَ بَحْرٌ لَيْسَ يَنْحَصِرُ

وَاخْتِمْ بِخَيرٍ لَنَا إِنَّا عَبِيْدُكَ لَا نَرْجُوْ سِوَاكَ فَمِنْكَ النَّفْعُ وَالضَّرَرُ

ثُمَّ الرِّضَا عَنْ أَبِي بَكْرٍ خَلِيْفَتِهِ مَنْ قَامَ مِنْ بَعْدِهِ لِلدِّيْنِ يَنْتَصِرُ

وَعَنْ أَبِي حَفْصٍ الْفَارُوقِ صَاحِبِهِ مَنْ قَوْلُهُ الْفَصْلُ فِي أَحْكَامِهِ عُمَرُ

وَجُدْ لِعُثْمَانَ ذِي النُّورَيْنِ مَنْ كَمُلَتْ لَهُ الْمَحَاسِنُ فِي الدَّارَيْنِ وَالظَّفَرُ

كَذَا عَلِيٌّ مَعَ ابْنَيْهِ وَأُمِّهِمَا أَهْلُ الْعَبَاءِ كَمَا قَدْ جَاءَنَا الْخَبَرُ

سَعْدٌ سَعِيْدٌ ابْنُ عَوْفٍ طَلْحَةٌ وَأَبُوْ عُبَيْدَةٍ وَزُبَيْرٌ سَادَةٌ غُرَرُ

وَحَمْزَةُ وَكَذَا الْعَبَّاسُ سَيِّدُنَا وَنَجْلُهُ الْحَبْرُ مَنْ زَالَتْ بِهِ الْغِيَرُ

وَالْآلُ وَالصَّحْبُ وَالْأَتْبَاعُ قَاطِبَةً مَا جَنَّ لَيْلُ الدَّيَاجِي أَوْ بَدَا السَّحَرُ

In the Name of Allah, the Lord of Mercy, the Giver of Mercy

Wa lillāhi al-Asmā'i al-Ḥusnā fa-idʿūhu bihā.

"Allah has the Most Beautiful Names. So call upon Him by them."[116]

Allāhumma innī as'aluka yā...

Allah, I ask You that You are:

Allah *(Allāh)*, the Lord of Mercy *(al-Raḥmān)*, the Giver of Mercy *(al-Raḥīm)*, the King *(al-Malik)*, the Most Holy *(al-Quddūs)*, the All-Perfect *(al-Salām)*, the Source of Serenity *(al-Mu'min)*, the Guardian *(al-Muhaymin)*, the Honourable *(al-ʿAzīz)*, the Compeller *(al-Jabbār)*, the Supreme *(al-Mutakabbir)*, the Creator *(al-Khāliq)*, the Inventor *(al-Bāri')*, the Shaper *(al-Muṣawwir)*, the Oft-Forgiving *(al-Ghaffār)*, the All-Dominant *(al-Qahhār)*, the Ever Giving *(al-Wahhāb)*, the Provider *(al-Razzāq)*, the Opener *(al-Fattāḥ)*, the All Knowing *(al-ʿAlīm)*, the Grasper *(al-Qābiḍ)*, the Expander *(al-Bāsiṭ)*, the Debasing *(al-Khāfiḍ)*, the Elevating *(al-Rāfiʿ)*, the Ennobling *(al-Muʿizz)*, the Humbling *(al-Mudhill)*, the All-Hearing *(al-Samīʿ)*, the All-Seeing *(al-Baṣīr)*, the Judge *(al-Ḥakam)*, the Just *(al-ʿAdl)*, the Most Kind *(al-Laṭīf)*, the All-Aware *(al-Khabīr)*, the Forbearing *(al-Ḥalīm)*, the Sublime *(al-ʿAẓīm)*, the Most Forgiving *(al-Ghafūr)*, the Most Thankful *(al-Shakūr)*, the Most High *(al-ʿAliyy)*, the Most Great *(al-Kabīr)*, the Protector *(al-Ḥafīẓ)*, the Overseer *(al-Muqīt)*, the Reckoner *(al-Ḥasīb)*, the Majestic *(al-Jalīl)*, the Noble *(al-Karīm)*, the Watchful *(al-Raqīb)*, the Responding *(al-Mujīb)*, the Expansive *(al-Wāsiʿ)*, the All-Wise *(al-Ḥakīm)*, the Most Loving *(al-Wadūd)*, the Glorious *(al-Majīd)*, the Resurrecter *(al-Bāʿith)*, the Witness *(al-Shahīd)*, the True *(al-Ḥaqq)*, the Trustee *(al-Wakīl)*, the Mighty *(al-Qawiyy)*, the Firm *(al-Matīn)*, the Ally *(al-Waliyy)*, the Praiseworthy *(al-Ḥamīd)*, the

---

116 *al-A'rāf*, 180.

بِسْمِ اللهِ الرَّحْمٰنِ الرَّحِيمِ

﴿وَلِلَّهِ ٱلْأَسْمَآءُ ٱلْحُسْنَىٰ فَٱدْعُوهُ بِهَا﴾

اَللّٰهُمَّ إِنِّيْ أَسْأَلُكَ يَا اَللّٰهُ، يَا رَحْمٰنُ، يَا رَحِيمُ، يَا مَلِكُ، يَا قُدُّوسُ، يَا سَلَامُ، يَا مُؤْمِنُ، يَا مُهَيْمِنُ، يَا عَزِيزُ، يَا جَبَّارُ، يَا مُتَكَبِّرُ، يَا خَالِقُ، يَا بَارِىءُ، يَا مُصَوِّرُ، يَا غَفَّارُ، يَا قَهَّارُ، يَا وَهَّابُ، يَا رَزَّاقُ، يَا فَتَّاحُ، يَا عَلِيمُ، يَا قَابِضُ، يَا بَاسِطُ، يَا خَافِضُ، يَا رَافِعُ، يَا مُعِزُّ، يَا مُذِلُّ، يَا سَمِيعُ، يَا بَصِيرُ، يَا حَكَمُ، يَا عَدْلُ، يَا لَطِيفُ، يَا خَبِيرُ، يَا حَلِيمُ، يَا عَظِيمُ، يَا غَفُورُ، يَا شَكُورُ، يَا عَلِيُّ، يَا كَبِيرُ، يَا حَفِيظُ، يَا مُقِيتُ، يَا حَسِيبُ، يَا جَلِيلُ، يَا كَرِيمُ، يَا رَقِيبُ، يَا مُجِيبُ، يَا وَاسِعُ، يَا حَكِيمُ، يَا وَدُودُ، يَا مَجِيدُ، يَا بَاعِثُ، يَا شَهِيدُ، يَا حَقُّ، يَا وَكِيلُ، يَا قَوِيُّ، يَا مَتِينُ، يَا وَلِيُّ، يَا حَمِيدُ،

Enumerating *(al-Muḥṣī)*, the Initiator *(al-Mubdi')*, the Repeater *(al-Muᶜīd)*, the Giver of Life *(al-Muḥyī)*, the Giver of Death *(al-Mumīt)*, the Ever Living *(al-Ḥayy)*, the Sustainer *(al-Qayyūm)*, the Existent *(al-Wājid)*, the Extolled *(al-Mājid)*, the One *(al-Wāḥid)*, the Absolute *(al-Ṣamad)*, the Most Able *(al-Qādir)*, the Most Powerful *(al-Muqtadir)*, the Advancer *(al-Muqaddim)*, the Postponer *(al-Mu'akhkhir)*, the First *(al-Awwal)*, the Last *(al-Ākhir)*, the Manifest *(al-Ẓāhir)*, the Hidden *(al-Bāṭin)*, the Liege *(al-Wālī)*, the Exalted *(al-Mutaᶜālī)*, the Benign *(al-Barr)*, the Ever Relenting *(al-Tawwāb)*, the Avenger *(al-Muntaqim)*, the Pardoning *(al-ᶜAfuww)*, the Compassionate *(al-Ra'ūf)*, the Owner of dominion *(Mālik al-mulk)*, the Possessor of majesty and generosity *(Dhū al-jalāli wa al-ikrām)*, the Equitable *(al-Muqsiṭ)*, the Uniting *(al-Jāmiᶜ)*, the Self-Sufficient *(al-Ghaniyy)*, the Sufficer *(al-Mughnī)*, the Preventer *(al-Māniᶜ)*, the Giver of Harm *(al-Ḍārr)*, the Giver of Benefit *(al-Nāfiᶜ)*, the Light *(al-Nūr)*, the Guide *(al-Hādī)*, the Innovator *(al-Badīᶜ)*, the Eternal *(al-Bāqī)*, the Inheritor *(al-Wārith)*, the Director *(al-Rashīd)*, the Enduring *(al-Ṣabūr)*, the Forgiver of sin *(Ghāfir al-dhanb)*, the Accepter of repentance *(Qābil al-tawb)*, the Severe in punishment *(Shadīd al-ᶜiqāb)*, the Source of all bounty *(Dhū al-ṭawl)*, the Source of all favours *(Dhū al-faḍl)*, the One of ascensions *(Dhū al-maᶜārij)*, the Owner of the Glorious Throne *(Dhū al-ᶜarshi al-ᶜaẓīm)*, the Tender *(al-Ḥannān)*, the Bountiful *(al-Mannān)*, the Noble *(al-Karīm)*, the Settler of Debts *(al-Dayyān)*, the Lord of the heavens and Earth *(Rabb al-samāwāti wa al-arḍ)*, the Innovator of the heavens and Earth *(Badīᶜ al-samāwāti wa al-arḍ)*, the Originator of the heavens and Earth *(Fāṭir al-samāwāti wa al-arḍ)*, the Light of the heavens and Earth *(Nūr al-samāwāti wa al-arḍ)*, the Holder of the heavens and Earth *(Qayyim al-samāwāti wa al-arḍ)*, the Maintainer of the heavens and Earth *(Qayyām al-samāwāti wa al-arḍ)*, the Sustainer of the heavens and Earth *(Qayyūm al-samāwāti wa al-arḍ)*, the Owner of the heavens and Earth *(Mālik al-samāwāti wa al-arḍ)*.

يَا مُحْصِي، يَا مُبْدِىءُ، يَا مُعِيدُ، يَا مُحْيِي، يَا مُمِيتُ، يَا حَيُّ، يَا قَيُّومُ، يَا وَاجِدُ، يَا مَاجِدُ، يَا وَاحِدُ، يَا صَمَدُ، يَا قَادِرُ، يَا مُقْتَدِرُ، يَا مُقَدِّمُ، يَا مُؤَخِّرُ، يَا أَوَّلُ، يَا آخِرُ، يَا ظَاهِرُ، يَا بَاطِنُ، يَا وَالِي، يَا مُتَعَالِي، يَا بَرُّ، يَا تَوَّابُ، يَا مُنْتَقِمُ، يَا عَفُوُّ، يَا رَؤُوفُ، يَا مَالِكَ الْمُلْكِ، يَا ذَا الْجَلَالِ وَالْإِكْرَامِ، يَا مُقْسِطُ، يَا جَامِعُ، يَا غَنِيُّ، يَا مُغْنِي، يَا مَانِعُ، يَا ضَارُّ، يَا نَافِعُ، يَا نُورُ، يَا هَادِي، يَا بَدِيعُ، يَا بَاقِي، يَا وَارِثُ، يَا رَشِيدُ، يَا صَبُورُ، يَا غَافِرَ الذَّنْبِ، يَا قَابِلَ التَّوبِ، يَا شَدِيدَ الْعِقَابِ، يَا ذَا الطَّوْلِ، يَا ذَا الفَضْلِ، يَا ذَا الْمَعَارِجِ، يَا ذَا الْعَرْشِ الْمَجِيدِ، يَا حَنَّانُ، يَا مَنَّانُ، يَا كَرِيمُ، يَا دَيَّانُ، يَا رَبَّ السَّمٰوَاتِ وَالْأَرْضِ، يَا بَدِيعَ السَّمٰوَاتِ وَالْأَرْضِ، يَا فَاطِرَ السَّمٰوَاتِ وَالْأَرْضِ، يَا نُورَ السَّمٰوَاتِ وَالْأَرْضِ، يَا قَيِّمَ السَّمٰوَاتِ وَالْأَرْضِ، يَا قَيَّامَ السَّمٰوَاتِ وَالْأَرْضِ، يَا قَيُّومَ السَّمٰوَاتِ وَالْأَرْضِ، يَا مَالِكَ السَّمٰوَاتِ وَالْأَرْضِ.

Allāhumma innī ʿabduk, ibnu ʿabdik, ibnu amatik, nāṣiyatī bi-yadik, māḍin fiyya ḥukmuk, ʿadlun fiyya qaḍā'uk, as'aluka bi-kulli ismin huwa lak: sammayta bihī nafsak, aw anzaltahu fī kitābik, aw ʿallamtahu aḥadan min khalqik, aw ista'tharta bihī fī ʿilmi al-ghaybi indak, an tajʿala al-Qur'āna al-ʿaẓīma rabīʿa qalbī, wa nūra baṣarī, wa jalā'a ḥuznī wa dhahāba hammī; wa sallā Allāhu ʿalā sayyidinā Muḥammadin wa ʿalā ālihi wa sallam – fī kulli lamḥatin wa nafasinʿ adada mā wasiʿahū ʿilmu Allāhi taʿālā.

Allah, I ask you with every name that is Yours: that you have called Yourself, or revealed in Your Book, or taught one of Your slaves, or favoured for Yourself in the realm of the unseen, that You make the Glorious Qur'an the spring of my heart, the light of my sight, the leave of my sadness, and the removal of my worry. Allah, exalt and send greetings of peace to our Master Muhammad and his family, at every moment and with every breath, in an amount equal to the knowledge of Allah the Exalted.

اَللّٰهُمَّ وَأَسْأَلُكَ بِكُلِّ اسْمٍ هُوَ لَكَ، سَمَّيْتَ بِهِ نَفْسَكَ، أَوْ أَنْزَلْتَهُ فِي كِتَابِكَ، أَوْ عَلَّمْتَهُ أَحَدًا مِنْ خَلْقِكَ، أَوِ اسْتَأْثَرْتَ بِهِ فِي عِلْمِ الْغَيْبِ عِنْدَكَ؛ أَنْ تَجْعَلَ الْقُرْآنَ الْعَظِيمَ رَبِيعَ قَلْبِي، وَنُورَ بَصَرِي، وَجِلَاءَ حُزْنِي، وَذَهَابَ هَمِّي وَغَمِّي، وَصَلَّى اللّٰهُ عَلَى سَيِّدِنَا مُحَمَّدٍ وَعَلَى آلِهِ وَسَلَّمَ - فِي كُلِّ لَمْحَةٍ وَنَفَسٍ عَدَدَ مَا وَسِعَهُ عِلْمُ اللّٰهِ تَعَالَىٰ.

Be Diligent with the Following Daily Words of Remembrance

Astaghfirullāha al-ʿAẓīm - 100 times.

I seek Allah's forgiveness, the Sublime.

Lā ilāha illā Allāh - 100 times.

'There is no god but Allah.'

Allāhumma ṣalli ʿalā sayyidinā Muḥammadin ʿabdika wa rasūlika al-nabiyyi al-ummiyyi wa ʿalā ālihī wa ṣaḥbihī wa sallim - 100 times.

'Allah, confer exaltations upon our Master Muhammad, Your slave and Messenger, the Unlettered Prophet; and upon all of his family and Companions.'

Reciting one part (thirtieth) of the Noble Qur'an. If one increases, it is better.

Subḥān Allāh, al-ḥamdu lillāh, lā ilāha illā Allāh, Allāhu Akbar, wa lā ḥawla wa lā quwwata illā billāhi al-ʿAliyyi al-ʿAẓīm - from 100 to 400 times.

'Glorified is Allah in sanctity, praise is to Allah, there is no god but Allah, Allah is Greatest, and there is no might nor strength but through Allah the Most High, the Sublime.' These are the Lasting Good Deeds.

Surah al-Ikhlāṣ - 50 times, and the more the better.

Yā Ḥayyu yā Qayyūmu lā ilāha illā ant - 41 to 100 times after Fajr,

'Ever Living, Sustainer of all, there is nothing worthy of worship but You.' It gives life to the heart through faith.

Lā ilāha illā Allāhu waḥdahū lā sharīka lah, lahū al-mulku wa lahū al-ḥamd, yuḥyī wa yumīt, wa huwa Ḥayyun lā yamūt, bi-yadihī al-khayr, wa huwa ʿalā kulli shay'in Qadīr - 100 times after the ṣubḥ prayer.

اِتَّخِذْ لِنَفْسِكَ الْأَوْرَادَ التَّالِيَةَ كُلَّ يَوْمٍ

١ - أَسْتَغْفِرُ اللّٰهَ الْعَظِيمَ - ١٠٠ - مَرَّةٍ.

٢ - لَا إِلٰهَ إِلَّا اللّٰهُ - ١٠٠ - مَرَّةٍ.

٣ - اَللّٰهُمَّ صَلِّ عَلَى سَيِّدِنَا مُحَمَّدٍ عَبْدِكَ وَنَبِيِّكَ وَرَسُولِكَ النَّبِيِّ الْأُمِّيِّ وَعَلَى آلِهِ وصَحْبِهِ وَسَلِّمْ - ١٠٠ - مَرَّةٍ.

وَيَحْسُنُ أَنْ تَزِيدَ إِلَى (٥٠٠) مَرَّةٍ فَقَدْ قَالَ بَعْضُ الْعَارِفِينَ: مَنْ وَاظَبَ عَلَيْهَا (٥٠٠) مَرَّةٍ كُلَّ يَوْمٍ فَإِنَّهُ يَرَى النَّبِيَّ ﷺ.

وَإِذَا انْتَهَيْتَ إِلَى أَلْفِ مَرَّةٍ فَهُوَ خَيْرٌ وَأَوْلَى، لِمَا تَقَدَّمَ فِي الْحَدِيثِ (ص٤٦) أَنَّهُ يَرَى مَقْعَدَهُ فِي الْجَنَّةِ.

٤ - قِرَاءَةُ جُزْءٍ مِنَ الْقُرْآنِ الْكَرِيمِ وَإِذَا زِدْتَ فَهُوَ خَيْرٌ لَكَ.

٥ - سُبْحَانَ اللّٰهِ، وَالْحَمْدُ لِلّٰهِ، وَلَا إِلٰهَ إِلَّا اللّٰهُ، وَاللّٰهُ أَكْبَرُ، وَلَا حَوْلَ وَلَا قُوَّةَ إِلَّا بِاللّٰهِ الْعَلِيِّ الْعَظِيمِ - ١٠٠ - مَرَّةٍ إِلَى - ٤٠٠ - مَرَّةٍ، فَإِنَّهَا مِنَ الْبَاقِيَاتِ الصَّالِحَاتِ.

٦ - سُورَةُ الْإِخْلَاصِ - ٥٠ - مَرَّةٍ وَالزِّيَادَةُ خَيْرٌ.

٧ - يَا حَيُّ يَا قَيُّومُ لَا إِلٰهَ إِلَّا أَنْتَ - ٤١ إِلَى ١٠٠ - مَرَّةٍ بَعْدَ الْفَجْرِ فَإِنَّهَا لِحَيَاةِ الْقَلْبِ بِالْإِيمَانِ.

٨ - لَا إِلٰهَ إِلَّا اللّٰهُ وَحْدَهُ لَا شَرِيكَ لَهُ، لَهُ الْمُلْكُ، وَلَهُ الْحَمْدُ، يُحْيِي وَيُمِيتُ، وَهُوَ حَيٌّ لَا يَمُوتُ، بِيَدِهِ الْخَيْرُ وَهُوَ عَلَى كُلِّ شَيْءٍ قَدِيرٌ؛ بَعْدَ صَلَاةِ الصُّبْحِ - ١٠٠ - مَرَّةٍ.

'There is no god but Allah, only He, without associates. Praise and dominion are His. He gives life and death, and He is Ever Living and never dies. All goodness is in His Hand. He is Powerful over all things.'

Lā ilāha illā Allāhu al-Maliku al-Ḥaqqu al-Mubīn – 100 times.

'There is no god but Allah, the King, the true, the Clear.' Preferably, this should be said after the Ẓuhr prayer, for it is to facilitate one's affairs and relieve one's worries.

Additionally, be diligent with: *Yā Laṭīf* (O Most Kind) – 129 times a day.

Be diligent with the ḍuḥā prayer, reciting Surah Shams in the first unit and Surah Ḍuḥā in the second one. In the third, recite Surah Kāfirūn, and in the fourth Surah Ikhlāṣ. In the rest, recite whatever comes easily, or repeat the latter in the aforementioned order. On Thursdays, after the ḍuḥā prayer, say: Yā Samīʿ (O All-Hearing) – 500 times. It is a cause for Allah's answer and acceptance. Diligently adhere to the night tahajjud prayer. If you have memorized Surah Yā-Sīn and Surah Dukhān, then recite them therein. If you are someone who recites a lot in the night prayer, then make those two surahs among what you recite. If you only wish to recite Surah Yā-Sīn in the eight units, then split it up according to the following:

a. Recite from the beginning until: "...So give them good news of forgiveness and an honourable reward"[117] in the first unit.
b. Recite from: "It is certainly We Who resurrect the dead..."[118] until: "...and are [rightly] guided"[119] in the second.
c. Recite from: "And why should I not worship the One Who has originated me..."[120] until: "...Yet they will all be brought before Us"[121] in the third.

117 *Yā-Sīn*, 11.
118 *Yā-Sīn*, 12.
119 *Yā-Sīn*, 21.
120 *Yā-Sīn*, 22.
121 *Yā-Sīn*, 32.

٩ - لَا إِلٰهَ إِلَّا اللّٰهُ الْمَلِكُ الْحَقُّ الْمُبِينُ - ١٠٠ - مَرَّةٍ، وَالْأَحْسَنُ أَنْ تَجْعَلَهَا عَقِبَ صَلَاةِ الظُّهْرِ فَإِنَّهَا لِتَيْسِيرِ الْأُمُورِ، وَتَفْرِيجِ الْهُمُومِ.

وَوَاظِبْ عَلَى - ١٢٩ - مَرَّةٍ: يَا لَطِيفُ.

١٠ - وَوَاظِبْ عَلَى صَلَاةِ الضُّحَى، وَاقْرَأْ فِي الرَّكْعَةِ الْأُولَى: ﴿وَٱلشَّمْسِ وَضُحَىٰهَا﴾ ، وَفِي الثَّانِيَةِ سُورَةَ الضُّحَى، وَفِي الثَّالِثَةِ: ﴿قُلْ يَـٰٓأَيُّهَا ٱلْكَـٰفِرُونَ﴾ ، وَفِي الرَّابِعَةِ سُورَةَ الْإِخْلَاصِ. ثُمَّ فِي الْبَوَاقِي مَا تَيَسَّرَ لَكَ، أَوْ أَعِدْ ذَلِكَ بِنَفْسِ التَّرْتِيبِ.

وَفِي يَوْمِ الْخَمِيسِ بَعْدَ صَلَاةِ الضُّحَى تَذْكُرُ يَا سَمِيعُ - ٥٠٠ - مَرَّةٍ، فَإِنَّهَا لِلْإِجَابَةِ وَالْقَبُولِ.

١١ - وَاظِبْ عَلَى صَلَاةِ التَّهَجُّدِ فِي اللَّيْلِ، وَإِذَا كُنْتَ تَحْفَظُ سُورَةَ يسٓ وَالدُّخَانِ فَاقْرَأْهُمَا فِي صَلَاةِ اللَّيْلِ، وَإِذَا كُنْتَ مِمَّنْ يَقْرَأُ كَثِيرًا فِي صَلَاةِ اللَّيْلِ فَلَا مَانِعَ أَنْ تَجْعَلَهُمَا مِنْ جُمْلَةِ مَا تَقْرَأُ، وَإِذَا أَرَدْتَ أَنْ تَقْتَصِرَ عَلَى قِرَاءَةِ سُورَةِ يسٓ فِي الرَّكَعَاتِ الثَّمَانِيَةِ مِنْ صَلَاةِ التَّهَجُّدِ فَلْيَكُنْ عَلَى التَّرْتِيبِ الْآتِي:

١ - تَقْرَأُ فِي الرَّكْعَةِ الْأُولَى مِنْ أَوَّلِ السُّورَةِ إِلَى قَوْلِهِ تَعَالَىٰ: ﴿فَبَشِّرْهُ بِمَغْفِرَةٍ وَأَجْرٍ كَرِيمٍ﴾ .

٢ - وَفِي الثَّانِيَةِ مِنْ قَوْلِهِ تَعَالَىٰ: ﴿إِنَّا نَحْنُ نُحْيِ ٱلْمَوْتَىٰ﴾ ، إِلَى قَوْلِهِ تَعَالَىٰ: ﴿وَهُم مُّهْتَدُونَ﴾ .

٣ - وَفِي الثَّالِثَةِ مِنْ قَوْلِهِ تَعَالَىٰ: ﴿وَمَا لِىَ لَآ أَعْبُدُ ٱلَّذِى فَطَرَنِى﴾ ، إِلَى قَوْلِهِ

d. Recite from: "There is a sign for them in the dead earth..."[122] until: "...Each is travelling in an orbit of their own"[123] in the fourth.
e. Recite from: "Another sign for them is that We carried their ancestors..."[124] until: "...nor can they return to their own people"[125] in the fifth.
f. Recite from: "The Trumpet will be blown..."[126] until: "...This is the Straight Path"[127] in the sixth.
g. Recite from: "Yet he already misled great multitudes of you..."[128] until: "...which are under their control?"[129] in the seventh.
h. Recite from: "And We have subjected these [animals] to them..."[130] until the end in the eighth.

Once you have concluded the prayer, say: *Astaghfirullāh* (I seek Allah's forgiveness) – 70 times, and *Yā Ṣamad* (O Absolute One) – 125 times. This is beneficial to accomplish your goals and aspirations. Then say: *Allāhumma lā tamqutnī* (Allah, do not scorn me) – three times.

Say the following in the prostrations of the night prayer:

Subḥān Dhī al-mulki wa al-malakūt, Subḥān Dhī al-ʿizzati wa al-jabarūt, Subḥān al-Ḥayyi alladhī lā yamūt, Subbūhun Quddūsun Rabbunā wa Rabbu al-malā'ikati wa al-rūḥ; Allāhumma innī aʿūdhu bi-riḍāka min sakhaṭik, wa aʿūdhu bi-ʿafwika min ʿiqābik, wa aʿūdhu bi-muʿāfātika min ʿuqūbatik, wa aʿūdhu bi-raḥmatika min ʿadhābik, wa aʿūdhu bika mink, jalla wajhuka al-karīm, lā uḥṣī thanā'an ʿalayk, anta kamā athnayta ʿalā nafsik.

Glory be to the Owner of dominion and kingship. Glory be to the Owner of

---

122 *Yā-Sīn*, 33.
123 *Yā-Sīn*, 40.
124 *Yā-Sīn*, 41.
125 *Yā-Sīn*, 50.
126 *Yā-Sīn*, 51.
127 *Yā-Sīn*, 61.
128 *Yā-Sīn*, 62.
129 *Yā-Sīn*, 71.
130 *Yā-Sīn*, 72.

تَعَالَىٰ: ﴿جَمِيعٌ لَّدَيْنَا مُحْضَرُونَ﴾ .

٤ - وَفِي الرَّابِعَةِ مِنْ قَوْلِهِ تَعَالَىٰ: ﴿وَءَايَةٌ لَّهُمُ ٱلْأَرْضُ﴾ ، إِلَى قَوْلِهِ تَعَالَىٰ: ﴿وَكُلٌّ فِى فَلَكٍ يَسْبَحُونَ﴾ .

٥ - وَفِي الخَامِسَةِ مِنْ قَوْلِهِ تَعَالَىٰ: ﴿وَءَايَةٌ لَّهُمْ أَنَّا حَمَلْنَا ذُرِّيَّتَهُمْ﴾ ، إِلَى قَوْلِهِ تَعَالَىٰ: ﴿وَلَآ إِلَىٰٓ أَهْلِهِمْ يَرْجِعُونَ﴾ .

٦ - وَفِي السَّادِسَةِ مِنْ قَوْلِهِ تَعَالَىٰ: ﴿وَنُفِخَ فِى ٱلصُّورِ﴾ ، إِلَى قَوْلِهِ تَعَالَىٰ: ﴿هَٰذَا صِرَٰطٌ مُّسْتَقِيمٌ﴾.

٧ - وَفِي السَّابِعَةِ مِنْ قَوْلِهِ تَعَالَىٰ: ﴿وَلَقَدْ أَضَلَّ مِنكُمْ جِبِلًّا﴾ ، إِلَى قَوْلِهِ تَعَالَىٰ: ﴿فَهُمْ لَهَا مَٰلِكُونَ﴾ .

٨ - وَفِي الثَّامِنَةِ مِنْ قَوْلِهِ تَعَالَىٰ: ﴿وَذَلَّلْنَٰهَا لَهُمْ﴾ ، إِلَى آخِرِ السُّوْرَةِ.

ثُمَّ مِنْ بَعْدِ فَرَاغِكَ مِنَ الصَّلَاةِ اسْتَغْفِرِ اللهَ - ٧٠ - مَرَّةٍ، وَقُلْ: يَا صَمَدُ - ١٢٥ - مَرَّةٍ، فَإِنَّهُ مُفِيدٌ لِمُهِمَّاتِكَ وَمَقَاصِدِكَ، ثُمَّ قُلْ: اَللّٰهُمَّ لَا تَمْقُتْنِي - ثَلَاثًا -.

١٢ - قُلْ فِي سُجُودِ قِيَامِ اللَّيْلِ: سُبْحَانَ ذِي الْمُلْكِ وَالْمَلَكُوْتِ، سُبْحَانَ ذِي الْعِزَّةِ وَالْجَبَرُوْتِ، سُبْحَانَ الْحَيِّ الَّذِيْ لَا يَمُوْتُ، سُبُّوْحٌ قُدُّوْسٌ، رَبُّنَا وَرَبُّ الْمَلَائِكَةِ وَالرُّوحِ، اَللّٰهُمَّ إِنِّي أَعُوذُ بِرِضَاكَ مِنْ سَخَطِكَ، وَأَعُوذُ بِعَفْوِكَ مِنْ عِقَابِكَ، وَأَعُوذُ بِمُعَافَاتِكَ مِنْ عُقُوبَتِكَ، وَأَعُوذُ بِرَحْمَتِكَ مِنْ عَذَابِكَ، وَأَعُوذُ بِكَ مِنْكَ، جَلَّ وَجْهُكَ الْكَرِيمُ، لَا أُحْصِي ثَنَاءً عَلَيْكَ، أَنْتَ كَمَا أَثْنَيْتَ عَلَى نَفْسِكَ.

might and sovereignty. Glory be to the Ever Living Who never dies. He is the Sanctified, The Holy One, our Lord, and the Lord of angels and spirits. Allah, I seek refuge in Your pleasure from Your wrath, in Your pardon from Your punishment, in Your giving wellness from Your punishment, and in Your mercy from Your torment. I seek refuge in You from You. Majestic be Your Noble Face. I can never truly extol You – You are as You have extolled Yourself.

Disclaimer:
All the supplications and words of remembrance that are mentioned here are either sourced from prophetic narrations, traditions from the predecessors, or from the teachings of the imams of our nations, may Allah the Exalted be pleased with them all and infuse us with what He blessed them with.

Remain diligent, my brother, with these general words of remembrance. As for the special ones, then they must have their own special compendium. May Allah exalt our Master Muhammad every time he is remembered by the mindful, forgotten by the heedless, with every glance of an eye and breath taken, and as many times as equal to everything encompassed by Allah's Knowledge. Amen. Praise be to Allah, the Lord of the worlds.

تَنْبِيهٌ:

جَمِيعُ مَا ذَكَرْتُهُ مِنَ الْأَدْعِيَةِ وَالْأَوْرَادِ فَهُوَ إِمَّا مُسْتَنَدٌ إِلَى الْأَحَادِيثِ النَّبَوِيَّةِ، أَوِ الْآثَارِ السَّلَفِيَّةِ، أَوْ تَعْلِيمَاتِ أَئِمَّةِ الْقَوْمِ رَضِيَ اللهُ تَعَالَى عَنْهُمْ أَجْمَعِينَ وَنَفَعَنَا بِمَا نَفَعَهُمْ.

فَوَاظِبْ يَا أَخِي عَلَى هَذِهِ الْأَوْرَادِ الْعَامَّةِ، أَمَّا الْخَاصَّةُ فَهِيَ تَحْتَاجُ إِلَى رِسَالَةٍ خَاصَّةٍ.

وَصَلَّى اللهُ عَلَى سَيِّدِنَا مُحَمَّدٍ كُلَّمَا ذَكَرَهُ الذَّاكِرُونَ، وَغَفَلَ عَنْ ذِكْرِهِ الْغَافِلُونَ، فِيْ كُلِّ لَمْحَةٍ وَنَفَسٍ عَدَدَ مَا وَسِعَهُ عِلْمُ اللهِ تَعَالَىٰ - آمِين، وَالْحَمْدُ لِلهِ رَبِّ الْعَالَمِينَ.

Appeals of Salvation

اِسۡتِغَاثَاتُ

In the Name of Allah,
the Lord of Mercy, the Giver of Mercy

“ My God, the Answer of those who plead,
By the truthful Prophets, the guide, the trustworthy one,

Expand my chest and ease our affairs;
Give us aid, O Almighty, Most Powerful one of all.

My God, the Hope of those who beg Him,
By the exact, truthful, aphoristic Speech, clear to all;

By the Light of Your Face, the splendor which
Radiates the Throne, and spreads through the cosmos;

By Your majestic nature, O Ancient One,
And by the light that shines in the hearts of the believers;

By the invocations of the Beloved, most noble,
The Master of both realms, the pride of the boastful;

By the Chosen One's face – its graceful light –
By the brilliant radiance of that honourable brow;

Through his prostrating under the Throne of Allah,
It was said to him, “Intercede for all the slaves!”

By the humility and abjectness of the pious,
And the wailing and the weeping of the infatuated;

By the brokenness and neediness of Your Friends,
And the crying exhale of the devoted worshippers;

By the supplication and extolment of the loyal folk,
By those slaves of Yours who poured forth prostrating;

By the incandescent lamps of the purified ones' hearts,
And by the dawning of the prosperous ones' faces;

بِسْمِ اللّٰهِ الرَّحْمٰنِ الرَّحِيمِ

يَا إِلٰهِي يَا مُجِيبَ السَّائِلِينَ   بِالنَّبِيِّ الصَّادِقِ الْهَادِي الْأَمِين
اِشْرَحِ الصَّدْرَ وَيَسِّرْ أَمْرَنَا   وَأَعِنَّا يَا قَوِيُّ يَا مَتِينُ
يَا إِلٰهِي يَا رَجَاءَ الْمُرْتَجِينَ   بِالْكَلَامِ الْمُحْكَمِ الْحَقِّ الْمُبِين
بِضِيَاءِ وَجْهِكَ النُّورُ الَّذِي   نَوَّرَ الْعَرْشَ وَعَمَّ الْعَالَمِينَ
بِصِفَاتٍ لَكَ جَلَّتْ يَا قَدِيمُ   وَ بِأَنْوَارِ قُلُوبِ الْمُؤْمِنِينَ
بِابْتِهَالَاتِ الْحَبِيبِ الْأَكْرَم   سَيِّدِ الْكَونينِ فَخْرِ الْفَاخِرِينَ
بِبَهَاءِ نُورِ وَجْهِ الْمُصْطَفَى ﷺ   وَضِيَاءِ وَسَنَا ذَاكَ الْجَبِينَ
بِسُجُودٍ تَحْتَ عَرْشِ اللّٰهِ إِذْ   قِيلَ اشْفَعْ فِي الْعِبَادِ أَجْمَعِينَ
بِخُشُوعٍ وَخُضُوعِ الْأَتْقِيَا   وَنَحِيبٍ وَّ أَنِينِ الْعَاشِقِينَ
بِانْكِسَارٍ وَّ افْتِقَارِ الْأَوْلِيَا   وَ زَفِيرٍ وَ بُكَاءِ الْعَابِدِينَ
بِدُعَاءٍ وَّ ثَنَا أَهْلِ الْوَفَا   بِعِبَادٍ لَكَ خَرُّوا سَاجِدِينَ
بِمَصَابِيحِ قُلُوبِ الْأَصْفِيَا   وَبِإِشْرَاقِ وُجُوهِ الْمُفْلِحِينَ

By the prayers of the worshippers – those earning Your love,
By the piety of those who single You – and You single them – out;

By the manifesting closeness of the depths of the night,
And by slaves who stood in the night for You, devoted;

By the manifesting presence at the times of conversing,
And the overflowing openings of knowledge in certitude;

By Your gifts which You have made special,
And gave them to Your Prophets and Your Messengers;

Gift us with proximity and pure love from You,
And connection to You, with certitude of the certain.

As well as witnesses that manifest at all times,
Most beautifully, O Deliverer of those lost in terror.

We call upon You in humility and abject need,
So answer the call of the broken and the destitute.

If we be the most disobedient, sinful folk,
You are the Benign, the Best of those who forgive.

If instead our erring becomes far too great,
Still, the ocean of Your forgiveness floods all sinners.

You allowed the extravagant sinner to feel greedy:
You prohibited that we ever despair of Your mercy!

Tis You Who said, "My Mercy precedes My
Wrath!" This is inscribed in the Preserved Tablet.

Tis You Who said, "My Mercy engulfs
All things! Be not among those who are hopeless!"

Tis You Who said, "Ask of His Bounty!"
O Most Generous, You are Most Giving to he who asks.

بِدُعَاءِ الْعُبَّادِ أَصْحَابِ الْوِدَادِ   وَ بِتَقْوَى الْمُخْلِصِينَ الْمُخْلَصِينَ

بِتَجَلِّي الْقُرْبِ فِي وَقْتِ السَّحَرِ   بِعَبِيْدٍ لَكَ قَامُوا قَانِتِينَ

بِتَجَلِّي الْأُنْسِ أَوْقَاتِ الْوِصَالِ   وَ فُيُوْضِ الْفَتْحِ بِالْعِلْمِ الْيَقِينَ

بِعَطَايَاكَ الَّتِي خَصَّصْتَهَا   فَمَنَحْتَ الْأَنْبِيَاءَ وَالْمُرْسَلِينَ

هَبْ لَنَا قُرْبًا وَ حُبًّا صَادِقًا   وَ وِصَالًا وَ يَقِينَ الْمُوقِنِينَ

وَ شُهُودًا لِلتَّجَلِّي دَائِمًا   بِالْجَمَالِ يَا مُغِيثَ الْوَالِهِينَ

قَدْ دَعَوْنَاكَ بِذُلٍّ وَافْتِقَارٍ   فَاسْتَجِبْ لِلْمُنْكَسِرِ وَالْمُسْتَكِينَ

إِنْ نَكُنْ أَعْصَى الْعُصَاةِ الْمُذْنِبِينَ   أَنْتَ بَرٌّ أَنْتَ خَيْرُ الْغَافِرِينَ

أَوْ تَكُنْ زُلَّاتُنَا قَدْ عَظُمَتْ   بَحْرُ غُفْرَانِكَ طَمَّ الْمُذْنِبِينَ

أَنْتَ أَطْعَمْتَ الْعِبَادَ الْمُسْرِفِينَ   قَدْ نَهَيْتَ أَنْ نَكُونَ قَانِطِينَ

أَنْتَ قُلْتَ رَحْمَتِي قَدْ سَبَقَتْ   غَضَبِي ذَلِكَ فِي اللَّوْحِ الْمُبِين

أَنْتَ قُلْتَ رَحْمَتِي قَدْ وَسِعَتْ   كُلَّ شَيْءٍ لَا تَكُونُوا يَائِسِينَ

أَنْتَ قُلْتَ وَاسْأَلُوا مِنْ فَضْلِهِ   يَا كَرِيمُ أَنْتَ مُعْطِي السَّائِلِينَ

We ask You out of dire need and necessity,
So answer the call of the needy and that of the sinners.

We knock at the doors of Your pardon, Merciful One,
Leave us not disappointed, lost without response.

We have honest faith in You, and good expectations,
And we turn towards You, every one of us at once.

We extend our hands towards You, hoping for
Your favour – it is hoped for by any one who has hope.

My Lord, show mercy to our humiliation, so forgive us;
Save us, O Saviour of every abject beggar.

Enshroud us, Noble One, with concealment
That does not expose us – You are the Best of coverers.

Conclude our affairs well, Best Responder;
Resurrect us among Your righteous bondsmen.

May God's prayers of exaltations eternally
Along with His peace – persisting forever with time –

Be especially for you, Imam of the Prophets.
And also for the Household, the pride of the pure folk.

Likewise for your Companions, the moons of guidance,
And for your loved ones, then for those who follow them.

And upon us and upon all our forefathers,
And upon all our offspring, then our close ones.

And for those who pray with this poem of
Reciters, listeners, and every single Muslim. ”

قَدْ سَأَلْنَاكَ بِفَقْرٍ وَّاضْطِرَارٍ   فَاسْتَجِبْ لِلْفُقَرَاءِ وَالْمُذْنِبِينَ

وَطَرَقْنَا بَابَ عَفْوٍ يَا رَحِيمُ   لَا تَدَعْنَا خَائِبِينَ خَاسِرِينَ

وَظَنَنَّا فِيكَ مِصْدَاقَ الظُّنُوْنِ   وَالْتَجَأْنَا لَكَ طَرًّا أَجْمَعِينَ

وَبَسَطْنَا أَيْدِيًا نَرْجُو بِهَا   فَضْلَكَ الْمَرْجُوَّ لِكُلِّ الْمُرْتَجِيْنَ

رَبِّ فَارْحَمْ ذُلَّنَا وَاغْفِرْ لَنَا   وَأَجِرْنَا يَا مُجِيرَ الضَّارِعِينَ

وَاسْبِلِ السِّتْرَ عَلَيْنَا يَا كَرِيمُ   دُونَ هَتْكٍ أَنْتَ خَيْرُ السَّاتِرِينَ

وَاخْتِمْنَا بِالْخَيْرِ يَا نِعْمَ الْمُجِيبُ   وَاحْشُرْنَا فِي الْعِبَادِ الصَّالِحِينَ

وَصَلَاةُ اللهِ تَتْرَى دَائِمًا   مَعَ سَلَامٍ أَبَدٍ فِي الْآبِدِينَ

لَكَ تُهْدَى يَا إِمَامَ الْأَنْبِيَاءِ   وَلِأَهْلِ الْبَيْتِ فَخْرِ الطَّاهِرِينَ

وَلِأَصْحَابِكَ أَقْمَارِ الْهُدَى   وَلِأَحْبَابِكَ ثُمَّ التَّابِعِينَ

وَعَلَيْنَا وَعَلَى آبَائِنَا   وَعَلَى أَبْنَائِنَا وَالْأَقْرَبِينَ

وَلِمَنْ يَدْعُو بِهَذَا النَّظْمِ مِنْ   قَارِئٍ أَوْ سَامِعٍ وَالْمُسْلِمِينَ

❁ ❁ ❁

This compendium is authored by the humble slave of Allah, the one most needy of his Needless Lord, during the days of his sacrosanct proximity. Allah the Exalted ennobled him with it in the City of Light (*al-Madīnah al-Munawwarah*); its lights shine brightly by the light of the Chosen One ﷺ.

Allah alone I do plead, and by the worth of the Beloved to Him I do seek His proximity, that He does not forbid us from entering the Door of Peace for sending peace upon the Master of Creation ﷺ. May He favour us with being his neighbours in the most perfect state.

May Allah confer His exaltations and greetings upon our Master Muhammad, his family, and his Companions with every glance and every breath, as many times as is equal to what is encompassed by the knowledge of Allah the Sublime. *Āmīn.*

كَتَبَهُ عَبْدُ اللهِ الْفَقِيرُ لِمَوْلَاهُ الْغَنِيِّ، أَيَّامَ مُجَاوَرَتِهِ الشَّرِيفَةِ، الَّتِي أَكْرَمَهُ اللهُ بِهَا فِي الْمَدِينَةِ الْمُنَوَّرَةِ بِأَنْوَارِ الْمُصْطَفَىٰ ﷺ.

وَاللهَ تَعَالَىٰ أَسْأَلُ، وَبِجَاهِ الْحَبِيبِ عِنْدَ اللهِ تَعَالَىٰ وَبِكَرَامَتِهِ أَتَوَسَّلُ؛ أَنْ لَّا يَقْطَعَنَا عَنْ دُخُولِ بَابِ السَّلَامِ لِأَجْلِ السَّلَامِ عَلَىٰ سَيِّدِ الْأَنَامِ ﷺ وَأَنْ يَتَفَضَّلَ عَلَيْنَا بِمُجَاوَرَتِهِ الْكَرِيمَةِ عَلَىٰ أَكْمَلِ الْأَحْوَالِ.

وَصَلَّى اللهُ عَلَىٰ سَيِّدِنَا مُحَمَّدٍ وَّعَلَىٰ آلِهِ وَصَحْبِهِ وَسَلَّمَ تَسْلِيمًا فِي كُلِّ لَمْحَةٍ وَّنَفَسٍ عَدَدَ مَا وَسِعَهُ عِلْمُ اللهِ الْعَظِيمِ - آمِين.

❁ ❁ ❁

The Muhammadan Ballad
By Imam al-Būṣīrī ﵁

❝ Praise is Allah's, the Originator of the creation from nothingness;
Then prayers of praise be upon the timelessly Chosen One.

Pray, my Lord, and send Your blessings always eternally
Upon Your Beloved, the Choicest best among all of creation.[131]

Muhammad is the noblest one among Arabs and non-Arabs;
Muhammad is the best of those who have walked upon the Earth.

Muhammad spreads forth all goodness – he is its gatherer –
Muhammad is the possessor of excellent grace and nobility.

Muhammad is the crown jewel of Allah's Messengers;
Muhammad is the truthful in his speech, honest with his words.

Muhammad is firm in his pledge, he preserves it;
Muhammad is of goodly character and noble, virtuous morals.

Muhammad had his clay form infused with light;
Muhammad remains as light since ancient timeless times.

Muhammad is a just judge, of prestigious status;
Muhammad is the ore of all bounty and every adage.

Muhammad is the best of Allah's creation from Muḍar;
Muhammad is the choicest best of all Allah's Messengers.

Muhammad's religion is true, his is what we adhere to;
Muhammad is a dawning banner of truth upon the cosmos.

---

131 This couplet is to be recited after every other couplet.

القَصِيدَةُ المُحَمَّدِيَّةُ

لِلْإِمَامِ الْبُوصَيْرِيِّ رَضِيَ اللهُ عَنْهُ

(اَلْحَمْدُ لِلّٰهِ مُنْشِئِ الْخَلْقِ مِنْ عَدَمٍ　　ثُمَّ الصَّلَاةُ عَلَى الْمُخْتَارِ فِي الْقِدَمِ)

مَوْلَايَ صَلِّ وَسَلِّمْ دَائِمًا أَبَدًا　　عَلَى حَبِيبِكَ خَيْرِ الْخَلْقِ كُلِّهِمِ

[تُكَرَّرُ بَعْدَ كُلِّ بَيْتٍ]

مُحَمَّدٌ أَشْرَفُ الْعَرَبِ وَالْعَجَمِ　　مُحَمَّدٌ خَيْرُ مَنْ يَمْشِي عَلَى قَدَمِ

مُحَمَّدٌ بَاسِطُ الْمَعْرُوفِ جَامِعُهُ　　مُحَمَّدٌ صَاحِبُ الْإِحْسَانِ وَالْكَرَمِ

مُحَمَّدٌ تَاجُ رُسْلِ اللهِ قَاطِبَةً　　مُحَمَّدٌ صَادِقُ الْأَقْوَالِ وَالْكَلِمِ

مُحَمَّدٌ ثَابِتُ الْمِيثَاقِ حَافِظُهُ　　مُحَمَّدٌ طَيِّبُ الْأَخْلَاقِ وَالشِّيَمِ

مُحَمَّدٌ جُبِلَتْ بِالنُّورِ طِينَتُهُ　　مُحَمَّدٌ لَمْ يَزَلْ نُورًا مِنَ الْقِدَمِ

مُحَمَّدٌ حَاكِمٌ بِالْعَدْلِ ذُوْ شَرَفٍ　　مُحَمَّدٌ مَعْدِنُ الْإِنْعَامِ وَالْحِكَمِ

مُحَمَّدٌ خَيْرُ خَلْقِ اللهِ مِنْ مُضَرٍ　　مُحَمَّدٌ خَيْرُ رُسْلِ اللهِ كُلِّهِمِ

مُحَمَّدٌ دِيْنُهُ حَقٌّ نَدِينُ بِهِ　　مُحَمَّدٌ مُشْرِقٌ حَقًّا عَلَى عَلَمِ

Muhammad's mention gives spirit to our souls;
Muhammad – all nations are obliged in gratitude to him.

Muhammad is the world's adornment and its brilliance;
Muhammad alleviates calamity and uplifts darkness.

Muhammad is a master, his endeavours are most honourable;
Muhammad – the Merciful distilled him with bounty.

Muhammad is singled out by the Creator, his choicest one;
Muhammad is free from all blameworthy accusation.

Muhammad is the smiling host, honouring his guest;
Muhammad – his neighbour, by Allah, is not overlooked.

Muhammad blessed this world when he was sent;
Muhammad came with revealed signs and divine wisdom.

Muhammad is our intercessor when we are resurrected;
Muhammad's light guides us away from darkness.

Muhammad stands upright for Allah with resolve;
Muhammad is the Seal to every Messenger before him. ”

مُحَمَّدٌ ذِكْرُهُ رُوحٌ لِأَنْفُسِنَا   مُحَمَّدٌ شُكْرُهُ فَرْضٌ عَلَى الْأُمَمِ

مُحَمَّدٌ زِينَةُ الدُّنْيَا وَبَهْجَتُهَا   مُحَمَّدٌ كَاشِفُ الْغُمَّاتِ وَالظُّلَمِ

مُحَمَّدٌ سَيِّدٌ طَابَتْ مَنَاقِبُهُ   مُحَمَّدٌ صَاغَهُ الرَّحْمٰنُ بِالنِّعَمِ

مُحَمَّدٌ صَفْوَةُ الْبَارِي وَخِيرَتُهُ   مُحَمَّدٌ طَاهِرٌ مِنْ سَائِرِ التُّهَمِ

مُحَمَّدٌ ضَاحِكٌ لِلضَّيْفِ مُكْرِمُهُ   مُحَمَّدٌ جَارُهُ وَاللهِ لَمْ يُضَمِ

مُحَمَّدٌ طَابَتِ الدُّنْيَا بِبِعْثَتِهِ   مُحَمَّدٌ جَاءَ بِالْآيَاتِ وَالْحِكَمِ

مُحَمَّدٌ يَوْمَ بَعْثِ النَّاسِ شَافِعُنَا   مُحَمَّدٌ نُورُهُ الْهَادِي مِنَ الظُّلَمِ

مُحَمَّدٌ قَائِمٌ لِلّٰهِ ذُو هِمَمٍ   مُحَمَّدٌ خَاتِمٌ لِلرُّسْلِ كُلِّهِمِ

Printed in Great Britain
by Amazon

44239460R00098